The Digital Revolution has spawned a seemingly infinite number of books addressing the Internet, social media and their meaning for our society and the future, with considerable repetition between them. In *Ethics and Religion in the Age of Social Media*, Kevin Healey and Robert H. Woods, Jr. provide a critical and original take on our digital dilemmas, and use their "prophetic rage" to shine a bright new light on the important issues at hand. I strongly recommend this absorbing book.

— Robert W. McChesney, University of Illinois at Urbana-Champaign

This insightful book offers proverbial wisdom to make ethical communication possible in a digital world where finding common ground is a challenge, tribalism is increasing, and civil discourse is decreasing. With clarity and insight, this engaging and thought-provoking book provides a masterful blueprint for restoring virtue and values to a media and information saturated society. Supported with research and wisdom, Healey and Woods's eye-opening observations are valuable to students beginning their study communication or leaders who will determine whether we are a society adrift in a digital sea of disconnected data, or dreamers and poets inspired by the good, the beautiful, and the true.

— Steven A. Beebe, PhD, Regents' and University Distinguished Professor Emeritus, Past President, National Communication Association

An amazing and thought-provoking book. An unbelievable effort. Genuinely a refreshing and different examination of the industry.

— Jason Alan Snyder, Global Chief Technology Officer, McCann Worldgroup

By highlighting the religious undertones of Silicon Valley, writers Healey and Woods dismantle the blind faith some harbor for technology as a savior to society. They also provide a critique of the tech industry that manages to make room for hope in technology's future. The relationship between religion and technology is one that is eloquently explored in a way that draws parallels and parables any follower can learn from.

— Shamika Goddard, Founder, Tech Chaplaincy Institute at Union Theological Seminary

ETHICS AND RELIGION IN THE AGE OF SOCIAL MEDIA

Arguing that popular digital platforms promote misguided assumptions about ethics and technology, this book lays out a new perspective on the relation between technological capacities and human virtue.

The authors criticize the "digital catechism" of technological idolatry arising from the insular, elite culture of Silicon Valley. In order to develop digital platforms that promote human freedom and socio-economic equality, they outline a set of five "proverbs" for living responsibly in the digital world: (1) information is not wisdom; (2) transparency is not authenticity; (3) convergence is not integrity; (4) processing is not judgment; and (5) storage is not memory. Each chapter ends with a simple exercise to help users break through the habitual modes of thinking that our favorite digital applications promote. Drawing from technical and policy experts, it offers corrective strategies to address the structural and ideological biases of current platform architectures, algorithms, user policies, and advertising models.

This book will appeal to scholars and graduate and advanced undergraduate students investigating the intersections of media, religion, and ethics, as well as journalists and professionals in the digital and technological space.

Kevin Healey (Ph.D., University of Illinois) is associate professor of communication at the University of New Hampshire. He writes and teaches religion, ethics, and digital culture. Kevin received the Communication Ethics Teaching Award from the National Communication Association in 2018 and the University Teaching Excellence Award from the University of New Hampshire in 2017. His essays appear in *Salon*, *Huffington Post*, and *Religion Dispatches*, as well as in numerous academic books and journals. This book is supported by his participation in a three-year Public Theologies of Technology and Presence grant program sponsored by the Institute of Buddhist Studies and the Henry Luce Foundation. Kevin lives in Durham, New Hampshire, with his wife Cristina, their daughter Madeline, and their dog Charlie.

Robert H. Woods Jr. (Ph.D., Regent University) is professor of communication and media at Spring Arbor University in Spring Arbor, Michigan. He teaches and writes about communication theory, media and culture, and ethics. Robert served as the President of the Religious Communication Association (RCA) and was named Scholar of the Year by the RCA in 2013. He is the network administrator for the Christianity and Communication Studies Network (www.theccsn.com). His articles appear in numerous scholarly journals, and he has authored, co-authored, and edited a dozen academic books. He lives in Washington State with his wife, Rebekah, their three dogs, and two cats.

ETHICS AND RELIGION IN THE AGE OF SOCIAL MEDIA

Digital Proverbs for Responsible Citizens

Kevin Healey and Robert H. Woods Jr.

Routledge
Taylor & Francis Group

NEW YORK AND LONDON

First edition published 2020
by Routledge
52 Vanderbilt Avenue, New York, NY 10017

and by Routledge
2 Park Square, Milton Park, Abingdon, Oxon, OX14 4RN

Routledge is an imprint of the Taylor & Francis Group, an informa business

© 2020 Taylor & Francis

The right of Kevin Healey and Robert H. Woods Jr. to be identified as authors of this work has been asserted by them in accordance with sections 77 and 78 of the Copyright, Designs and Patents Act 1988.

Library of Congress Cataloging-in-Publication Data
A catalog record for this title has been requested

ISBN: 978-1-138-33498-4 (hbk)
ISBN: 978-1-138-33500-4 (pbk)
ISBN: 978-0-367-82418-1 (ebk)

Typeset in Bembo
by Aptara, India

CONTENTS

FOREWORD

This sophisticated book is moral philosophy in the Counter-Enlightenment tradition, though its approach to ethics can be located even more deeply in the history of ideas. The genealogy of this tradition takes us to Judeo-Christian ethics of the first century AD and the sacred Vedas in ancient India. Moral philosophy in Counter-Enlightenment terms could be restated as the Jewish trajectory from Martin Buber to Emmanuel Levinas. But for the technological world of digital platforms, the eighteenth century is the decisive modern revolution. I locate *Digital Proverbs* within this intellectual history in order to illuminate its importance among the multiple analyses of Silicon Valley. This unique interpretation of today's technoculture is formidable and will be enduring because it represents so keenly the Counter-Enlightenment paradigm.

In the eighteenth-century Enlightenment, human beings were considered sovereign as ends in themselves and self-determination became the highest good. René Descartes established this version of rational being by identifying the essence of the self as a thinking substance. The sciences are to be constructed by statistical precision, and rational choice becomes the foundation of deontological and utilitarian ethics. Following Descartes's rationalism, moral principles are derived by disembodied reason. Kant assimilated ethics to logic. In John Stuart Mill, individual liberty has priority over the moral order, and therefore ethics is exterior. Ethical systems that depend on these approaches are formalistic, grounding reason in an apparatus of neutral standards outside of society and culture.

Digital Proverbs eschews the rational choice tradition and represents the Counter-Enlightenment's philosophy of language instead. Healey and Woods operate with a different conceptual foundation, a linguistic trajectory that enables them to develop normative discourse instead of rules and abstract principles.

There was substantial opposition to linear rationality during the eighteenth century, but it can be illustrated through Giambattista Vico and Jean-Jacques Rousseau.

Vico, as Professor of rhetoric at the University of Naples for four decades, contended that philology ought to preoccupy philosophers because language was quintessentially human. Vico's *New Science* was a detailed account of the history of language and cultural customs, while his *Study Methods of Our Time* was a humanities masterpiece in contrast to Descartes's mathematics. Rousseau is also Counter-Enlightenment. In his *Essay on the Origin of Language,* writing allows us to create social and political systems beyond immediate responses to the environment. Though he did not resolve it satisfactorily, Rousseau in *The Social Contract* correctly identifies the freedom-and-moral-order conundrum in literature and history as more fundamental than the subject-object dichotomy in Cartesian epistemology.

The Counter-Enlightenment starts over intellectually with the human lifeworld, with human existence rather than individual autonomy. Its vigorous humanities commitment inspires nineteenth-century intellectuals to emphasize language. And with the linguistic trajectory from Ferdinand de Saussure to Ernst Cassirer's *Philosophy of Symbolic Forms,* the philosophy of language is developed systematically. For Cassirer, symbolization is not merely central to cognition, but recomposing events into a narrative constitutes human existence. For Suzanne Langer, the philosophy-of-language tradition from the Counter-Enlightenment is *Philosophy in a New Key.* The new question at the centerpiece of philosophical inquiry is the manner in which language represents the meaning and purpose of human existence. Rather than individual rights as the integrating norm, obligations to one another define our collaborative action. Humans-in-linguistic-relation is the key to understanding ethics. Implementing the truth that the symbolic realm is intrinsic to the human species, *Digital Proverbs* in its prophetic critique identifies Silicon Valley's technocratic worldview—the tenets of faith that underlie its discourse of efficiency and messianic progress.

As Hans-Georg Gadamer elaborates in his *Truth and Method,* language in the Counter-Enlightenment legacy is a primal competence through which humanity discloses the fundamental conditions of its humanness. Therefore, natural language, rather than the artificial language of mathematical logic, is the mode of human understanding. Instead of technology's statistics, or the linear induction and hierarchical deduction of Enlightenment epistemology, *Digital Proverbs* develops a cogent discourse ethics from the natural languages of human interaction. Healey and Woods present a stunning array of symbolic formations that together comprise their digital humanism, such as proverbs and corollaries, prophetic critique, disinformation campaigns, false distinctions, priestly propaganda, weaponized information, and authentic communication.

The quality of this book's discursive moral philosophy becomes apparent when comparing it to Norbert Wiener's classic *The Human Use of Human Beings: Cybernetics and Society.* Wiener's positivism mathematically integrates physiological, hydraulic, and electronic systems in his legendary *Cybernetics.* Following the second law of thermodynamics, information is defined as the negative logarithm of entropy with information, of necessity, commanding in order to control. In *The Human Use of Human Beings,* six years later, Wiener was intellectually perturbed about the command-control character of communication in his theory, but his concern presumed autonomous subjectivity outside the theory itself. The elementary philosophy of language that his cybernetics represents compelled him by its logic to sacrifice in theory what he takes back by exhortation. His statistical mechanics promoted the mistaken view since the Enlightenment that technological products are a means to trans-technological ends, rather than develop an approach to technology in which ends and means are integrated into the theory itself. The rationalist tradition in Wiener's *Cybernetics*, in effect, eliminates the fallacious conflation of means and ends by denying it. But in defining away the distinction between these two domains, Wiener's positivistic cybernetics confronts a conundrum: Can a theory without an a-theoretical realm contain itself? *The Human Use of Human Beings* can therefore be accurate in what it denies and wrong in what it affirms.

Resembling Silicon Valley today, Wiener's *Cybernetics* places humankind in the contradictory position of creating a world that condemns its makers for their deficiencies in controlling it. Humanity produces the mechanisms for its own erasure. Robert Mejia uses the evil twin idea from mythology to describe the creation of the controlled, therefore artificial self, in Wiener's *Cybernetics*. The possibilities of an evil-twin doppelgänger mean that originating agents assist in their own demise. They first create an innovative scenario, and then upon its completion a doppelgänger is constituted as more capable. Humans produce the very entity that makes them obsolete.

Healey and Woods's discourse ethics avoids both the conundrum and the doppelgänger paradox. *Digital Proverbs* differs fundamentally from the individualistic producer-product binary that Wiener's positivism represents. In discourse ethics, there is no unitary subject that produces and uses tools. Disclosures of phenomena and those to whom they are disclosed are co-original. Narratives of interaction are the opposite of the rational-choice individualism that Wiener reclaims in *The Human Use of Human Beings*.

University of Oxford philosopher Luciano Floridi is a notable contemporary in the Wiener tradition, and *Digital Proverbs* illustrates how the limitations of his analysis are overcome. Floridi's *Philosophy of Information, Ethics of Information,* and *The Fourth Revolution* describe the digital revolution (technosphere) as an information environment (infosphere) in which humans are embedded with both natural and artificial agents as informational organisms (inforgs).

In Floridi's inforg in the infosphere, with the brain as a data processor and the body a technological apparatus of information energy, the body is effaced in favor of epistemic projections of the mind. He reifies the mind-body dichotomy, a dualism so uncritically dominant in the West, that to perpetuate it without critique limits his relevance to the fundamental issues. Healey and Woods's digital humanism, in contrast to mind-body dualism, is able to engage the complicated debates over history about mental causation and bodily behavior.

Despite the prodigious reconstructions in the Wiener genealogy, the challenge remains to account for the human-technology interface in radically different terms. *Digital Proverbs* rejects the subject-object dichotomy, the opposition of primary mind to secondary body, the presumption of technological determinism in Silicon Valley's Singularity convergence, and the persistence of the optimism-pessimism debate. *Digital Proverbs* refutes these conceptual misdirections. Its discursive moral philosophy constructs an integrated digital humanism that embraces technological possibility while foregrounding human values.

In the philosophy of language that this book illustrates, understanding expands our existential horizon and deepens our humanity, not only to see more but to see differently. Explanations *why* are center stage, as distinct from explanations of *what* something is or *how* it functions. Because Healey and Woods know intellectual history, their prophetic critique engages enduring issues on the human agenda. They are astute in contributing to moral philosophy, with Habermas's communicative rationality given depth and specificity in their developing an alternative consciousness to the technocratic worldview. *Digital Proverbs* achieves that rare scholarly finesse in which resistance thinking simultaneously imagines new ways of being.

Clifford G. Christians,
University of Illinois-Urbana

ACKNOWLEDGMENTS

This book is the culmination of many years of work. Arguably, it began when we decided to co-edit our previous volume on the prophetic critique of popular media. Our exploration of the proverbs began in earnest at the 2013 meeting of the National Communications Association in Washington, D.C., with a presentation titled, "Information Is Not Wisdom, Convergence Is Not Integrity: Proverbs for an Era of Digital Humanism." Those two proverbs became the focus of an article in *Explorations in Media Ecology*, followed by an article in *Journal of Media Ethics* titled "Storage Is Not Memory, Processing Is Not Judgment." The full list of five proverbs, including transparency is not authenticity, first appeared in a special issue of the journal *Religions* in 2015. Various iterations of our critique of Silicon Valley culture appear in *Nomos Journal*, *Journal of Television and New Media*, *Journal of Information, Communication and Ethics in Society*, and *Journal of Religion, Media and Digital Culture*. Variations on these ideas also appear in popular venues like *Huffington Post*, *Salon*, and *Religion Dispatches*. These references are cited throughout the book. Suffice it to say, the present book draws from previously published material, though it goes well beyond those earlier instantiations.

As was the case with our previous book, we are deeply indebted to our intellectual mentor Clifford G. Christians, whose work in the area of media ethics is exemplary and whose wisdom and integrity are unmatched. We would also like to thank the many outstanding colleagues who have generously donated their time and effort to review and provide feedback on early drafts of this book. These individuals include Amy Bix, Patricia Condon, Nora Draper, Michelle Gibbons, Renee Heath, Karolyn Kinane, and Jason Snyder. The photographs appearing in Chapters 3 and 5 are provided courtesy of Karolyn Kinane and Amy Snow, respectively. Thanks to Karolyn and Amy for the use of these images.

This book project is supported in part by Public Theologies of Technology and Presence, a three-year grant program offered through the Institute of Buddhist

Studies and the Henry Luce Foundation. We offer special thanks to Steven Barrie-Anthony for his stewardship of this innovative program and to the cohort of brilliant grantees whose ideas and energy have kept wind in our sails.

Special thanks to Marsha Daigle-Williamson for her skillful copyediting, extreme flexibility, and quick turnaround time with edits. Thanks also to John Muether for preparing an index that serves readers well. Spring Arbor University's library staff (Elizabeth Walker-Papke, Karen Parsons, Kami Moyer, Susan Panak, and Robbie Bolton) provided timely research support during the several years that this project took shape.

We also thank our institutions (University of New Hampshire and Spring Arbor University) for their continued support of this work and other related projects that fed into this one. Our department chairs, directors, deans, vice presidents, and provosts supported release time and made funds available to help work on this book.

We are grateful for Routledge Publishing and gifted advocates like Laura Briskman, Brian Eschrich, and Nicole Salazar. These colleagues demonstrated patience and professionalism as we worked to meet deadlines, and went above and beyond the call of duty in support of this work.

Finally, we would like to thank our spouses, Cristina Healey and Rebekah Woods, for their constant support and encouragement during the past few years, especially when we were in the midst of an argument, or stuck in the creative process, at which point they reminded us to take a deep breath and count our many blessings. They give us space to work and room to breathe. They are partners in every sense of the word.

A PERSONAL NOTE TO READERS

Thanks for taking time to consider the ideas presented in this book. Regardless of what brought you here, we are grateful for your time—an increasingly precious commodity in our "that-was-so-eight-seconds-ago" culture. We recognize that digital distractions make it difficult to pay attention to longer forms of writing. As fans of good reads, we worked hard to fill these pages with our favorite ideas and examples. In terms of style and tone, we try to walk a fine line between conversational and scholarly. And to escape the tedium of parsing out individual experiences, we opted for "we" and "our" to maintain a singular voice, figuring you would not care whether the example was one of Kevin's or Robert's as long as it was a good one. We hope all of this, and more below, warrants at least eight more seconds.

Why This Book? Why Now? (Or, a Tale of Two Authors' Prophetic Rage)

Although we share a lot in common, your authors come from several different camps. One of us (Kevin) is a religiously unaffiliated, registered Independent who leans strongly Democratic, while the other (Robert) is a committed evangelical Christian who is a registered Republican. In many academic circles, such differences would bar us from friendship, let alone a decade's worth of collaboration. But if politics can make strange bedfellows, so too can prophetic rage.

Our partnership began through a common mentor, Clifford G. Christians (University of Illinois at Urbana-Champaign). Cliff's call for "prophetic witness" in the face of our technological society ignited our friendship and became a guiding concept for our subsequent work. Like the prophets of old, much of our work has been fueled by rage. Not rage as in "cocksureness" but in a growing restlessness that something is wrong with the world. More specifically, an agitated awareness that something is wrong with a growing technological mindedness that privileges strident individualism over moral responsibility and elevates technical skill and efficiency over non-instrumental virtues such as moderation and humility. This techno-mindedness, in turn, fosters a messianic belief in the collection and dissemination of information as the path to societal progress and personal happiness—as if any problem we face could be solved with just a little more information. Enough to enrage, and bind, any two prophets.

As we realized fairly early on in our collaboration, these concerns are not just for those on the Left or the Right but are of central concern to all people, all parties, and all religions interested in fostering a humane collaboration between people and machines that does not subvert human dignity to profit and efficiency. This made bridge-building across our camps easy and eventually resulted in a set of key questions that formed the foundation of this book, including, "What is the vision that I hold for the future of our digital economy and how should things be different? Can they be different? Are we serving as witnesses to technology that supports human flourishing and justice in the digital economy?"

Furthermore, addressing questions like these mean a commitment to understanding the importance of religious belief in American public life—even if one does not necessarily agree with those beliefs. There is power in belief. It is inspiring. It can motivate principled commitment to democratic debate and collaboration despite differences. It can also be frightening when it is clearly moving in the wrong direction, when it is sparking tribalism, animosity, greed, or hatred. Our collaboration, in large part, has thus been about showing how seemingly secular endeavors like Silicon Valley tech companies are full of belief and ritual in ways that are inseparable from American religious history. We cannot understand where tech is taking us, or who is taking us there, if we do not understand the cultural, religious, and spiritual dimensions of technical development. This is something that is generally missing from media and religion scholarship. We are seeking to put it clearly on the map.

Our Central Arguments: The Moral Catechism and Five Proverbs

In a nutshell, we suggest that the most popular digital platforms tend to promote a set of ideological biases (or "digital worldview") that we call the "moral catechism of Silicon Valley." Make no mistake about it, this catechism is as much like any other set of religious rites and rituals that re-define who we are, how we should act, and what kinds of human beings we should be. In the process of setting forth certain do's and don'ts for proper digital living, the catechism falsely equates technological capacities with specific human virtues, for example, equating information with wisdom and transparency with authenticity, to name a few.

In response, to develop digital platforms that promote human freedom and socio-economic equality, we must maintain a clear distinction between technological (instrumental) capacities and the (non-instrumental) capacity for human virtue. Toward these ends, we outline a set of guiding principles or "proverbs" aimed at confronting Silicon Valley's moral catechism and fostering a more humane digital environment that include the following: (1) information is *not* wisdom; (2) transparency is *not* authenticity; (3) convergence is *not* integrity; (4) processing is *not* judgment; and (5) storage is *not* memory. You get the idea. Silicon Valley's catechism says the opposite: information *is* wisdom; transparency *is* authenticity, and so on. We disagree.

While the proverbs say "no" to the catechism, we also provide a positive path forward by coupling each proverb with a corollary, statements to which we can say "yes": (1) inform wisely; (2) strive for authentic transparency; (3) integrate divergent elements; (4) process judiciously; and (5) remember the virtue of forgetting. Note that we do not consider these five proverbs and their corollaries to be exhaustive, but as a starting point for a broader conversation about safeguarding human dignity and democratic processes.

On their own, information processing and data storage cannot guarantee the achievement of virtues found in the proverbs above, let alone replace them. So, in consultation with technical and policy experts, we offer specific corrective strategies to address the structural and ideological biases of current platform architectures, algorithms, user policies, advertising models, and regulatory frameworks that undermine our ability as humans to cultivate virtues such as those identified in the proverbs. Through our diverse approach, we avoid political and religious partisanship. While avoiding a cynical rejection of all innovation, we call for what media ethicist Clifford G. Christians (1989) calls "normative technologies," which are technical systems and platforms that amplify human virtue rather than vice. By issuing this call, we fully embrace the potential benefits of emerging technologies.

Moreover, a key argument that weaves itself through this book's tapestry is that when it comes to the digital economy, we need to have our heads on straight and think about what we are doing *before* we do it. We need to be mindful before we launch that new app, as we launch it, and after we launch it. We need to avoid replacing the *ought* with the *is* and meaning with measurement.

We need, first and foremost, to be human. We need to remember what it means to be human, to remember what makes us fully human. That is why we devote so much time to articulating basic virtues like wisdom, judgment, authenticity, integrity, and memory. The need for such virtues will not go away, no matter what new gadgets or platforms arise. Such virtues are the anchors, the pivot points, the north stars, of any conversation that aims to envision a just future of human flourishing.

In the final analysis, despite the many challenges ahead, your authors refuse to adopt an attitude of cynicism and despair about the nature of commercial media. Through the forward-looking thrust of our approach and its redemptive possibilities, we intend to demonstrate that critical engagement with digital culture is essentially a hopeful, and hope-filled, endeavor for generations to come.

How to Read This Book

If you are reading this book, you are probably a student or professor. You might be majoring in Communication, or you might be teaching a course on pop culture within a Religious Studies program. Hopefully some of you reading this are journalists, media critics, software engineers, and other working professionals. In any case, you are likely seeking an alternative intellectual lens through which to engage an emerging digital economy that is still in its infancy.

Keep in mind that all good arguments are nuanced. In any nuanced book, it is easy to take a word or phrase or even a paragraph out of context and assume wrongly that you have understood the gist of the argument. You will notice that we spend a lot of time articulating a view of technology with which we fundamentally disagree. Pay close attention to whose views we are describing. Notice the context of those descriptions. Do we follow up with a refutation, a revision, a counter-argument? What are we really saying about wisdom and information? About memory and storage? There are many moving parts to this book. Try to see how these parts interact, and why we have structured the book as we do. Do not lose the forest for the trees.

You may be tempted to focus on the clear case studies at the end of each chapter dealing with a particular proverb. Of course, we have included those precisely because they are easy to latch on to. While we do offer case studies of particular people, products, and policies, the point of this book is not to provide end-all, be-all solutions. There is no simple fix to ensure justice in the digital economy. On-the-ground, day-to-day examples and practices must also be coupled with broadscale initiatives. Otherwise, we still end up with a small group of winners and a whole lot of losers in the digital economy. As you read, let your mind work between these two dimensions: short-term practices and long-term, broadscale initiatives. We hope to demonstrate to you how the two are deeply connected.

One thing that is certain about the future of technology is that it is largely unpredictable. We might think we know where things are headed, and then some start-up in a garage in Palo Alto changes everything. We think we know what the impact of a new device, or service, or platform might be. But then, years later, we realize things did not turn out that way; other problems arose that we did not anticipate. We were tempted, at such times, to fix the problems caused by previous technologies with new technologies.

Our point is less to prescribe specific technical or policy solutions in the here and now and more to proclaim, to pronounce, prophetically, that as we move forward into the digital future we must keep our eyes trained on those fixed points that keep us from veering radically off course.

Remember that we humans are happiest when we aspire to our highest virtues. Remember that those include wisdom and integrity. Keep asking what those words mean. Keep asking whether, and how, we can embody them at every step in the technical process so that our technical society is still a human, humane one for all.

Here is to the current and budding prophets among us. Keep moving forward, eight seconds at a time.

Kevin Healey and Robert H. Woods Jr.
Summer 2019

INTRODUCTION

In 2017, two professors at the University of Washington, Jevin West, assistant professor at the Information School, and Carl T. Bergstrom, biology professor, offered a course titled "Calling Bullshit: Data Reasoning in a Digital World." Fed up with "crystals-and-homeopathy aunts," "casually racist" uncles, and the fake news that fueled their rants, the goal of the course was to teach people how to think critically about digital propaganda (Bergstrom and West 2017; Townsend 2017). Bergstrom and West were concerned that democratic processes were being undermined by an improper understanding of Big Data, including how algorithms were "overfitting data" to serve partisan ends. The class filled up within one minute of opening for registration and received media attention from across the country (Townsend 2017).

The fervor surrounding this course caught our attention. At first, we thought it was a hoax or at least a PR stunt to promote a new book. After all, no respectable university would allow such a word be used in its curriculum, right? But when the sting of realizing that our own courses would never fill so quickly eventually wore off, we agreed that this course was exactly what individuals needed to help make better sense of their daily digital propaganda and to start taking greater responsibility for promoting a more hopeful future. As one of our academic friends remarked, "This course's title captures what deceivers do. We all know it when we see or hear it and can usually sniff it out, but few of us have the time, skills, or courage, to speak up and act out. After all, doing so just might ruin the fun!"

Charting a Course Beyond the Digital Propaganda

Our book certainly shares Bergstrom and West's concerns about digital culture's impact on responsible civic engagement and public discourse. But just as important, we are also concerned about how such practices can undermine human dignity and virtue, amplifying the negative effects of digital culture on democratic processes as we increasingly hand over basic moral decision-making to machines—and, of course, their engineers—in nearly every aspect of life.

Within Silicon Valley there is an emerging digital anthropology that characterizes human beings as re-evolving, or de-evolving, as the case may be. The current human being is simply too inefficient, too inconsistent, and too lacking in processing speed, transparency, integrity, and algorithmic precision to accurately judge or solve our greatest societal problems in a timely manner. Silicon Valley's solution? "Let us re-make human beings in our own image." In this techno-centric worldview, solving problems (even if they are the wrong problems to solve) and making progress (even if the progress is going in the wrong direction) in efficient ways (assuming faster is always better) are the "holy trinity" that will ultimately save humanity. The end goal is to make human beings, and unapologetically so, "more than human" (Weintraub 2015).

The religious overtones at this point are glaring, even for the most apathetic agnostic. A key premise in this book is that digital platforms encode a set of quasi-religious ideological biases that we call the "moral catechism of Silicon Valley." A *catechism* is a summary of principles maintained by a particular religion or church in the form of rites, rituals, and practices designed to reinforce followers' continued support in its core doctrines and mission. As we present throughout, Silicon Valley's moral catechism falsely equates technological capacities with specific human virtues. Implicit in tech elites' rhetoric, in platform architectures, and elsewhere is a five-point creed: (1) information *is* wisdom; (2) transparency *is* authenticity; (3) convergence *is* integrity; (4) processing *is* judgment; and (5) storage *is* memory. More will be said about each of these core assumptions or tenets in individual chapters later in this book (see Chapters 3–7).

In response to Silicon Valley's moral catechism, and to develop digital platforms that enhance rather than undermine responsible civic engagement and human dignity, we argue that we must first maintain a clear distinction between technical capacities and the capacity for human virtue. To this end, we offer a series of proverbs and corollary principles that directly challenge the five-point creed above. A *proverb* is a short, pithy statement that embodies key, and often unstated, assumptions about what is ultimately real, true, good, and beautiful in the world and is worth pursuing.

It is worth noting that, as a global-historical phenomenon, proverbs have long served to guide public debates by appealing to the universal truths embodied in the various wisdom traditions. The vitality of the proverb has persisted even with the advent of the personal computer (Simpson 1992, pp. x–xi). While proverbs are obviously of long-standing interest to linguists, scholars in other areas have taken an interest in them to address pedagogical and cross-cultural concerns. For example, business educators have proposed using proverbs to teach finance to Chinese-speaking students, while management scholars have suggested the use of proverbs in cultivating context-sensitive leadership where local communities desire more egalitarian working conditions (Biktimirov and Feng 2006; Bernard and Fernandez 2012).

To be clear, we are not neo-Luddites or technology haters. We use Facebook, Twitter, WordPress, Photoshop, and every other tool you can imagine currently in use (and will use those that are soon to be invented). Before entering academia, one of us had a career as a website producer for top-tier media companies in New York City, a place known by techies as "Silicon Alley." We embrace and celebrate the immense potential of digital technology. To be sure, technical affordances such as information processing and data storage clearly have the potential to contribute to the achievement of human virtues like wisdom, judgment, and memory. But on their own, despite their creators' best intentions, they cannot guarantee the achievement of such virtues, let alone replace them, as the catechism assumes. Thus, by stating our analyses in religious terms, for example, the Church of Google, we seek to draw attention to the dangers of a "blind faith in technology" and the "market fundamentalism" that follows close behind (Carr 2010, p. 149; Vaidhyanathan 2011a, p. 1).

Furthermore, by addressing the catechism's implications in consultation with students, colleagues, technical and policy experts, this book explores existing and emerging strategies for addressing the structural and ideological biases of current platform architectures, algorithms, user policies, advertising models, and regulatory frameworks. Our goal is not necessarily to offer a complete set of solutions but a set of core principles to guide our thinking about digital technologies. In this way, we can understand what is working within existing solutions and you, the reader, can use such insights to develop new solutions and strategies that we cannot see at the time of this writing. Together we can yet help usher in an era of *digital humanism*—one in which our technologies truly enhance rather than undermine the quality of civic leadership and engagement.

The Moral Catechism of Silicon Valley

At a recent dinner party, our hosts' eight-year-old daughter came in to say goodnight just as the dessert was being served. After a quick kiss on the check, her parents reminded her to say her prayers before she went to bed. About ten minutes later, the little girl returned to the table with a concerned look on her face.

"What's wrong?," her parents asked.

"I'm not quite sure how to pray anymore," she said.

A half-worried, half-humorous grin came over her parents' faces: "What on earth do you mean?" Now, almost in tears, the little girl asked: "Well, is Google God'?

"Did something happen today at school that makes you ask this?" her parents asked.

The little girl explained that her class was learning about the history of the Internet. During the lesson, her teacher had basically argued that Google can do no evil, is very powerful, exists everywhere in the world at one time, never sleeps, knows everything, remembers all, and can live forever. "When I said that's what we learned about God in Sunday School," she explained, "the teacher just smiled. So, what's the difference between Google and God?"

In almost perfect unison her parents turned toward us. They knew we were working on this book and hoped we could chime in with something simple yet elegant, maybe even profound. One of us turned to the other and said, tongue-in-cheek,

"Well, God only requires one password that can never be hacked. And the upload speeds are instantaneous!" Of course, sarcasm is rarely a helpful response to an eight-year-old's sincere question. So, we did what most professors do when buying time: we turned the question around and asked, "What do *you* think is the difference?"

The little girl's face lightened as all eyes at the table now fell on her. After a few seconds passed, she proudly proclaimed: "I'm not sure yet. I know some things are the same about them. But there are some *bbbiiiggg* differences too!" From the mouth of babes, as the saying goes.

When Technology and Religion Collide

At the heart of this young girl's question is the heart of this book, namely, calling into question Silicon Valley's unique blend of free market libertarianism and do-it-yourself spirituality. The religious dimensions of digital culture pre-date the Internet not just by decades but by centuries. Silicon Valley's ideology is characterized by a mixture of Christian end-times theology and Gnosticism on the one hand, and East Asian concepts and practice derived from Buddhism and Hinduism on the other (Healey 2015).

Described as "informationism" by some and "Californian ideology" by others, Silicon Valley's moral catechism harbors a rosy worldview that assumes a messianic march of personal happiness and social progress in the collection and dissemination of information (Schultze 2002, p. 21; Barbrook and Cameron 1995). Corporate leaders such as Google's former director of engineering Ray Kurzweil espouse a view of our technological future that is infused with end-times themes such as the much anticipated human-computer convergence called "the Singularity." This much anticipated human-machine merger is essentially a "rapture for nerds" (Lanier 2011, pp. 16–17). In the end(times), we need only hope for a future in which we are "all watched over by machines of loving grace," whose benevolent algorithms will care for us and ritualistically absolve us from sinful intentions (see Turner 2006, pp. 38–39). In this future, technology sits enthroned as Redeemer King and unbelievers are damned to digital purgatory.

Proponents of this religion of technological optimism make up a tribe whose holy city is Silicon Valley and whose churches include, as you might have guessed, the Church of Google and the Church of Facebook. CEOs, "Chief Mindfulness Officers," and software engineers operate as the Zen Masters, Gurus, and priests who make possible high-speed human access to the digital divine or to the limitless flow of information and instantaneous communication worldwide.

When asked in an interview what the perfect search engine would be like, Google co-founder Brin replied, "It would be like the Mind of God" (quoted in Vaidhyanathan 2011b). Though striking, the comment is a logical extension of Silicon Valley's catechism. When technology becomes a faith unto itself, software engineers serve as its high priests. Driven by this same omniscient ethos, Facebook CEO and chairman Mark Zuckerberg—leader of a digital kingdom serving two billion—wants Facebook users to play a similar role to "pastors in churches." He believes Facebook can be used to unite what he sees as a "divided" society, and make users feel like they are "part of something bigger" (Sulleyman 2017).

This Silicon Valley quasi-religious rhetoric is not new. Andrew Carnegie and Henry Ford often framed their vision of business in theological terms (Vaidhyanathan 2011b). What sets the Silicon Valley elites apart is its almost singular emphasis on information as the vehicle for technological and social progress, epitomized by Google's official mission statement, "To organize the world's information and make it universally accessible and useful" (http://www.google.com/about/company/). Employees suggest that this goal gives their work a sense of moral purpose. Reflecting on her experience at the company, Google's Sheryl Sandberg recalls, "I went to Google because Google had a higher mission, which is to make the world's information freely available" (Auletta 2010, p. 86).

Trust in the benefits of information is an essential component of the reigning digital "orthodoxy" among technology enthusiasts (Lanier 2011, p. 22). If the Singularity serves as rapture for nerds, then mottos like those proposed by Google represent a techno-centric version of liberation theology. While Google and Facebook elevate this faith to new heights, their missions represent the culmination of a cultural preoccupation with the "efficiency of information exchange" that dates back at least to the Industrial Revolution (Carr 2010, p. 167).

In short, in its embrace of engineering, Silicon Valley corporate culture recapitulates the idea that intelligence comes from a series of discrete, mechanized steps and processes and can be measured and consistently, or ritualistically, repeated. Yet an unflagging trust in the benefits of information and efficiency tends not to enhance human freedom but to entrench individuals within complex technological, economic, and political systems that treat them merely as a technical means to an end that requires us to remind ourselves constantly, "You are not a gadget" (Lanier 2011).

Core Tenets of Silicon Valley's Moral Catechism

Our description of Silicon Valley's ideology as a catechism is thus fitting. It describes not just strictly held economic principles that aim toward increased revenue streams but also a set of sweeping assumptions about technology and human beings that posit digital technologies as the guarantors of human virtue and catalysts of salvation in a democratic society. What we describe as the "moral catechism of Silicon Valley" may be represented in the following five-point creed, or core tenets and assumptions of faith that misleadingly equate specific technological operations with specific human virtues:

1. *Information is wisdom.* Captured by descriptions like "informationism," tech culture assumes that the proliferation of information online is unquestionably beneficial. As we will show, corporate mission statements and elite pronouncements often harbor an implicit assumption that the accumulation of information is tantamount to the cultivation of wisdom, as if the solution to any problem presented only requires the gathering of more information.

2. *Transparency is authenticity.* The catechism assumes that widespread dissemination of all types of information, including information previously kept private by individuals or organizations, is unquestionably beneficial. The more we expose about ourselves, and the more we learn about others (whether they want us to or not), the more we all become comfortable with being our "true" selves.

3. *Convergence is integrity.* Technical convergence makes previously separate functions available on a single device. Your phone is also a radio, a computer, and a television. The catechism assumes that as technologies converge, the different aspects of our lives will do the same. Digital media allows our roles as consumers, citizens, workers, and family members to converge, making it possible to blend these roles into one coherent identity.

4. *Processing is judgment.* Algorithmic processing is an important element in most digital platforms, from Facebook's News Feed to Google's search results. The catechism assumes that algorithmic processing can function as an efficient substitute for human judgment, for example, in making editorial decisions about content, or in making legal decisions about crimes committed.

5. *Storage is memory.* The catechism assumes that data storage is equivalent to the extension of human memory. With increased storage capacity, individuals no longer have to worry about forgetting the most important events in their lives. Social media platforms like Facebook offer timelines of user behavior and algorithmically driven "memories" that pop up with apparent spontaneity in one's News Feed.

The problem with a catechism like the one above is that, by definition, it is largely unquestioned. It is not meant to be questioned but instead is taken for granted. You will not find these tenets displayed on billboards or painted on the walls of Silicon Valley corporate offices. They operate in the background of our thinking, and we are reminded of them explicitly only when we stray too far from them. The assumptions of digital culture, as embodied in the catechism above, are religious at their core. They answer the basic questions that any religion must about the nature of human beings and the world we live in, about mortality, morality, and meaning. Thus, when we refer to "the dogma of free-market fundamentalism," or to the assumption of market infallibility as a "catechism," such concepts are more than merely metaphorical. They are instead contributions to a "theology of culture" that identifies the "faith" of a culture as idolatrous when centered on that which is not truly of ultimate concern. Such analysis is crucial as the idols of technology and economic self-interest have come to define the culture and moral catechism of Silicon Valley.

In response to such assumptions in the catechism stands an alternate vision that aims to "embrace and champion values and goals such as liberty, creativity, and democracy" (https://www.google.com/about/company/). Since technical protocols, policies, and hardware that support the catechism tend to become locked in over time, making change more difficult, a sense of urgency is justified. As the speed of technical change increases, so does our need for a different kind of critique that recognizes the religious undertones and nuances associated with the catechism, while remaining committed to preserving human freedom and promoting individual and corporate responsibility.

Moreover, as evidenced above, conversations about digital culture often tend to devolve into debates between celebrants and skeptics, each representing the twin vices of naiveté and cynicism. A hopeful critique of Silicon Valley's moral catechism must therefore avoid the celebratory assumption that digital technologies will cure all ills if we simply allow the market to work its magic. On one hand, we cannot naively assume that human flourishing will arise naturally from any established political-economic system. On the other hand, we cannot fall into despair that digital technology is taking us all to hell in a handbasket. There are important tensions between market capitalism and democratic values, and those tensions can be productive. Markets are powerful tools. The question is how to integrate new technologies into our lives in ways that maintain, rather than undermine, the basic values underpinning our social and political commitments.

We believe the kind of approach needed as described above is found in prophetic media critique. Prophetic media critique is based, in large part, on Walter Brueggemann's idea of the "prophetic imagination," which avoids the dual extremes of naive idealism and dystopian fear (Brueggemann 2001, p. 7). Walter Brueggemann served as a North American Old Testament scholar and professor at Columbia Theological Seminary in Decatur, Georgia. For Brueggemann, the prophetic vocation today is to demonstrate *resistance thinking*—that is, thinking that resists the status quo and dominant forces of our technological culture while simultaneously helping others imagine alternative, hope-filled ways of thinking and being. Such critics face an uphill battle, however, since they strike at a global and most "holy" epicenter of cultural and economic trends: California's Silicon Valley.

In Search of a Prophetic and Hopeful Media Critique

Prophetic critique stands in contrast to the priestly propaganda of mainstream media. As a major source of popular mythologies, media function like ecclesiological structures, or religious institutions. The word "myth" comes from *mythos*, which refers to a story that people in a particular community use to understand themselves. Media perform a priestly function in that they confirm and exploit what a community wants to believe about itself. The Latin word *pontifex*, which in Roman culture referred to a high priest or chief of priests, literally translates as a builder of bridges. Media perform rituals and build bridges that connect us to our culture's broader beliefs.

In the pre-digital broadcast era, investigative infotainment shows like *60 minutes* or *20/20* confirmed our culture's belief in the need to unmask villains and protect individuals from evil corporations. Meanwhile, movies like *Rocky* confirmed the belief that rugged individualism and self-determination are the ways to overcome hardships in life. Even today, mainstream news programs, magazines, and advertisements tend to promote the beliefs that newer is better and higher connectivity speeds will guarantee human progress. In such messaging, purchasing the latest release of a service or device is often portrayed as a religious rite of passage into a higher or more evolved state of being. Like real priests, priestly media let us take part in rites and rituals about happiness, success, romance, and other such mythologies.

In this sense, as French sociologist Jacques Ellul explains, priestly media are propaganda: they tell people what they want to believe more than they try to challenge the status quo or change individual beliefs. Commercial media are generally not interested in speaking truth to power or shining light on corrupt and oppressive organizations, except in cases where doing so might benefit their brand or bottom line. Ultimately, they are concerned with economic gain. Popular, priestly media tell stories to maintain old and gain new audiences, or converts, to their messages and products. In the process, they tend to reinforce the existing cultural system's beliefs about its own power and goodness (Ellul 1971).

In contrast, in a prophetic framework, popular media, as culture-forming industries and social institutions, can become sites of struggle, or spaces of action, where individuals demonstrate their resistance toward our culture's techno-centric, dominant consciousness. When we exercise prophetic imagination, we possess an "alternative consciousness" to the dominant consciousness, or techno-centric worldview, of society (Brueggemann 2001, p. 16). This alternative consciousness has two important functions.

First, it serves to critique and dismantle the dominant consciousness of its parent culture. Second, it struggles against the ongoing risk that alternative consciousness will be co-opted or domesticated to serve the interests of the dominant worldview (Brueggemann 2001, pp. 13–14). The primary task of prophetic imagination, then, is to expose the thinking that props up the existing social order, or technological order. In Old Testament terms, Moses was "not engaged in a struggle to transform a regime; rather, his concern was with the consciousness that undergirded and made such a regime possible" (Brueggemann 2001, p. 28).

The shift from a broadcast era to cable news and social media has, paradoxically, created new opportunities for prophetic critique even as it amplifies priestly, tribal rhetoric. Comedian John Oliver's successful HBO program *Last Week Tonight* (an offshoot of Jon Stewart's *The Daily Show*) won multiple awards for its scathing critiques of the tobacco, coal, and tech industries. In many ways Oliver's show is an exemplary form of prophetic critique. Unfortunately, audiences for such shows tend to be fragmented into political or demographic tribes. In some cases, the tribalism of cable news shows crosses a red line, for example, when viewers led successful campaigns to pull advertising from and ultimately cancel Glenn Beck and Bill O'Reilly's shows in the wake of these hosts' controversial comments on immigration, race, or, in O'Reilly's case, accusations of sexual harassment. A few news programs continue to maintain a semblance of bipartisan objectivity, such as *PBS NewsHour*, which regularly hosts conversations between left-leaning analyst Mark Shields and conservative columnist David Brooks. But in maintaining such balance, the show arguably forfeits the prophetic role in favor of the priestly.

The emergence of social media has further complicated matters. Facebook, Google, and the latter-owned YouTube have become indispensable platforms for the distribution of all content—whether film, music, news, or cable programming. As we discuss in later chapters, while these platforms have aided the ascendance of innovative forms of news reporting and analysis, they are also implicated in the most egregious forms of tribal propaganda and state-sponsored disinformation campaigns. In this context, transformation first and foremost requires the recognition of the dominant (techno) consciousness that is Silicon Valley's moral catechism.

In addition to Brueggemann's prophetic imagination, we are also indebted to media scholar Clifford G. Christians's notion of "prophetic witness." By recognizing that each medium has a unique grammar, Christians argues, we can develop a "normative" technology based on principles of openness and conviviality rather than mere technical efficiency (Christians 1989). The goal here is not to reject but to transform our media environment, "enabling a critical consciousness to prosper" (Christians 1997, p. 78). For this reason, Christians's call for prophetic witness refers not to Old Testament capital-P prophets like Jeremiah or Isaiah who predict the future but to small-p prophets from any religious or non-religious framework who speak "a true word, with pathos, with an unquenchable concern for justice" (Christians 1989, p. 137). Everyday prophets in the small-p sense "speak to the oppressiveness of technocratic culture" in order to redirect history toward human empowerment (Christians 1997, p. 77). Through prophetic witness, we are able to reject technical idolatry, that is, the elevation of technology to the status of a sacred object or ultimate source of wisdom, intelligence, and social progress. Instead, we aim to guide the emerging technical environment so that it might encourage, rather than obstruct, the realization of "authentic Being" (Christians 1997, p. 77).

Characteristics of Prophetic Media Critique

Motivated by a concern for equality, human dignity, and social justice, prophetic media critique seeks to expose the "hypocrisy, hubris, and pride" of those in positions of power (Schultze 2003, p. 339). At the same time, it seeks to nurture those voices that question the misguided faith and overt idolatry of mainstream culture. The prophetic voice seeks to "cut through the idolatrous attitudes, intentions, and desires which are driving technology forward" (Christians 1997, p. 78). Such an approach is consistent with the aims of critical scholarship and includes six major characteristics that can be applied to Silicon Valley's moral catechism:

1. *Prophetic critique sees media technologies as value-laden, not morally neutral.* Technical development fundamentally alters the moral landscape in which human beings live. They disrupt existing moral ecologies. This is provocatively illustrated in the film *The Gods Must Be Crazy*, in which local tribespeople discover a Coca-Cola bottle that dropped from an airplane (1980). While dazzled by the creative and practical possibilities of a strong, clear object that fell from the sky, the community experiences violence and jealousy on an unprecedented scale. Thus, while

a new technology may be functionally neutral (i.e., used as an artist's tool or as a weapon), it nevertheless has an ecological bias in that it amplifies latent moral tensions and may even introduce new dilemmas. The presumption that technology is neutral weakens the human capacity for moral discernment and hastens the process through which technologically centered values of necessity and efficiency displace human-centered values of community, empathy, and justice.

2. *Prophetic critique prioritizes the human over the technological.* Prophetic critique prioritizes the preservation of human dignity in the face of increasingly complex technological, political, and economic systems. It insists that the capacity to achieve values such as justice, equality, and truth is not located within technology but always within human beings. As one critic reminds us, "People, not machines, made the Renaissance" (Lanier 2011, p. 46). We must rely ultimately on human conscience, and not the presumed sophistication of markets and technologies, to guide us toward wise judgments. Technology's main effect is to amplify the manifest and latent dynamics within existing human communities (Toyama 2015, p. 29). Without proper attention to the human context of development, new technologies will tend to augment privilege and power where it exists, despite their potential to redress social inequities.

3. *Prophetic critique is embodied.* In emphasizing the human over the technological, prophetic critique engages issues of social identity with regard to race, class, gender, economic status, and other lines of social difference. The prophetic voice is not impersonal or abstract: it has a face and a name, a body and a location. Prophetic critique highlights the limits of a media form's positive potential as well as its negative effects, putting a human face on each. It reminds us that overarching values such as truth and justice cannot be derived from impersonal market forces, complex algorithms, or networked "clouds" but must instead be achieved through the sweat-and-tears struggle of embodied social actors. For this reason, throughout this book we include examples from professionals, students, and activists whose life's work highlights the potential of technology to amplify human virtue.

4. *Prophetic critique seeks to catalyze human virtue, personally and collectively.* The prophetic voice calls out individuals and communities for veering away from their own stated values. It calls for a return to those values or, in many cases, a fuller realization of values partially achieved. With regard to media, prophetic critique examines the ways in which technologies and political-economic systems uphold or fail to uphold the basic values that communities and cultures claim to hold dear. In this sense, the prophetic voice issues a call to be true to ourselves as individuals and communities. It is a call for authenticity and integrity in personal relationships as well as in large-scale systems of communication, and the wisdom, courage, and judgment such a call demands. Importantly, given the rise of "fake news" and state-waged propaganda campaigns, prophetic critique maintains adherence to the virtue of truth and honesty, including a recognition of empirical evidence derived from scientific methods.

5. *Prophetic critique assumes the universality of human virtue.* Prophetic critique calls for a return to concepts that all cultures hold dear: wisdom, judgment, and integrity. Such concepts apply in a range of cases, from individual media use to community networking and even global media policy. Moral life is developmental in character. Fittingly, this book draws from models of psychological and spiritual development that discern these concepts across religious and political boundaries. We are especially indebted to social-psychological research that integrates the spiritual insights of the great wisdom traditions, namely, Robert A. Emmons's (1999) *The Psychology of Ultimate Concerns* and Polly Young-Eisendrath and Melvin Miller's (2000) *The Psychology of Mature Spirituality.* While some postmodern and post-structural philosophers warn that universalist theories can be Westernizing, colonizing, neglectful of diversity, or paternalistic, we see greater risk in the appropriation of psychology by commercial advertising, marketing, and public relations. Commercial organizations have methodically constructed their own universalist models of the human mind in an effort to manipulate users' emotions and behavior. The pragmatic necessity of a pluralistically enlightened universalism—one driven by a concern for human dignity rather than profit—is especially salient in today's digital culture (see Benhabib 2002).

6. *Prophetic critique involves risk.* Finally, while prophetic critique may be a pragmatic necessity, it is one that always involves risk. In part this risk is personal, since speaking prophetically invites not only criticism but sometimes violence. The risk is also ethical and indeed spiritual. In the context of commercial media environments, which thrive on partisan and divisive rhetoric, prophetic critique may easily devolve into mere demagoguery, self-interested assertions, or cynicism. In fact, many of the disinformation campaigns and conspiracy theories that circulate online succeed precisely because they adopt the veneer of prophetic critique. Such campaigns not only exploit our thirst for authentic prophetic critique but also succumb to the vices of deception, usually motivated by fear or greed. Thus, we take a spiritual risk when we speak in, or give credence to, a voice that is prophetic in tone: we may lose sight of truth or succumb to anger. False prophets abound, and especially in the digital world. This is a paradox we must acknowledge if we wish to address the imbalances of digital culture.

The Prophet and the Bodhisattva

We are concerned with avoiding the philosophical and ethical risks that often accompany prophetic media critique. To stay clear of what Martin Luther King Jr. called "internal violence of the spirit," we need a place to channel our critical, prophetic rage at the injustices we discern in the moral landscape (King 1961, p. 46).

Let us admit that when one hears the phrase "prophetic critique," images of doom and gloom come to mind. After all, a prophet's words "are often slashing, designed to shock rather than to edify" (Brueggemann 2001, p. 28). Few of us are in the mood for anything deeply prophetic on a regular basis. The prophets are watchmen and watchwomen. They do not hesitate to draw attention toward our own or our leaders' hypocritical actions and attitudes. They attack idolatry, pride, and complacency. They speak out against those who would "eat my people's flesh," who would make "widows their prey" (Mic. 3:3; Isa. 10:2; see also Amos 8:4–6; Isa. 3:15, 10:1–2, 59:8–9, 14–15; see also Buber 1985).

But in the process of drawing our attention to impending doom, prophets simultaneously hold out a glimmer of hope for redemption and the possibility of a better future. Prophetic critics neither *reject* mainstream media mythologies nor aim merely to *deconstruct* them; rather, they aim to imaginatively "*reconstruct* tribal liturgies of shared understanding and to reassert tribal expressions of hope" that cut across ideological divides and speak to wider audiences (Schultze 2003, p. 204). Using his or her own "prophetic imagination," the prophetic critic casts an alternative framing story (or alternative consciousness) that confronts the dominant consciousness. The prophetic voice aggressively challenges our culture's dominant narrative at the sub-ideological level while groups on the Right and Left push for their own agendas. The prophetic critic imagines a different and presumably better world and considers whether technology is moving us toward or away from it. In some instances, the prophetic critic illuminates the existing roadblocks and helps the community to imagine an alternative vision of social reality that is in tune with its most humane beliefs and sentiments. In other cases, the prophetic critic brings individuals "to a point of despair and thereby frees them to imagine a new alternative" without giving them that alternative just yet (Vest 2006).

To assist in the prophetic imagination of new alternatives, throughout this book we pair a clear rejection of Silicon Valley's catechism with specific practices, policies, and products that may steer the ship in a more sustainable direction. Along these lines, we draw particular inspiration from Charles Strain's (2014) book *The Prophet and the Bodhisattva*. Citing Jesuit priest Daniel Berrigan and Buddhist monk Thich Nhat Hanh as exemplars and visionaries, Strain argues for integrating the prophetic voice of Judeo-Christian theology with the contemplative practices of Buddhism.

Considering the pervasiveness of Buddhist and other East Asian ideas in Silicon Valley culture, theoretical bridge-building with these traditions likewise makes pragmatic and theoretical sense. Indeed, critical strains within both academic scholarship and Buddhism posit enlightenment as a "quest for liberation from ignorance and domination" (Hubbard and Swanson 1997, p. 305). We should strive, in other words, to be both the prophet and the Bodhisattva. We need the wise and vocal (prophetic) critic who is visible and socially engaged—and enraged—and who points us toward redemption, and the quiet practitioner who cultivates equanimity through the solitude of prayer and meditation (Strain 2014, pp. 82–83). We need the prophetic voice who is angered by injustice and says, "No, there is a better way!" and the Bodhisattva whose quiet practice generates a compassionate vision of possibility to which we say, "Yes, and here is the path to a better way!"

This balance is difficult to imagine, never mind achieve. The Bodhisattva without the prophet risks complacency with systemic injustice. Many of the same Silicon

Valley companies espousing the benefits of contemplation or mindfulness of the kind associated with the Bodhisattva tradition are producing platforms and engaging in business practices that entrench ideologies of oppression. At the same time, as some media criticism demonstrates, when not tempered by mindful practice the prophetic voice risks devolving into cynicism, resignation, and despair, perhaps even hatred. Much critical scholarship tends to focus on institutional and policy reform, while neglecting these subjective dimensions of political-economic reality. Institutional reform cannot hope to address human suffering in the long term if social actors are motivated primarily by the "three poisons" of greed, aggression, and delusion (Loy 2013, pp. 404, 417). By offering a science and theory of ideology with politically liberating potential, Buddhist concepts have much to offer critical scholarship.

For these reasons, Buddhism's concern for personal transformation and the Judeo-Christian concern for social justice "need each other" if we are to address both individual and structural sources of suffering (Loy 2013, p. 401). For this reason, in the main chapters of the book we pair each of our five proverbs outlined above with a corollary, or a positive statement that is illuminated through prophetic critique. For example, while we skeptically reject the Silicon Valley proverb that information is equivalent to wisdom as stated in our proverb "information is not wisdom," we nevertheless celebrate the possibility that information *can* serve as a key component of this important virtue. What we seek, in other words, is the positive corollary stated as follows: information *in service of* wisdom, or inform wisely. Through this both/and approach, we can yet promote an "alternative consciousness" in which our technologies truly enhance rather than undermine the quality of civic leadership and engagement.

In response to Silicon Valley's moral catechism, the following digital proverbs and their corollaries allow for an alternative technological consciousness premised on flesh-and-blood human beings as the central concern of political and social life.

1. *Information is not wisdom; inform wisely.* Wisdom involves the ability to understand the significance of what we see, hear, or otherwise perceive. The mere presence of bits and bytes of information does not necessarily entail understanding. It may hinder the cultivation of wisdom if our capacity to discern its meaning does not keep pace with the increasing rate of its proliferation. Wisdom, as the ability to understand the significance of information in its appropriate historical, economic, political, and cultural contexts, requires a number of other virtues, including judgment and prudence. We must exercise such virtues to ensure that information systems develop in service of wisdom, not at its expense.

2. *Transparency is not authenticity; strive for authentic transparency.* Authenticity is not merely the outward revelation of one's thoughts or feelings. It is dependent on other virtues like prudence and forbearance. Sometimes transparency catalyzes authenticity, but sometimes it may undermine it. A judicious measure of privacy, even secrecy, is necessary for the authentic development of persons, organizations, and nations. There is no simple formula (or algorithm) for an authentic

life or authentic democracy. Human judgment is part of the process. Journalists, for example, must exercise judgment when data are hacked and released by WikiLeaks. The ability to access and expose information can be wielded like weapon. As part of a disingenuous propaganda strategy, weaponized information can undermine authentic communication. We must exercise prudent judgment to ensure that responsible data transparency will serve the goal of authentic human flourishing.

3. *Convergence is not integrity; integrate divergent elements.* The assumption that convergent devices like smartphones make it easier to balance our different social roles may serve the interests of commercial producers. But such devices often make it more difficult to balance our responsibilities as parents, employees, and citizens. The convergence of smaller, discrete sets of data into vast, aggregated Big Data sets often leads to privacy violations and discrimination. Where convergence does promote an experience of integrity, it is often a bounded one that serves as a measure of socio-economic privilege. To assume that convergence necessarily entails greater integrity for all cedes power to those who make important design, content, and policy decisions. Personal and collective integrity are matters of negotiation where there is no simple technological solution. We will leverage the concept of "contextual integrity" to show how wisdom and prudent judgment can guide technical and data convergence in ways that respect individual privacy and promote political-economic justice.

4. *Processing is not judgment; process judiciously.* The algorithms with which we live are programmed by software engineers whose primary concerns reflect the motivations of commercial organizations. Software engineers and CEOs serve as special types of moral gatekeepers in the digital economy. Even setting aside commercial interests, algorithmic processing is always a process of encoding specific values and judgments in anticipation of hypothetical situations. It represents a kind of pre-judgment. Though not without benefit, it cannot replace the contextual exercise of human judgment, which is always social, relational, and embodied. Processing may enhance human judgment, provided that our technical systems are adequately transparent to public scrutiny through genuine processes of democratic debate.

5. *Storage is not memory; remember the virtue of forgetting.* Memory is much more than a matter of data storage. It is a process, and a relational one at that. Memories develop over time and can change each time they are recalled. The process of forming and calling upon memories involves a number of related virtues: judgment, wisdom, even courage. The types of data storage that computers provide are not without benefit. But storage, by itself, is not the same as memory. What should be stored? By whom? Who should have access? When? Under what conditions? For how long? These types of questions are political in the sense that they involve negotiations between individuals and groups (indeed, nations) with different goals and interests. Here again, data storage may serve the interests of personal and collective memory provided we address the aforementioned questions wisely.

Structure and Organization of the Book

The exposition of these five proverbs highlights inequities of power and class privilege obscured by techno-utopian rhetoric. Part One includes two chapters that describe the current state of these inequities and their historical origins. Chapter 1 describes the crisis in digital media, explaining how the underlying ideology of digital culture manifests in today's pressing issues like privacy violations, political fragmentation, and technology addiction. This crisis is not always easy to recognize because it is partly a crisis of complacency and capitulation to the commercial status quo. Chapter 2 examines the historical roots of this crisis, especially the history of American religion and mass media, and demonstrates how the current crisis shares a familiar past with other technological innovations over the past 100 years.

Part Two (Chapters 3–7) is the core of the book, and here we articulate each of the five proverbs and their corollaries presented above. Each chapter accomplishes three main tasks. First, we demonstrate that social marketing campaigns, public pronouncements, and/or popular reception of digital technologies and the news they deliver reflect adherence to one or more of the five tenets of Silicon Valley's catechism, whether explicitly or implicitly. Second, we develop a normative understanding of the virtues in each proverb, drawing from literature in moral-developmental theory, wisdom studies, memory studies, contemplative studies, and religious ethics. Third, we offer one or two specific personal practices that can help individuals in sustaining their spirit and cultivating their moral imagination. Contemplative practices like meditation, prayer, and even arts-based pedagogy help to nurture the self. In the context of information overload and constant connectivity, such practices, often developed in solitude, allow us to remember who we are and to imagine another world beyond one poisoned by greed and delusion. This aspect of engagement is not so much about articulating and following rules or laws. For the practitioner, the process and the practice of virtue are themselves the point. One practitioner calls this "being peace" (see Strain 2014, p. 91). The levelheadedness we cultivate through such practices provides us with the intellectual space, and spiritual resilience, to critique the world around us and to articulate strategies for moving forward, without falling into the twin traps of rage and despair.

Part Three articulates an overarching strategy for steering the ship in a more workable direction with long-term solutions. Even if we accept that digital media forms an integral part of human flourishing, some technologies' designs and regulatory frameworks may do better than others in building "an ethically responsive and economically sustainable architecture of human flourishing" (Healey 2015, p. 208). Along with personal practice, therefore, the cultivation of moral imagination involves social engagement to transform one's technical environment. To this end, we explore exemplary policies, products, and solutions for developing normative technologies that are consistent with collectively shared values. We examine specific corrective strategies that address the structural and ideological biases of current platform architectures, algorithms, user policies, advertising models, and regulatory frameworks.

In this way, we can envision technical environments that enhance, rather than under-mine, the achievement of human flourishing.

Finally, as explained in the Conclusion, we propose a framework for applying Martin Luther King Jr.'s philosophy of non-violence to the ethical development of technological products and policies. King offers six specific principles for caring for oneself and others in a spirit of love and compassion. By concluding with these broad, time-tested principles, we hope to inspire researchers and professionals to steer the ship toward an era of digital humanism—one that that embraces technological possibility while insisting that its pursuit requires the foregrounding of human virtues that cannot be outsourced even to the most speedy and elaborate networks and processors.

Conclusion

Jevin West and Carl T. Bergstrom's University of Washington course, "Calling Bullshit: Data Reasoning in a Digital World," continues to be standing room only each semester it is offered. We remain envious. We also remain committed to our shared belief in calling out Silicon Valley's misleading communication practices and to promoting an alternative technological vision premised on the embodied human being as the central concern of political and social life, rather than the abstraction of our data-driven online identities.

In sum, this book is especially timely given the current critical juncture in media history. Recent demographic shifts and the emergence of new media technologies have generated new possibilities for public engagement in the public sphere. Younger generations are weary of hypocrisy and partisanship and readily embrace social net-working technologies that challenge established media and social institutions. The current juncture, therefore, has implications for the future role of civic engagement in public life. It is not only an opportunity to move beyond mere partisan tribalism, it is also an opportunity for philosophical critiques of communication and media to find a place in the public sphere. Time is of the essence: as happened during the birth of radio broadcasting, ongoing technological and policy decisions will likely set the course of political discourse for decades to come. A critique of the kind proposed in this book can preserve and revitalize the overarching values of democratic citizen-ship, corporate responsibility, and social justice as we continue to progress through the digital age.

References

Auletta, Ken. *Googled: The End of the World as We Know It.* New York: Penguin Books, 2010.

Barbrook, Richard, and Andy Cameron. "The Californian Ideology." Alamut. September 18, 1995. http://www.hrc.wmin.ac.uk/hrc/theory/californianideo/main/t.4.2.html.

Benhabib, Seyla. *The Claims of Culture: Equality and Diversity in the Global Era.* Princeton, NJ: Princeton University Press, 2002.

Bergstrom Carl T., and Jevin West. "Calling Bullshit: Data Reasoning in a Digital World." Course Syllabus, University of Washington. Fall 2017. http://callingbullshit.org/syllabus.html.

Bernard, April, and Adonis Diaz Fernandez. "Yoruba Proverbs as Cultural Metaphor for Understanding Management in the Caribbean." *International Journal of Cross Cultural Management* 12, no. 3 (2012): 329–38.

Biktimirov, Ernest N., and Jingtao Feng. "Different Locks Must Be Opened with Different Keys: Using Chinese Proverbs for Teaching Finance to Chinese-Speaking Students." *Journal of Teaching in International Business* 17, no. 3 (2006): 83–102.

Brueggemann, Walter. *The Prophetic Imagination*. 2nd ed. Minneapolis, MN: Fortress Press, 2001.

Buber, Martin. *The Prophetic Faith*. New York: Collier Books, 1985.

Carr, Nicholas. *The Shallows: What the Internet Is Doing to Our Brains*. New York: W.W. Norton, 2010.

Christians, Clifford G. "Technology and Triadic Theories of Mediation." In *Rethinking Media, Religion and Culture*, edited by Stewart M. Hoover, 65–84. Thousand Oaks, CA: Sage, 1997.

———. "A Theory of Normative Technology." In *Technological Transformation: Contextual and Conceptual Implications*, edited by Edmund F. Byrne and Joseph C. Pitts, 123–40. Boston, MA: Kluwer Academic, 1989.

Ellul, Jacques. *Propaganda: The Formation of Men's Attitudes*. New York: Knopf, 1971.

Emmons, Robert A. *The Psychology of Ultimate Concerns: Motivation and Spirituality in Ultimate Concerns*. New York: Guilford Press, 1999.

The Gods Must Be Crazy. Directed by Jamie Uys. C.A.T. Films. South Africa: New Realm, 1980.

Google. "About." https://www.google.com/about/company/.

Healey, Kevin. "Disrupting Wisdom 2.0: The Quest for 'Mindfulness' in Silicon Valley and Beyond." *Journal of Religion, Media and Digital Culture* 4, no. 1 (May 14, 2015): 67–95.

Hubbard, Jamie, and Paul Loren Swanson, eds. *Pruning the Bodhi Tree: The Storm over Critical Buddhism*. Honolulu: University of Hawaii Press, 1997.

King, Martin Luther, Jr. "Love, Law, and Civil Disobedience." In *A Testament of Hope: The Essential Writings of Martin Luther King, Jr.*, edited by James M. Washington, 43–53. San Francisco: Harper & Row, 1986.

Lanier, Jaron. *You Are Not a Gadget: A Manifesto*. New York: Vintage Books, 2011.

Loy, David R. "Why Buddhism and the West Need Each Other: On the Interdependence of Personal and Social Transformation." *Journal of Buddhist Ethics* 20 (2013): 401–21.

Schultze, Quentin J. *Habits of the High Tech Heart: Living Virtuously in the Information Age*. Grand Rapids, MI: Baker Books, 2002.

———. *Christianity and the Mass Media in America: Toward a Democratic Accommodation*. East Lansing, MI: Michigan State University Press, 2003.

Simpson, John. *The Concise Oxford Dictionary of Proverbs*. 2nd ed. New York: Oxford University Press, 1992.

Strain, Charles R. *The Prophet and the Bodhisattva: Daniel Berrigan, Thich Nhat Hanh, and the Ethics of Peace and Justice*. Eugene, OR: Wipf and Stock, 2014.

Sulleyman, Aatif. "Mark Zuckerberg Wants Facebook Users to Be Like Church Pastors." *The Independent*. June 27, 2017. https://www.independent.co.uk/life-style/gadgets-and-tech/news/facebook-mark-zuckerberg-social-network-users-church-pastors-morality-responsibility-divided-society-a7810296.html.

Townsend, Tess. "These University of Washington Professors Are Teaching a Course on Bullshit." *Vox*, Recode. February 19, 2017. https://www.recode.net/2017/2/19/14660236/big-data-bullshit-college-course-university-washington.

Toyama, Kentaro. *Geek Heresy: Rescuing Social Change from the Cult of Technology*. New York: PublicAffairs, 2015.

Turner, Fred. *From Counterculture to Cyberculture: Stewart Brand, the Whole Earth Network, and the Rise of Digital Utopianism*. Chicago: University of Chicago Press, 2006.

Vaidhyanathan, Siva. *The Googlization of Everything (And Why We Should Worry)*. Berkeley, CA: University of California Press, 2011a.

———. "Berkman Center: Siva Vaidhyanathan on the Googlization of Everything." *Berkman Klein Center*. March 7, 2011b. https://cyber.harvard.edu/events/2011/02/vaidhyanathan.

Vest, John. "The Prophetic Pathos of *Crash*." The Martin Marty Center for the Public Understanding of Religion. March 23, 2006. https://divinity.uchicago.edu/sightings/prophetic-pathos-crash-john-w-vest.

Weintraub, Karen. "How Technology in Our Bodies Will Make Us 'More Than Human'." *National Geographic*, November 7, 2015. https://news.nationalgeographic.com/2015/11/151107-cyborg-human-brain-enhancement-technology-science.

Young-Eisendrath, Polly, and Melvin Miller, eds. *The Psychology of Mature Spirituality: Integrity, Wisdom, Transcendence*. London: Routledge, 2000.

PART I

1

THE CURRENT CRISIS IN DIGITAL MEDIA

In October 2012, stuntman Felix Baumgartner jumped from a 24-mile-high space capsule, becoming the first human in free fall to break the sound barrier. His jump broke previous records set by retired Air Force Colonel Joe Kittinger, who provided guidance to Baumgartner during the mission. Like Kittinger before him, the daredevil faced an early crisis as he began to enter, but quickly recovered from a dreaded tailspin. "At a certain R.P.M.," he explained, "there's only one way for blood to leave your body, and that's through your eyeballs. That means you're dead." While the jump was "harder than I expected," Fearless Felix landed safely in New Mexico four minutes and twenty seconds later (Tierney 2012b).

The mission, dubbed "Red Bull Stratos," was financed by the popular drink company and marked the culmination of a marketing relationship that began in 1988 (Badenhausen 2012). It involved the assistance of 300 technical and medical experts, including former NASA employees. A project five years in the making, scientists observing Stratos collected data for the benefit of pilots and astronauts. Meanwhile, in line with its other co-branded initiatives like Infiniti Red Bull Racing, the namesake company commodified Stratos by offering merchandise like T-shirts, hats, and backpacks. The mission yielded "tens of millions of dollars in global exposure" for the brand in what was "perhaps the greatest marketing stunt of all time" (Heitner 2012). *Forbes* magazine notes that "another winner came out of Sunday's jump besides Red Bull: the Internet"—more specifically YouTube, which broke its own record for concurrent live video streams as eight million viewers tuned in (Badenhausen 2012).

On Tailspins and Technical Leaps of Faith

Stratos symbolizes a broader trend, traceable to the late 1980s and early 1990s, in which the twin themes of commercialism and technical bravado combine. Then-President Bill Clinton and Vice President Al Gore along with conservative

Republicans hitched their ideological wagon to the techno-libertarian dream of Silicon Valley. Their enchantment with cyberspace integrated the spirit of American exceptionalism, faith in free markets, and a view of computer networks as nature's next evolutionary leap. The surprising resonance between progressive and conservative ideologies culminated in the mid-1990s passage of the Telecommunications Act of 1996, which represents the joint effort of technology elites like Swiss-born American philanthropist Esther Dyson and conservatives like Newt Gingrich (McChesney 2013, p. 105). In fact, Gingrich described the policy as part of a divinely inspired "mission" (Turner 2006, p. 231).

This celebratory entrance of technical and political elites into the so-called New Economy constituted a leap of faith not unlike the breathtaking feat of Fearless Felix. While Colonel Kittinger praised Baumgartner for his courage, we might ask whether the combination of *technophilia*, or a strong enthusiasm for technology, and commercialism tends more toward an ethos of recklessness—one cultivated not simply through technical expertise but also by an apparatus of psychological and ideological coercion. Indeed, Baumgartner suffered panic attacks while training in his claustrophobic space suit, at one point fleeing the country by plane to avoid an endurance test. Psychologists worked with him to mitigate fears that appear to have been well-founded, considering his near-death tailspin (Tierney 2012a).

Rather than encouraging competition and market diversity, Silicon Valley's techno-centric ideology has triggered an economic tailspin of industry consolidation and a rapid decline of public interest values. This development has important implications since specific protocols, applications, and platforms tend to become "locked in" for generations along with any unforeseen consequences. In the digital era, the process of technological lock-in resembles Baumgartner's tailspin both in terms of the difficulty of restoring balance and of the danger posed by the potential loss of lifeblood. Giving in to techno-utopian ideology regularly leads to a willingness to jump recklessly into new technical environments, but the consequences of such imprudence are not uniformly distributed. In our culture of digital monopolies, users become locked into a limited range of commercial providers who, in turn, generate profit by extracting user data—the lifeblood of the digital economy—and packaging it for sale to marketers, government agencies, and banks. Such techniques entrench social stereotypes and exacerbate class inequality even as profits boom.

In recent years, critics have implicated digital technologies in a range of problems from psychological distraction to global financial crises. Several critics refer to an emerging "anti-net backlash." These critics identify problems and suggest solutions at different levels from modifying our personal habits to implementing technical and legal remedies. A common thread in all these critiques is that digital culture is driven by an overarching ideology, described in our book's introductory chapter as "the California Ideology" (Barbrook and Cameron 1998). As we demonstrate in this chapter, this ideology along with its "moral catechism" has significant psychological, moral, and spiritual dimensions. We begin with the epistemological dimensions of this ideology, that is, how Silicon Valley thinks about concepts like knowledge, progress, and expertise. We then move to consider its psychological, moral, and spiritual dimensions before concluding with reflections on how the virtue of prudence can redirect our focus away from solely instrumental or technical skills to non-instrumental values such as moderation, discernment, and humility that help confront the crisis.

The Crisis Is Ideological

The guiding principle of techno-utopianism (supported by a never-ending stream of "proof of progress" data) is that everything always has, always does, and always will continue to get better and better, forever and ever, amen. This "mythos of the digital sublime" depends on an inability to recognize the reality of limitations on anything: growth, potential, money, or natural resources (Schultze 2002, p. 116). Within this techno-religious worldview, if for some inexplicable reason our way of life is derailed, or evidence of our vulnerability is brought to our attention, it is only a temporary setback, just another problem to be overcome through the modern miracle of technological advancement. To be sure, not everyone accepts or adheres to this philosophy; people abstain and resist. What we are identifying here is a relative center of gravity, a defining ethos that makes resistance and abstinence meaningful and necessary in the first place.

Public confidence in a techno-centric way of life is based, in part, on the belief that technology can deliver on its promises by always satisfying our hungers, whatever their type or size, in the most convenient and efficient ways (Pacey 1983). Proof of progress is no farther away than the rote retelling of the most recent technological hurdles scaled: from the first manufactured automobile, to the first talking motion picture, to the first computer small enough to fit on our lap. When computer-processing speed doubles every 18 months, we marvel at our culture's ability to make our lives more efficient. Silicon Valley's "symbol brokers" rely on proof of progress in language like "fastest," "easiest," and "most efficient" to stir consumer frenzy and reinforce our belief in our system's superiority (Schultze 2002, p. 116). As the system rewards our extravagant demands with immediate supply, our identification with its power to deliver us from boredom and anonymity is strengthened (Boorstin 1992, pp. 3–6). "Get it now" and "Why wait?" are common mantras that reinforce our obsession with efficiency and immediacy, often measured in the seconds required to deliver the satisfaction. Immediate gratification is so foundational that it is often portrayed as something we are entitled to as citizens.

In most cases, however, proof-of-progress data are flawed. They are self-confirming, focusing on the wonder of human achievement while failing to show that progress in one area may be accompanied by less positive developments in another. Progress is taken out of context to support personal or corporate agendas (Pacey 1983, p. 14). For example, increases in openness and connectivity worldwide are used to demonstrate the power of Facebook's mission ("to give people the power to build community and bring the world closer together"), but such increases also come with corresponding reductions in privacy and security. For every technological benefit supporting proof of progress, there may be a technological burden that gets buried in in the sea of high fives and virtual victory laps.

Undoubtedly, technological advancement fosters improvements in our quality of life, including greater comfort, luxury, convenience, and choice, all of which function as proof of progress and efficiency. But instead of seeing technological advancement and conspicuous digital consumption as "superficial indulgences" that contribute to major changes in social structures, personal identity, and bankruptcy, Silicon Valley enthusiasts promote them as a "strangely democratic and unifying force." In this light, a technological purchase is not simply "one-dimensional or shallow," narcissistic, or fragmenting. Besides, if what we want is peace on earth, then "a unifying system" that transcends religious, cultural, and caste differences" is what we need (Cohen 2002; see also Twitchell 2003). And, thankfully, this is the system, at least "on paper," that Silicon Valley promises.

In addition to a belief in progress, Silicon Valley's reigning ideology elevates expert knowledge over other ways of knowing. Hardware and software programmers, network administrators, and the like enjoy greater material wealth and elevated social status in the system. At places like Google and Facebook, "merit" means one's ability to create good software. Within this culture of expertise, a clear knowledge gap exists between technological, specialized forms of knowing, on the one hand, and more general and moral perspectives that rely on wisdom, on the other. Information managers "specialize" by relying on ostensibly detached, presumably objective, quantitative ways of knowing. Their job is to effectively manage and transmit information in bits and bytes, not to be responsible for using the information they transmit for good. The focus is on making something new, asking "What's next?" without pausing to consider the effects of "What is?"

We are reminded of Jeff Goldblum's character, Dr. Malcolm, in Steven Spielberg's now classic film *Jurassic Park* (1993) when he remarks, "The lack of humility before nature that's being displayed here staggers me." Granted, he was talking about cloning dinosaurs at the time, but the same kind of logic explains this knowledge gap and Silicon Valley's technological hubris. Dr. Malcolm continues: "Your scientists were so preoccupied with whether or not they could, that they didn't stop to think if they should." In other words, when the ethical "ought" (i.e., should we be doing this, or is this the right thing to do?) is subjugated to the ethical "is" (i.e., is it scientifically possible to do this, or is it technically possible to do this?), the ethic of efficiency and progress rules the day and trumps all other ethical standards. The clear consequence of a society "lacking any clear 'oughts' is a religion of quick decisions and instant deletes" (Schultze 2002, p. 28). These kinds of instrumental values act tyrannically as "a spiritual guillotine, decapitating other values" that have cultural and transcendent staying power (Shriver 1972, p. 537). A society committed to instrumental values "eliminates all moral obstructions to their ascendency" (Christians et al. 1993, p. 171).

More importantly, perhaps, beliefs in progress, experts, and unlimited resource often mask, or obscure, the politics of science and technology. To the extent that scientific and technical development reflects the views and prerogatives of experts and elites, our technical environment will augment the power and privilege of some at the expense of others. Digital behemoths like Google and Apple have only recently begun to acknowledge the real-world implications of Silicon Valley's lack of racial, gender, and age diversity, not to mention the broader socio-economic disparities that their business models can exacerbate. In this context, the "myth of inevitability" around information technologies "performs an important role in their institutionalization, and in the broader effort to shape the future toward certain ends" (Gates 2011, p. 6). This myth assumes that the course of technological development is pre-ordained, set in stone, or otherwise unchangeable, as a form of techno-divine Providence.

Often, the rhetoric of inevitability is used by designers, inventors, or other proponents of a new technology. But it might also be found in pessimistic detractors. In either case, the assumption that the course of technological development is unchangeable and predictable carries the implication that since there is nothing we can do about it, there is no need (or, it is a waste of valuable time) to try to stop a new technology from developing or even to try to ensure that it is designed, developed, and deployed ethically and sustainably. One example of the clear course of inevitability relates to the implementation of body cameras for law enforcement officers. When policy makers or tech leaders describe the widespread availability, use, or implementation of a technology as a foregone conclusion, as simply a matter of time, or as something inescapable (usually for the better), this feeds into the myth of inevitability (Gates 2011, p. 6). However, while certain aspects of technical development may be inevitable, other important aspects are not. The future is not inevitable but contingent and contestable. A global information network of some kind may have been inevitable, but the World Wide Web was not. Social networking technologies may have been inevitable, but Facebook certainly was not.

These are subtle but hugely important distinctions. Especially on the part of civil authorities, the assumption of inevitability "encourages public acquiescence, while suppressing alternative, less technocratic ways to address complex social problems" (Gates 2011, p. 6). As such, assumptions that impact the design, implementation, regulation, and use of technology can be seen as "a form of social control" (Gates 2011, p. 6). Without proper attention to the human context of development and implementation (the politics of science and tech), emergent technologies may ultimately augment privilege for the few and power for the technocratic state.

Google is arguably the most successful organization to build a commercial enterprise based on these assumptions about the value of information and expertise. As noted in the Introduction, its mission is "to organize the world's information and make it universally accessible and useful." As a product, for instance, Google Glass was not successful. But it has near-monopoly control of the search-engine market and has leveraged that success to branch into other development areas like artificial intelligence, geospatial mapping, self-driving cars, smartphones, and more. As critics point out, though, Google's mission assumes a lot: first, that it is possible to collect and organize all of the world's information; second, that it is beneficial to do so; third, that commercial organizations can and should do so with all due haste.

As we discuss later in the book (Chapter 6), Google further posits that algorithms can and should process such information in order to render it meaningful and useful. More problematically, Google also claims that the efficiency and accuracy of these algorithmic processes places it above moral reproach. It is, according to its corporate proponents, built to be good (Vaidhyanathan 2011, pp. 44–50).

At issue here is the assumption that data and algorithmic processing are objective in the sense of being morally neutral and free from the emotional baggage of human experience. We do not deny the importance of the norm of objectivity *per se*. It is useful within certain narrow parameters. Before we leave the house, we want to know whether it is raining or not. We expect the weather report to be accurate and objective: it is either raining or it is not. We want an objective report on the final score of an important game. But objectivity as a normative value has come to enjoy a much wider range of applicability than it should.

This is clear in the early history of professional journalism, where the norm of objectivity emerged to buttress the power of commercial newspapers during the industry's crisis of credibility. If papers simply report the facts, so the story went, it does not matter if there are twenty papers in a city or a single company with monopoly control of the market. Over time, however, the problems associated with so-called objective "he said, she said" reporting have become clear. They tend to serve the agenda-setting interests of powerful elites, usually politicians and business owners. If the misapplication, or over-application, of objectivity in news reporting tends to benefit commercial news organizations, so too does it benefit established social, political, and economic institutions in the realms of scientific research and data processing. The increasingly blurry line between science and commerce makes this problem all the more pressing, as evidenced in the controversial user experiments jointly conducted by university researchers and commercial organizations like Facebook and the dating website OkCupid (see Chapter 4).

It is worth noting that the ideology of data and expertise reaches a crisis point just as its counter-extreme gains ascendency in public discourse: namely, a tendency among politicians and voters to abandon the very notion of objective, empirical truth altogether in favor of various cults of personality in which might makes right. These may be two sides of the same coin. Technologies are "neither good nor bad, nor neutral," as one historian famously put it (Kranzberg 1986, p. 545). Instead, they are "thoroughly cultural forms" that reflect the "ideological conflicts of the societies that produce them" (Gates 2011, p. 4). What we are arguing for here is "strong" objectivity, defined as "actively acknowledging and accounting for one's biases, values, and attitudes" (Leavy 2017, p. 38). There are some things about which we should not be neutral or objective. We should be outraged at injustice and infuse our work with the concern for justice. But we should do so ethically and with integrity.

The Crisis Is Psychological

In his 2017 essay "Building Global Community," Facebook founder and CEO Mark Zuckerberg emphasized his company's long-standing social mission, positioning himself as an authority on the "personal, emotional, and spiritual needs" we all share (Zuckerberg 2017). Facebook, he wrote, is well-positioned to cultivate social structures necessary for the moral validation, personal development, and sense of purpose that are prerequisites of a "healthy society" (Zuckerberg 2017). As executives like Zuckerberg capture and process information about users' behavior and feelings, they assume a powerful gatekeeping role. Even with noble intent, gatekeeping can undermine users' well-being if conducted on the basis of misguided understandings of human psychology.

As discussed in Chapters 4 and 5 of this book, Facebook's platform architectures and user policies encode specific ideas about authenticity and integrity. These ideas are ones that Mark Zuckerberg has articulated over the years in interviews and in his own Facebook posts. But his pronouncements about these core concepts contradict positions held by contemporary psychoanalytic theorists. Zuckerberg, who has no qualifications as a psychologist or psychiatrist, willingly conducts "psychoanalysis outside the clinic" (Frosh 2010). In doing so he stands on fragile ethical ground. Facebook's policy decisions are rooted in a naive understanding of human psychology that assumes the beneficence of commercial markets and defines psychological well-being in ways that are consistent with the company's commercial interests. Further, the company's public statements demonstrate a strategy of disavowal that absolves it from responsibility when its appropriation of psychoanalytic concepts goes awry. Contrary to Zuckerberg's stated goals, Facebook's discursive performance of psychoanalysis outside the clinic likely undermines users' cultivation of authenticity and integrity while unwittingly exacerbating preexisting socio-economic inequalities.

Of course, the conduct of psychoanalysis "outside the clinic" is not unique to Facebook. Companies like OkCupid and Uber similarly defend psychological experiments by appealing to the goals of enhanced user-control or increased product efficiency (Scheiber 2017). The problem is not necessarily that such extra-clinical experiments directly cause psychological harm to users. Most users engage such platforms responsibly, and other research shows that many users leverage Facebook's tools to engage in self-soothing behavior with therapeutic effect (although research does suggest that certain platforms may exacerbate issues among individuals prone to depression or narcissism) (Ancient et al. 2013). Questions about the well-being of users are important, of course. But they tend to sideline more complicated questions about how commercial platforms might amplify the latent narcissism, fantasies of grandiosity, and contemptuous sense of privilege pervasive among Silicon Valley elites.

Power often operates unconsciously. As one observer remarks, "Whenever we believe we know something," we tend to become "tripped up uncomfortably by our wish to know it. This wish always has unconscious components" (Frosh 2010, p. 6). There are important social-psychological implications to the pervasive cultural belief in progress and expertise. Silicon Valley elites not only harbor a belief in the possibility of total, perfect knowledge of the world; they fancy themselves as uniquely capable of achieving that goal through technical expertise. On the contrary, psychosocial theory argues that "nothing can be known reliably, given that the unconscious disrupts everything" (Frosh 2010, p. 9). In this sense, tech executives' public statements (like Zuckerberg's above) represent "the discourse of the Master," that is, the claim of expertise, of omniscience, and "the hope of mastery" (Frosh 2010, pp. 9–11). Such hope, however sincere, is dangerous if unchecked.

Facebook's self-positioning as engineer-analyst vis-à-vis the user-patient is another instance of the historical appropriation of psychoanalysis by governmental and corporate bureaucracies.

Given the history of psychoanalysis' "collusion with oppressive regimes" (Frosh 2010, p. 157), psychoanalytic concepts are always at risk of becoming "part of the state apparatus" (Frosh 2010, p. 191). Zuckerberg's vision reflects a normative vision of autonomous individuals interacting within the political-economic context of affluent liberal societies. This vision is underscored by Zuckerberg's depiction of himself as the prototypical Facebook user (Hoffmann et al. 2016, p. 10). Insofar as Facebook's site architecture reflects that presumptuous vision, its ongoing development amounts to a process of "coding the privileged self" (Healey and Potter 2017).

To the extent that scholars wish to understand the psychological implications of digital media, it is imperative to resuscitate psychoanalytic theory's critical function of "radical social critique" before it becomes "accommodated into technologies of social control" (Frosh 2010, pp. 12–13). Critical scholarship must examine how such systems impinge on subject formation through "the economy of the psyche" (Butler 2005, p. vii). The question is not how to exclude psychological research from development, but how to engineer digital platforms that deploy psychoanalytic theory "creatively and yet with integrity," in a way that recognizes the potential consequences and aims toward emancipatory ends (Frosh 2010, p. 192). Engaging that question seriously may yield digital media platforms that afford greater agency among users and greater integrity for the political-economic systems in which we live.

The Crisis Is Moral

Armed with their catechism, Silicon Valley leaders argue that government regulation is largely unnecessary and opposition from outsiders is often misguided because, as Zuckerberg reminds critics, "We have a different worldview than some of the folks who are covering this" (Perrigo 2018). At a conference in 2009, Google's executive chairman Eric Schmidt was asked whether lawmakers should introduce new regulations in light of the company's increasing market power. A similar question was asked of Zuckerberg nearly a decade later as he appeared before congress to answer questions about Facebook's role in Russia's interference in the 2016 presidential election. Both leaders responded in essentially the same way. Yes, regulation was important, and they welcomed so-called partnerships with government since they are not able to address all the complicated issues they face by themselves.

However, both leaders argued that Google's and Facebook's guiding mission statements and values, respectively, amounted to a form of *self*-regulation. Their products, in other words, were designed to be good and will therefore always yield beneficial results because their product design is nearly flawless. For centuries, some theologians made similar arguments about the nature of God to help explain the problem of evil in the world: because God by his nature is good, no evil can flow from him, and whatever he wills is inherently good. Evil is thus a result of outside forces (see Wright 2013; Meister and Dew 2017).

But to reduce moral goodness to a matter of engineering precision, as these tech leaders do, is an argument against politics. It relieves powerful organizations of any social responsibility by suggesting that technological development is inevitable and inherently progressive. It is a perspective that locates the capacity for ethical behavior not in human judgment but in the emergent intelligence of abstract technological systems. Company mottos like Google's "Don't be evil," then, point to a troublesome view of ethics that undermines the company's brand image of childlike playfulness and beneficence. And in a new take on the Tower of Babel plot in the Book of Genesis, Facebook's mission promises to give users the "power" to elevate human potential by sharing *themselves* globally and instantaneously, thus "making the world more open and connected" (Zuckerberg 2017). Quoting Christian theologian Reinhold Niebuhr, one observer notes that "the pretensions of virtue are as offensive to God as the pretensions of power" (Vaidhyanathan 2011, p. 77). As such, Silicon Valley's most egregious "sin" may very well be that of hubris or pride—one of the seven capital sins described in Dante's *The Divine Comedy* (Vaidhyanathan 2011, p. 76).

The catechism of Silicon Valley holds markets and technologies as sacrosanct, outside the bounds of legitimate critique. Proponents view digital technologies as benign and morally neutral or, more often, as uniquely capable of cultivating human virtue. This view is bolstered by rhetoric that displaces human agency and responsibility, even as elites shape its development and use. This problem is not new but is endemic to capitalism. Prior to computer systems, consumer surveillance took the form of credit ratings, which represented a form of "moral accounting" enacted by elites and internalized by citizen-consumers (Vaidhyanathan 2011, p. 71). Computerized automation does not remove this aspect of moral judgment, yet its air of scientific objectivity and technological efficiency helps to obscure processes of moral gatekeeping.

In the digital economy, as in previous eras, business practices function as rituals that solidify privileged forms of subjectivity (constructions of the self) among elites and industry insiders. Silicon Valley subculture is exclusive in terms of gender, race, age and socio-economic status. Boards of directors, employees, and conference attendees are overwhelmingly white and male. Ageism is rampant, and tech culture has long been characterized by "a belief that the young were agents of salvation" (Vaidhyanathan 2011, p. 72). In San Francisco, attacks on techies wearing Google Glass and protests against employees riding Google buses are manifestations of growing class tensions. This lack of diversity among developers and executives leads to a skewed vision of what products and solutions are important. The digital economy reflects the interests of the privileged self.

This atmosphere of privilege and entitlement gives rise to an attitude of contempt, rather than compassion, toward employees and users. Anecdotes abound illustrating the contemptuous attitudes of tech elites. Despite his personal interest in Buddhist and Hindu practices (Robinson 2013, p. 87), Steve Jobs famously described fellow employees as "shitheads." In a message to users in which he openly admitted and celebrated his site's user-data experimentation, OkCupid's Christian Rudder included an illustration of a guinea pig on which he had scrawled the label "you."

Such anecdotes indicate not that a few individuals have single-handedly shaped the digital economy to reflect their personal vices, but rather that, to the extent that it has been commercialized, an ethos of contempt is endemic to the digital economy itself. The personal character of those who achieve success reflects that underlying dynamic, yet most employees and users are unaware of its broader socio-economic impacts because they are indirect and manifest most intensely in underprivileged, hence invisible, communities at home and abroad. While tech employees in Silicon Valley benefit from on-site yoga classes and meditation rooms, the walls of Apple's factories in China are adorned with such quotations from Foxconn CEO Terry Gou as "Growth, thy name is suffering" and "A harsh environment is a good thing" (Chan 2013, p. 89).

As U.S.-based leaders internalize market values, they tend to ignore or refuse responsibility for labor conditions at home and overseas; the environmental impact of e-waste; the use of commercial platforms to enable human trafficking; the impact of revenge porn on young women; and other market externalities (McChesney 2013, p. 28). Users, whose data comprise the lifeblood of the information economy, are held in contempt by commercial imperatives that require managers and developers to treat them as a means to an end. Legal and rhetorical strategies for nudging users toward greater personal transparency amount to a process of soft coercion (Healey 2014, p. 200). The collective implications of this process are emerging. Data aggregation exacerbates socio-economic inequality as insurance companies, credit card companies, and retailers engage in price discrimination and the marketing of predatory financial instruments. Marketers divide users into class-based reputation categories that, over time, can become self-fulfilling prophecies. Among users themselves, the affordances of commercial platforms feed into a worldview premised not on hospitality but on exclusion, ostracization, maliciousness, and vengeance. Harassment and bullying have caused legal headaches for companies that had initially enjoyed financial support from investors.

In the final analysis, the presumed neutrality of data systems places the burden of ethical responsibility on users while absolving companies of responsibility. If the platform is morally neutral, it must be the user who is at fault when things go awry. For media scholars who aim to encourage moral behavior on the part of artists and professionals, fans, and citizens, this insight serves as an important reminder: while attending to the conduct of individuals, we must attend as well to the virtues and vices embodied in the broader political economy in which media institutions, technologies, and content emerge. We cannot simply assume that the virtuous conduct of individuals such as social media users, journalists, and software engineers is sufficient to revolutionize unjust political and economic systems. The goal of catalyzing virtue among media professionals is undermined insofar as the institutions in which they operate actively cultivate and exploit the vices of greed, aggression, or delusion. Every media system has a moral center of gravity, a point on the continuum between vice and virtue where content clusters. To the extent that greed drives media economics, the moral quality of its content, and its very architecture, suffers.

The Crisis Is Spiritual

When we treat a finite object as if it had infinite worth—as if it were, in fact, sacred—we are guilty of idolatry (Healey 2013; Brueggemann 2001, p. 11). We put on a pedestal, for our personal and collective worship, something that does not deserve such adoration. Doing so leads to deeply felt problems. Bridging the gap between psychology and spirituality, one scholar calls the study of such problems "the psychology of ultimate concerns" (Emmons 1999).

"The psychology of ultimate concerns" is a direct reference to the German existential philosopher Paul Tillich (1886–1965), a mid-twentieth-century Christian theologian widely considered one of the most influential theologians of the twentieth century. Tillich defined faith broadly as a matter of being grasped by an "ultimate concern" (Tillich 1964). This experience is common to all people, whether they are religious or not. Likewise, we all know how it feels to realize that someone or something we *thought* to be sacred turns out to be fallible, flawed, finite. When we attend thoughtfully to the theology of culture—its implicit, perhaps unconscious division of sacred from profane—our goal is similar to that of the psychologist: to diagnose faulty or unhealthy patterns of thought that negatively impact our well-being. The problematic beliefs described above, specifically, the ideology of information, the misappropriation of psychological research, the entrenched privilege and its architectures of contempt, impact our daily lives in profound ways that are sometimes obvious but more often quite subtle.

Over roughly three decades, Tillich diagnosed the "spiritual situation of our technical society" as one in which broad gains in technical prowess are followed by a loss of depth (Tillich 1988). The horizontal dimension expands too rapidly and at the expense of the vertical. The remainder of this book explores both the individual and collective dimensions of this loss of depth. For now, we consider the mundane experience of our spiritual situation in today's digital society. Roughly half a century ago Tillich wrote, "Today, more intensely than in preceding periods, man [*sic*] is so lonely that he cannot bear solitude. And he tries desperately to become a part of the crowd. Everything in our world supports him" (Tillich 1963, p. 8).

How prescient are Tillich's words. Connected devices have spawned a culture of availability in which we are available to everyone but ourselves, with a flood of sensational headlines decrying the psychic damage such gadgets have wrought. We should not be surprised then when each college semester many "digital natives" choose, with no prompting, to focus their class projects on Internet or smartphone addiction, crafting experiments in which their peers agree to give up their networked gadgets. Such experiments, or media fasts, typically end abruptly, with students complaining that they wish their friends would stick it out a bit longer, if only to help complete the assignment. Reflecting on her own experiment along these lines, one student of ours concluded her final paper with these thoughts:

> We were asked in class if we are able to take time to focus only on ourselves and be comfortable with having "you" time, such as taking a walk in the woods or going for a run in silence. … *For the first time in my life, I took into consideration that maybe I am scared to be fully isolated* (quoted with permission; emphasis added).

Swiss psychiatrist and founder of analytical philosophy Carl G. Jung argued that many of our cultural pathologies stem from fear of our own unconscious thoughts; the vast "undiscovered self" that constitutes the subject of any authentic spiritual quest (Jung [1957] 2006). This is the presence that draws near in those moments of restful contemplation that our hand-held devices so efficiently push out of reach. Yet it is in those moments of focused attention when we find an equanimity that bolsters our resistance to, and which may ultimately transform, the web of distraction that surrounds us.

This situation sounds dire. So why does it persist? Arguably, everyone suffers from the loss of spiritual depth and the consequent inability to cope with solitude. But that is a long-term argument. In the short term, some people do stand to gain. This point is well articulated by Old Testament scholar Walter Brueggemann in his now classic book *The Prophetic Imagination*. In the days of King Solomon, he notes, an abundance of material goods brought a sense of comfort and complacency which sidelined the prophetic voice of a potentially radical counter-culture.

The lessons of that story are still pertinent. As Brueggemann argues, all it takes to quell cries for justice and humility is *satiation*, or the controlled satiation of all hungers that rulers have leveraged throughout history. "It is difficult to keep a revolution of freedom and justice under way [*sic*] when there is satiation" (Brueggemann 2001, p. 32), he notes, stressing the satiated mind of non-marginalized groups as the lynchpin of political control. The privileged classes, alas, are the ones with power to address systemic injustice.

Under the reign of Solomon, explains Brueggemann, the people of Israel and Judah ate, drank, and "were happy" (1 Kings 4:20). The prophetic imagination was largely absent during the Solomonic reign (except for the prophet Ahijah, whom Solomon simply ignored) (1 Kings 11). But one is left to wonder about the apparent happiness of Solomon's community:

> It is at least thinkable that happiness characterized by satiation is not the same as the joy of freedom. It is evident that immunity to any transcendent voice and disregard of neighbor leads finally to the disappearance of passion. And where passion disappears there will not be any serious humanizing energy.
>
> (Brueggemann 2001, p. 38)

What joy of freedom is lost as we pass the hours playing the latest game or scrolling through our social media feeds? Perhaps our compulsive smartphone and Internet habits are less a matter of addiction *per se* and more a matter of what Brueggemann calls a "royal program of achievable satiation" (Brueggemann 2001, p. 42).

While the "pursuit of happiness" is among the foundational principles of Enlightenment notions of democracy, the ethos of consumer culture has always served to cultivate a shallow understanding of what constitutes this elusive goal. Consumerism is a kind of religion unto itself, and an optimistic one at that (Brueggemann 2001, p. 43). Advertisements teach us that we are merely one product, one service, one gadget away from true happiness. There is nothing mysterious about it. If we would only get working on such solutions, offering them in the marketplace at a reasonable price, we will please God himself with our material success. Moreover, we can do this by pulling ourselves up by our own bootstraps. We do not need neighbors or communities, never mind social programs.

Who stands to gain in today's version of Solomon's kingdom of abundance? Critics call out today's purveyors of royal consciousness by casting their arguments in religious terms. Media scholars and journalists refer in critical tones to the "Gospel of Google" (Vaidhyanathan 2011, p. 1), warning us of the dangers of "blind faith in technology" and "market fundamentalism" (Carr 2010, p. xiii). Technologist Jaron Lanier, the so-called father of virtual reality, argues further that Silicon Valley's techno-centric worldview asks human beings to "define themselves downward" while making computers seem smarter than they are (Lanier 2011, p. 19). Digital culture has lost touch with its humanistic roots, Lanier says, as he urges us to resurrect the values that energized the Internet's earliest pioneers. The "sweet faith in human nature" that guided the initial development of the Internet, he posits, "has been superseded by a different faith in the centrality of imaginary entities epitomized by the idea that the Internet as a whole is coming alive and turning into a superhuman creature" (Lanier 2011, p. 14).

Authors like Lanier and Siva Vaidhyanathan do not approach their work from a confessional, religious perspective. The critiques they offer are secular, not theological. Nevertheless, their work contributes handily to what we have described above as a "theology of culture," a psychology of ultimate concerns. They identify the underlying assumptions that lead technology companies to forsake social responsibility for hubris, sanctifying computerized clouds while striking at the dignity of flesh-and-blood individuals. The question arises: what alternate vision can we propose to cultivate the fundamentally human virtues of creativity, wisdom, and judgment?

Conclusion: A Call for Technological Prudence

Before jumping from his capsule, with all eyes watching, Felix Baumgartner remarked, "Sometimes you have to go up really high to understand how small you really are" (Tierney 2012b). After recovering from a tailspin and landing safely, he later observed, "When you stand up there on top of the world, you become so humble. It's not about breaking records any more. It's not about getting scientific data. It's all about coming home" (Tierney 2012b).

His remarks come as a welcome contrast to the hubris of many technology elites. Yet in the Stratos mission, as is too often the case, such humility was an unforeseen byproduct of personal and technical bravado. Rather than being an afterthought, such humility should be present in all stages of development. When it comes to questions of design, implementation, regulation, and use, prudence is the name of the game.

As a metaphor for unbridled technological development, we suggest that Baumgartner's initial anxiety was well-founded. While we should not take his early lead by fleeing in panic from whatever gadgets or platforms appear on the horizon, neither should we acquiesce to regimes of ideological coercion that allow us to jump with blind faith into the unknown as commercial entities and government agencies stand poised to roll out new technologies unprecedented in their scope of impact. Whether automated drones, self-driving cars, or ubiquitous body cameras, we find ourselves collectively on the small ledge where Baumgartner realized his own finitude. Once there, the question of balance is primary, since its lack portends a violent tailspin of grotesque consequence.

While Colonel Kittinger proudly described Baumgartner's feat as one of courage, that virtue cannot be reduced to a mere willingness to assume risk. It is instead a golden mean between the twin vices of cowardice and rashness. Courage takes a peculiarly flesh-and-blood form in the digital age. It is neither rash nor paralyzed by fear and despair. As the Irish-Iranian poet Kareem Tayyar suggests, "there is no reason to think that your best days are already behind you" (Tayyar 2015). We are wise to heed his cautions against both blind ambition and premature despair in the digital age.

Far from a Luddite rejection of newfangled tools, the call to technical prudence recognizes digital technologies as public goods with a potential to rejuvenate democratic life. Yet this call insists that development, use, and regulation should be subject to intensive scrutiny, particularly from the many reporters, whistleblowers, artists, and activists who are arguably more deserving of Kittinger's praise. Among others, that list includes the protestors who disrupted Silicon Valley's elite conferences; the women who initiated the #BlackLivesMatter movement; the organizers who have pressed for union rights among Uber drivers; the journalists who have thoughtfully reported on organizations from WikiLeaks to WeCopwatch. In courageous and prudent hands, the future may be one where technologies augment justice for all rather than privilege for the few.

References

Ancient, Claire, Alice Good, Clare Wilson, and Tineke Fitch. "Can Ubiquitous Devices Utilising Reminiscence Therapy Be Used to Promote Well-Being in Dementia Patients? An Exploratory Study." In *Universal Access in Human-Computer Interaction: Applications and Services for Quality of Life*, edited by Constantine Stephanidis and Margherita Antona, 426–35. New York: Springer, 2013.

Badenhausen, Kurt. "Felix Baumgartner Unlikely to Cash in on Red Bull Space Jump." *Forbes*, October 15, 2012. https://www.forbes.com/sites/kurtbadenhausen/2012/10/15/felix-baumgartner-unlikely-to-cash-in-on-red-bull-space-jump/#1cad19218ef7.

Barbrook, Richard, and Andy Cameron. "The Californian Ideology." Alamut. September 18, 1998. http://www.hrc.wmin.ac.uk/hrc/theory/californianideo/main/t.4.2.html.

Boorstin, Daniel J. *The Image: A Guide to Pseudo-Events in America.* New York: Vintage Books, 1992.

Brueggemann, Walter. *The Prophetic Imagination.* 2nd ed. Minneapolis, MN: Fortress Press, 2001.

Butler, Judith. *Giving an Account of Oneself.* New York: Fordham University Press, 2005.

Carr, Nicholas. *The Shallows: What the Internet Is Doing to Our Brains.* New York: W.W. Norton, 2010.

Chan, Jenny. "A Suicide Survivor: The Life of a Chinese Worker." *New Technology, Work and Employment* 28 (2013): 84–99.

Christians, Clifford G., John P. Ferré, and Mark Fackler. *Good News: Social Ethics and the Press.* New York: Oxford University Press, 1993.

Cohen, Patricia. "In Defense of Our Wicked, Wicked Ways," *The New York Times* [online], July 7, 2002. http://www.nytimes.com/2002/07/07/style/in-defense-of-our-wicked-wicked-ways.html.

Emmons, Robert A. *The Psychology of Ultimate Concerns: Motivation and Spirituality in Personality.* New York: Guilford Press, 1999.

Frosh, Stephen. *Psychoanalysis Outside the Clinic: Interventions in Psychosocial Studies.* London: Palgrave Macmillan, 2010.

Gates, Kelly A. *Our Biometric Future: Facial Recognition Technology and the Culture of Surveillance.* New York: New York University Press, 2011.

Healey, Kevin. "You Are Not a Gadget: Prophetic Critique in the Age of Digital Media." In *Prophetic Critique and Popular Media: Theoretical Foundations and Practical Applications,* edited by Robert H. Woods Jr. and Kevin Healey, 171–91. New York: Peter Lang, 2013.

———. "Coercion, Consent, and the Struggle for Social Media." *Explorations in Media Ecology* 13, nos. 3–4 (2014): 195–212.

Healey, Kevin, and Richard Potter. "Coding the Privileged Self: Facebook and the Ethics of Psychoanalysis Outside the Clinic." *Journal of Television and New Media* 19, no. 7 (2017): 660–76.

Heitner, Darren. "Red Bull Stratos Worth Tens of Millions of Dollars in Global Exposure for the Red Bull Brand." *Forbes*, October 15, 2012. https://www.forbes.com/sites/darrenheitner/2012/10/15/red-bull-stratos-worth-tens-of-millions-of-dollars-in-global-exposure-for-the-red-bull-brand/#318ee30e7df5.

Hoffmann, Anna Lauren, Nicholas Proferes, and Michael Zimmer. "'Making the World More Open and Connected': Mark Zuckerberg and the Discursive Construction of Facebook and Its Users." *New Media & Society* 20, no. 1 (July 2016): 1–20.

Jung, Carl G. *The Undiscovered Self.* 1957. Reprint ed., New York: Signet, 2006.

Kranzberg, Melvin. "Technology and History: 'Kranzberg's Laws'." *Technology and Culture* 27, no. 3 (July 1986): 544–60.

Lanier, Jaron. *You Are Not a Gadget: A Manifesto.* New York: Vintage Books, 2011.

Leavy, Patricia. *Research Design.* New York: The Guilford Press, 2017.

McChesney, Robert W. *Digital Disconnect: How Capitalism Is Turning the Internet Against Democracy.* New York: The New Press, 2013.

Meister, Chad, and James K. Dew Jr. *God and the Problem of Evil: Five Views.* Downer's Grove, IL: IVP Academic, 2017.

Pacey, Arnold. *The Culture of Technology*. Cambridge, MA: MIT Press, 1983.

Perrigo, Billy. "Mark Zuckerberg Says He Wants to Work with Sheryl Sandberg for Decades." *Time*, November 21, 2018. http://time.com/5461065/facebook-mark-zuckerberg-sheryl-sandberg/.

Robinson, Brett T. *Appletopia: Media Technology and the Religious Imagination of Steve Jobs*. Waco, TX: Baylor University Press, 2013.

Scheiber, Noam. "How Uber Uses Psychological Tricks." *New York Times*, April 2, 2017. https://www.nytimes.com/interactive/2017/04/02/technology/uber-drivers-psychological-tricks.html.

Schultze, Quentin J. *Habits of the High Tech Heart: Living Virtuously in the Information Age*. Grand Rapids, MI: Baker Books, 2002.

Shriver, Donald W. "Man and His Machines: Four Angels of Vision." *Technology and Culture* 13 (October 1972): 531–55.

Tayyar, Kareen. *Magic Carpet Poems*. Huntington Beach, CA: Tebot Bach Press, 2015.

Tierney, John. "Daredevil Sets Sight on a 22-Mile Fall." *New York Times*, October 8, 2012a. https://www.nytimes.com/2012/10/09/science/fearless-felix-baumgartner-to-try-to-become-first-sky-diver-to-break-sound-barrier.html.

———. "24 Miles, 4 Minutes and 834 M.P.H., All in One Jump." *New York Times*, October 14, 2012b. https://www.nytimes.com/2012/10/15/us/felix-baumgartner-skydiving.html.

Tillich, Paul. *The Eternal Now*. New York: Harcourt Brace, 1963.

———. *Theology of Culture*. New York: Oxford University Press, 1964.

———. *The Spiritual Situation in Our Technological Society*. Macon, GA: Mercer University Press, 1988.

Turner, Fred. *From Counterculture to Cyberculture: Stewart Brand, the Whole Earth Network, and the Rise of Digital Utopianism*. Chicago, IL: University of Chicago Press, 2006.

Twitchell, James B. *Living It Up: America's Love Affair with Luxury*. New York: Columbia University Press, 2003.

Vaidhyanathan, Siva. *The Googlization of Everything (And Why We Should Worry)*. Berkeley, CA: University of California Press, 2011.

Wright, N. T. *Evil and the Justice of God*. Downer's Grove, IL: IVP Books, 2013.

Zuckerberg, Mark. Building Global Community." Facebook. February 16, 2017. https://www.facebook.com/notes/mark-zuckerberg/building-global-community/10103508221158471/.

2

HISTORICAL ORIGINS OF THE DIGITAL CRISIS

By the summer of 2011, retired subway worker Robert Fitzpatrick spent most of his life savings promoting the end-times predictions of radio preacher Harold Camping, who warned that the world would end on May 21 of that year. Citing Camping's elaborate calculations, followers like Fitzpatrick held no doubt about the prediction. As the day came and went, Camping and his believers faced a wave of mockery from pundits. As Camping re-calculated in the wake of the media storm, even Fitzpatrick remained loyal. Sober voices suggested that Camping's story exemplifies a broader "prophecy upswing" that scholars should take seriously (Hagerty 2011).

At the same time, famed inventor, author, and futurist Ray Kurzweil appeared on television to promote his vision of a post-human future. According to Kurzweil, science will reverse-engineer the human brain by 2029, and by 2045 super-intelligent machines will merge with humans in a so-called "Singularity," making us effectively immortal. Critics highlighted the religious overtones of such predictions, suggesting that Kurzweil's "unwavering" certainty amounts to a kind of end-times "faith" (Stevens 2011). Others described Kurzweil as "proselytizing" (quoted in Stevens 2011) on behalf of the "the gospel of 'Singularity'" (Clements 2011). In a publicity shot that one reviewer labeled his "crazy man photo" (Maslin 2005), Kurzweil appears clutching a street preacher-style cardboard sign reading "The Singularity is Near." But Kurzweil told another reporter that he can afford such feats of self-deprecation because his ideas are "based on a detailed scientific analysis of the history of technology and not on faith" (Stevens 2011). Any comparison of Singularity to religion, he insists, is simply incorrect.

Such dismissals notwithstanding, there is a parallel between Camping and Kurzweil that is revealing. Without drawing any conclusions about the date of Christ's return or the potential benefits of artificial intelligence (AI), both men are getting something wrong fundamentally and in a way that we need to avoid. It is not that Christian theology is wrong for expecting Christ's return; nor is it wrong to expect that AI or virtual reality will bring about unprecedented experiences for humans. Rather, our concern is that both Camping and Kurzweil exhibit the vice of presumptuousness. Stated plainly, they have a lot of chutzpah.

Throughout the centuries, orthodox Christians have agreed that the Bible does not, in *Davinci Code*-like fashion, provide hidden codes predicting the day, hour, longitude, and latitude of Christ's return. Advocates of Kurzweil's vision espouse a vision that mirrors, in technological terms, the prophecy of Camping and other end-times preachers by framing their predictions as overly precise, inevitable, and authoritative. Moreover, Kurzweil's pursuit of immortality through technology is both a validation of end-times date-setting and an affront to orthodox Christian teachings about the source of human salvation. In the hands of technologists, software engineers, and corporate executives, such ideologies have troubling consequences. It is as if the elites of Silicon Valley are driven to win a competition with religious rebels as to who can introduce the most confusion to the most people. What chutzpah!

The comparison between Camping and Kurzweil is fitting, since the comparison illustrates the complex historical ties between media and religion. The aim of this chapter is to provide important historical context for the current crises in digital media, including the economic, ideological, and cultural roots of Silicon Valley's moral catechism (see Woods and Healey 2013; Healey 2015, 2017; Healey and Woods 2017). More specifically, we aim to show that the current crisis in digital media must be understood within the context of U.S. religious history. Since the founding of the American republic, market economics and religious zeal have influenced each other. Sometimes these forces amplify the virtues of each, but often they amplify their respective vices.

The most powerful tech companies are based in the United States and as such carry with them this complex history of virtue and vice. To be sure, from China to the European Union the world at large is pushing back at Silicon Valley's distinctly American ideology. But the beliefs underlying tech culture are deeply entrenched, and to understand the current crisis we must first understand its origins. To shed light on these beliefs, we begin our historical romp by exploring the ancient, modern, and Enlightenment roots of our current crises. We then consider several twentieth-century forces contributing to the co-mingling between religion and private enterprise that continues to influence conversations about the role of technology in public life.

Ancient and Modern Historical Contexts

To understand the distinctly American and religious sources of Silicon Valley's ideology, we begin with the Old Testament. One of the Old Testament's central concerns is how power can be, and is often, misused and abused when it remains in the hands of a select few. However well-intentioned a powerful elite may be, power brings privilege, which in turn brings naiveté and blindness to the concerns of everyday citizens. Silicon Valley is, in a sense, only the latest example.

Royal Consciousness

History is the story of the human disposition toward what Old Testament biblical scholar Walter Brueggemann calls "royal consciousness"—a set of beliefs driven by, and which ultimately serve, elite interests. From ancient Israel to modern-day Hollywood, every cultural system eventually becomes beholden to a dominant worldview. Brueggemann's re-telling of Old Testament narratives rings shockingly true in today's socio-economic context. With the abandonment of Moses's radical vision, the prevailing worldview in the kingdom of Solomon was characterized by, among other things, (1) an elaborate bureaucracy which, in imitation of the larger empires, served to institutionalize technical reason; and (2) a fascination with wisdom that, in addition to imitating the great regimes, represented an effort to rationalize reality, that is, package it in manageable portions (Brueggemann 2001, p. 31). Sound familiar?

Following German philosopher and economist Karl Marx, Brueggemann argues that the dominant religious worldview of a culture tends to provide justification for an otherwise unjust and exploitative political-economic environment. As we demonstrate throughout this chapter, media typically serve to catalyze this process by amplifying the voice of the status quo. Religious ideology supports both an "economics of affluence" and "politics of oppression," each supporting the other (Brueggemann 2001, p. 36). For instance, in King Solomon's kingdom, the pervasive sense of God's permanence became tightly linked to Jerusalem's political and economic success. As this happened, the sense of God's otherness or "over-againstness" subtly dissolved, and a "royal consciousness" emerged in which citizens—otherwise gripped by humility toward God—came to feel at ease in His presence. (Later in this chapter, we will see this theme return with the advent of market fundamentalism and the attendant hubris of Silicon corporate executives and their political allies.) An interesting, scathingly sardonic critique on the political exploitation of the theology of immanence is presented by former Pink Floyd front man, Roger Waters, in his recording, "What God Wants," taken from his Compact Disc, *Amused to Death*. The CD is a musical unfolding of the thesis from communication scholar, Neil Postman's (1985) book, *Amusing Ourselves to Death*.

Iron Cages and Cocoons

Now, fast forward from Moses and ancient Jerusalem to the historical advent of modernity (roughly 1500 CE). Sociologist Max Weber characterizes modernity as a process of differentiation between unique spheres of value: for example, science, law, and art. Most importantly, the sphere of science, guided by instrumental rationality, came to dominate. This process resulted in increased bureaucratization driven by concerns for efficiency and the imperatives of emergent complex systems. Weber described this process in colorful terms translated as a "shell hard as steel" or more famously as an "iron cage" ([1905] 2002, p. 121).

A similarly dire picture appears in the work of influential sociologist and lay Catholic theologian Jacques Ellul, who clearly took Weber's grim "iron cage" diagnosis to heart. Ellul's better-known work focuses on the drive toward efficiency, what he calls *la technique*. *La technique* is the impetus, the ultimate concern, that drives technologically advanced societies (Ellul [1948] 1967, p. 79; Ellul 1971, p. 25). *La technique* imposes its own standards of maximum efficiency on all aspects of modern life, to the point where technology, especially communications media, become "an engulfing universe" that surround us "as a cocoon." At a certain point, human beings "cannot have any relationship with the 'natural' world except through technological mediation" (Ellul 1978, p. 216). Such a society is so captivated by the drive toward technical efficiency that it will remove any moral obstacle to its ascendency, as "in ancient days men put out the eyes of nightingales in order to make them sing better" (Ellul [1948] 1967, p. 75). Still sounding familiar?

Are we trapped in a cage, a cocoon, of our own making? Are we digital nightingales, blinding ourselves that we might sing more sweetly on the pages of Instagram and Twitter? Perhaps. But many theorists argue that our cage, or cocoon, is not as solid as it may appear (Postone 1990, p. 170; Benhabib 1986, p. 248). Such theorists suggest that the negative or even pathological effects of instrumental reason are not endemic to modernity itself but are instead specific to the dynamics of market capitalism in its later stages. In a hopeful vein, the rationalization of society may actually be a step forward in human development. Weber's mistake was to overemphasize instrumental rationality to the point where too often we imagine it to have a life of its own, and one beyond our control. Even Ellul admitted ultimately that *la technique* is not an evil imposed from an external source. Instead our technical situation, of which communications media is its troublesome manifestation, is a reflection of our "fallen" nature as mere humans (Christians 1990, p. 336; Christians 2006, p. 154).

To answer our own rhetorical question, no, we are not victims trapped in cages or cocoons of historical inevitability. Our situation, as in the days of King Solomon, is a failure of priorities and judgment. It stems from our misjudgment regarding what are matters of ultimate concern. Perhaps we have lost our way. But perhaps our forbearers left breadcrumbs that might guide us back onto the path of human flourishing.

A New Religious Economy

Some of the breadcrumbs to help us get back on track were left by Enlightenment thinkers like James Madison and Thomas Jefferson, often referred to as the Founding Fathers of the American republic. To be sure, these men were not then, and are not today, beyond moral reproach. Jefferson literally drank tea brought to him by a slave, even as he penned the Declaration of Independence. Nevertheless, the concepts of liberty, freedom, and justice live on. In this section, we argue for an immanent critique of American founding ideals, in other words, a critique that asks us to recall, re-examine, and revive visionary ideals that we have still to achieve. This is the sort of critique that Martin Luther King Jr. made in his iconic "I Have a Dream" speech, where instead of rejecting American ideals, he demanded that we live up to them.

The Founders would be aghast at our idolatrous worship of markets and technology. The First Amendment's protections for religious equality and freedom of the press encapsulate a unique vision of a religious economy based on competition between multiple sects within a diverse and thriving media system. The First Amendment provides not only for a democratic press but also for an active and pluralistic religious conversation. Freedom of religion and freedom of the press overlap, together providing a check against the dominance of particular tribal or partisan views. It is precisely in such an environment that the prophetic role of religion, that is, one that challenges the powerful, the status quo, and the ruling elite with a call for truth and justice may be realized.

The tendency to acquiesce to market imperatives (an aspect of Ellul's *la technique*) was clear long before our country's founding documents were written. In the pre-Revolutionary American colonies, itinerant preacher George Whitefield embraced the communications techniques of a burgeoning consumer marketplace. He described his work as "trafficking for the Lord" (Lambert 2006, p. 128). Whitefield's itinerancy contributed both to a political revolution and to a new religious economy based on a consumerist model of competitive engagement. The pitfalls of Whitefield's brand of free-market religion include, among other vices, egregious self-promotion and cynical manipulation of the press. Yet the Founders saw the potential of this emerging marketplace and sought to establish a framework for amplifying its virtues while minimizing such potential vices.

Drawing from Adam Smith, the Founders argued for disestablishment, that is, the rejection of federally sponsored religious institutions like the Church of England. This would spur religious competition that, in turn, would whittle away error to reveal a "pure and rational religion" (Smith 1977, p. 315). Despite their indebtedness to Smith, a revered figure among free-market enthusiasts, the philosophical basis for the Founders' vision flies in the face of contemporary free-market enthusiasm. Smith did not single-mindedly promote unfettered, or unregulated, free markets as a cure-all. In reality, he outlined problems that arise when large institutions of any kind gain too much power, whether corporations (then called joint-stock companies), religious establishments, or governments (Krueger 2001). Such buildups of power are detrimental to markets and churches alike, Smith argued, because they subvert individual liberty as well as the public good. James Madison, who drafted key arguments for religious freedom leading to the First Amendment, drew heavily from these elements of Smith's work (Fleischacker 2002). Today, however, this nuanced history has been obscured by neoliberal narratives that reduce Smith's theories to the metaphor of the "invisible hand," an image Smith used only once in his 1776 work *The Wealth of Nations* but which has now come to symbolize the alleged equation of private gain with public good.

There is much the Founders failed to anticipate in their ambitious vision for the new republic. To be sure, the early nineteenth century is marked by a "democratization" of American Christianity inseparable from the emergence of the mass media (Hatch 1989; Schultze 2003).

In other words, competition surely arose but so did an unforeseen concentration of wealth and power. The thirst for riches, and the accompanying vice of ruthless self-interest, was clear in the early days when men set out to explore the territories west of the original colonies. Early American frontiersmen were, like the Internet's past and present entrepreneurs, mostly white men. Google's choice of the term "Explorer" for its early adopters of Glass—a voice-controlled device that looks like a pair of eyeglasses and displays information directly in the user's field of vision—extends the powerful metaphors historically associated with networked technologies, including "cyberspace" and the digital "frontier." Such metaphors evoke "America's libertarian imagination, with its primal identification of wilderness and freedom" (Davis 1998, p. 108).

Proponents have used such imagery to suggest that the Internet is, or should be, beyond the reach of government. But just as the open spaces of the Western frontier soon became "farmed and fenced" (Davis 1998, p. 108), the digital frontier became privatized and commercialized, despite popular notions that its essence was uniquely resistant to markets and bureaucracies.

The Business of Religion

This frontier mentality lends itself to a view of technology as neutral, if not inherently beneficial. In the mid-nineteenth century, religious and business entrepreneurs held fast to a "transmission model" of communication, which views technology as a mere means of moving ideas from one place to another. This view is morally problematic since it can lead to a naïvely idealistic view of new communication technology that imagines technology as good when in the hands of good people, and evil in the hands of so-called evil people. In many cases past and present, it results in an idolatrous veneration, if not worship, of technology as a modern god.

Christians, for example, were among the first to embrace the "intoxicating effects" of Samuel Morse's telegraph in 1844. Morse suggested that the purpose of the telegraph "was not to spread the price of pork but to ask the question 'What Hath God Wrought?'" (Carey 1989, p. 588). On May 24, 1844, Morse sent those very words—"What hath God wrought" (a Bible quotation from Numbers 23:23)—as the first-ever telegraph transmission. He sent it from the Supreme Court room in Washington, D.C., to his assistant, Alfred Vail, in Baltimore, Maryland. It set off a wellspring of religious fervor and a corresponding "rhetoric of the electrical sublime" (Carey 1989, p. 206).

For Christians worldwide, Morse's telegraph promised something that had been stripped from communal life by writing and later print, namely, a promise of "unity of interest, men linked by a single mind, and the worldwide victory of Christianity" (Czitrom 1982, p. 10). In the minds of many, "universal peace and harmony" were somehow now attainable (Czitrom 1982, p. 10). The establishment of telegraph connections with Europe in 1857 had further impact on the American imagination for universalism. The clerics saw God's guiding hand in the unfurling of this momentous development. The poets went so far as to call the telegraph "a loving girdle round the earth" (Standage 1998, p. 81). In the end, the new technologies were perceived as holding the promise of "the Universal Brotherhood of Universal Man" (Carey 1989, p. 208; see also Marvin 1987; Sawhney 1994). Religious enthusiasts quickly took the messianic promises of the telegraph to the next level. In April 1923, Reverend R. R. Brown ushered in the first Radio Church where he asked his listeners to join the "World Radio Congregation" (Ward 1994, pp. 228–29). And here's the pitch: Individuals in rural communities previously cut off from services, such as the farmer or the handicapped, could now "almost imagine being in church" (Gomery 1995, p. 238).

As religious sects began to achieve success in the religious marketplace by acquiescing to the political-economic status quo, they effectively muted their prophetic voice. Fundamentalists, to a large extent, abandoned the commitment to social action that had characterized the work of earlier evangelicals (Marsden 1980, p. 92), while the Social Gospel movement aimed to redeem market capitalism from within by conceiving of the church as a morally infused business enterprise (Moore 1994). In 1921, the *Handbook of Church Advertising* declared, "The objection will be raised that we are mixing faith with business, and that they won't mix. Too long has the world labored under this delusion. They must mix if civilization is to endure" (quoted in Moore 1994, p. 213).

In the emerging medium of radio broadcasting, progressives and conservatives alike refrained from social critique in favor of commercial palatability. The birth of electronic broadcasting initially brought a range of religious voices to the airwaves, but government policies generated a contentious debate between mainline and evangelical churches—both of whom sacrificed the prophetic elements of their faith to survive in an increasingly commercial environment (Moore 1994; Schultze 2003). A 1948 guidebook titled *Religious Radio: What to Do and How* warned, "Don't alarm listeners with long lists of what is wrong with the world. Don't speak dogmatically. Remember it's normality we're all striving for" (quoted in Moore 1994, pp. 234–35).

Soon television emerged as the next great means of evangelism. In the 1950s, TV allowed preachers like Billy Graham to "preach to more people in one night on TV than perhaps [the Apostle] Paul did in his whole lifetime" (Graham 1983, p. 8). Then, in the 1970s and 1980s, Christian television pioneers became leaders in the push toward satellite technology. As televangelist Jimmy Swaggart said of such technology, "For the first time in history God has given a handful of men [which included Jim Baker, Pat Robertson, Oral Roberts, and himself] the opportunity to reach tens of million with the gospel of Christ" (Swaggart 1984). Ben Armstrong, former executive director of the National Religious Broadcasters, once argued that the newest communication technologies would become a "revolutionary new form of the worshipping, witnessing church that existed twenty centuries ago" (Armstrong 1979, pp. 8–9). Armstrong called broadcasting one of the "major miracles of modern times" and envisioned a new church, more like the early church, where members lived in peace and harmony. "Radio and television have broken through the wall of tradition we have built up around the church" and "have restored conditions remarkably similar to the early church" (Armstrong 1979, pp. 172–73). Armstrong went so far as to wonder whether the angel referred to in Revelation 14:6 might be a communication satellite used by God to fulfill the prophecy of the last days (Armstrong 1979, p. 172).

For better or worse, the Christian Church increasingly imitated the communication theories and business practices of broadcasting industry, especially after World War II. Evangelicals, in particular, quickly adopted the "manipulation" mode of communication because it seemed to fit so well with the emphasis on the Great Commission (Matt. 28:18), which calls Christians to spread the Gospel message to all nations of the world. Since media were considered basically neutral, or amoral, evangelicals soon began using secular models of communication and marketing to reach the world for Christ (Schultze 1987). When mass media are in Christian hands, said one tele-evangelist, they can "redirect a nation to the paths of righteousness" (Schultze 1987, p. 250). Pope Paul VI, in his 1976 *Evangelii nuntiandi*, captured the spirit of this evangelistic impulse when he said of religious radio and television broadcasts, "The Church would feel guilty before the Lord if she did not use these powerful means that human skill is daily rendering more perfect" (Zukowski 1994, p. 176).

Not surprisingly, Christianity and its churches worldwide grew in both number and influence during the electronic era. This included a growing political influence in the United States as well through organizations such as Pat Robertson's Christian Coalition and Jerry Falwell's Moral Majority, each supported by their leader's national tele-evangelistic platforms. Despite such inroads, insiders noted that adopting secular models of communication and marketing, however unintentional, turned "Christian TV into commercials for Christ, veritable sales pitches" (Schultze 1992, p. 19). As one insider remarked, "with the overarching demand of the Great Commission looming over every evangelical enterprise, it is very easy to go for ratings instead of rationality, quantity rather than quality" (Myers 1989, p. 22).

As commercial imperatives select winners and losers in the religious economy, success is enjoyed by those versions of Christianity that comport with market ideology. Evangelicals' eventual domination of broadcasting, and willing partnership with political power, gave rise to what is often referred to as the Religious Right and Moral Majority. Some disillusioned insiders complained about the pressure to choose between the role of "prophet" and "advisor," but many remained comfortable in the latter role (Martin 1996, p. 229). Ironically, the success of evangelicals also had the effect of contributing to the dismantling of institutional religion, giving rise to a highly commodified "spiritual marketplace" that tends to further fragment the prophetic voice (Miller 2004; Roof 1999).

The Religion of Private Enterprise

As early twentieth-century religious leaders of the "electronic Great Awakening" began to adapt business models for religious ends, intellectuals and businessmen began meanwhile to adapt religious terminology to describe their own, more secular, goals. The line between business and religion became increasingly blurred. Social psychologists like Gustave Le Bon and Edward Bernays espoused methods by which elite leaders could manipulate the supposedly irrational mind of the public (Ewen 1996). As if channeling Ellul's notion of *la technique*, Le Bon rejected the notion that informed critical thinking was the key to democratic flourishing, insisting instead that "it is numbers, not values that count." Speaking to his fellow elites, he insisted, "we must become a cult, write our philosophy of life in flaming headlines, and sell our cause in the market" (Ewen 1996, p. 144).

In his history of the public relations industry, Stuart Ewen (1996) lambasts the "religion of private enterprise" that lurks behind this elite ideology (p. 246). Other historians agree. Christian media critic Quentin J. Schultze (2003) argues that advertising employs a "rhetoric of conversion" with clear roots in Christian popular theology and claims that advertisers are essentially "secular evangelicals"—even "the great evangelists of our age" (p. 313). Business became a religion unto itself.

To a considerable extent, newspapers in the nineteenth century had served as critics of both commercial and religious institutions, ruffling the feathers of each. But as commercialization pushed religious publishing toward moral sensationalism and entertainment, corporate concentration turned a once-lively partisan press into a wasteland of "yellow" journalism.

Professional journalism was born as an industry strategy to fend off government regulation and allow the trend toward commercialism to reach fruition (McChesney 2004, pp. 58–66). For most of the twentieth century, professional reporters have either held religion at arm's length or adopted a "broad truths" perspective in coverage, with the result of drawing the prophetic elements of religious faith within fairly narrow bounds (Silk 1995, pp. 49–55). The nature and quality of journalistic reporting changed as the industry commercialized and acquiesced to an emerging faith in the sacredness of the market.

By 1929, John Dewey noted, "we are living in a money culture. Its cult and rites dominate" (Dewey 1999, p. 5). Advertising and public relations assumed immense institutional power, and PR became "the secret religion of all religions" (Ewen 1996, p. 132). In response to the public's distaste for direct corporate propaganda, in the 1950s, business elites actively recruited religious leaders to mobilize against the New Deal and to preach the gospel of free enterprise. With corporate support, preachers like the Reverend James Fifield Jr. created a convincing public relations campaign for corporate America, articulating theological arguments for the compatibility of Christianity and capitalism (Kruse 2015, pp. 15–18). As one historian notes, Franklin Delano Roosevelt's programs "went head-to-head with the religion of private enterprise" (Ewen 1996, p. 246).

Quest Culture and the Spiritual Marketplace

In the latter half of the twentieth century, the decline of institutional religion led to a business-minded religion industry and a consumer-oriented "spiritual marketplace" focused on the quest for spiritual identity through media and retail products (Roof

1999). Many congregants of mainstream churches continued to attend out of habit but felt disconnected from their churches' underlying goals. Or, they shared those goals but felt that traditional institutions failed to express or fulfill them properly (Roof 1999, p. 62). Religious believers moved from "dwelling" within traditional institutions to "seeking" spiritual experience and meaning elsewhere (Wuthnow 1998, pp. 1–18). In some cases, new forms of practice such as Pentecostalism (which emerged in Los Angeles in the early 1900s with the Azusa Street Revival) (Dayton 1987; Robeck 2006) represented a return of emotion and an appreciation for mystery in religious experience. Overall, the development of "quest culture" stemmed from a kind of "wholeness hunger," an effort to overcome the fractured nature of modern life by reintegrating aspects of one's life and self (Roof 1999, pp. 62–63). Among conservatives, traditional denominational structures gave way to networks of para-church organizations and business-like megachurches that became deeply involved in Washington politics. For 1960s progressives, the counter-culture sought ecstatic experiences through the psychedelic music and drug experimentation. Changes in U.S. immigration laws generated interest in east-Asian philosophy (Roof 1999, p. 73), where counter-culture types found ideas that resonated with their experiences. Composer John Cage's avant-garde protest of heteronormative culture, inspired by the Zen teacher D. T. Suzuki, gave way to the more commercially palatable east-Asian flirtations of the Beatles, whose "hunger for transcendence" led them to Maharishi Mahesh Yogi and Paramahansa Yogananda's *Autobiography of a Yogi* (Turner 2006, p. viii). The latter was the sole book remaining on Steve Jobs' iPad when he took his last family trip to Hawaii in 2011 (Robinson 2013, p. 75).

Psychedelic proponent Timothy Leary and Grateful Dead lyricist John Perry Barlow were among the first proponents of cyberspace as a consciousness-expanding technology. Steve Jobs followed a similar path, drawing from Zen meditation, Hindu practices, and psychedelic experimentation to build the cult-status branding of Apple's digital products (Robinson 2013, pp. 86–87). Positing consciousness (i.e., the mind) as the site of potential revolution, such leaders distanced themselves from the "agonistic" politics of controversial activist groups like the Weathermen (Turner 2006, p. 35). At least initially, these tech leaders remained skeptical of corporate power and rejected crass commercialism, assuming that "the revolutionary nature of the technology could trump the monopolizing force of the market" (McChesney 2013, p. 105).

By the mid-twentieth century and beyond, conservatives and liberals alike wholeheartedly entered a questing mode, although in different ways. Evangelicals employed a creative use of music and performance in their church services and focused on the core theological truth of an individual's relationship with Jesus as a source of personal salvation. Progressives turned to secular music, technology, and East-Asian philosophies and practices. Though conservative evangelicals and counter-culture liberals differed in their socio-political values, their approaches each centered on concerns about the individual self. Questions such as "Who am I?" and "What is my purpose?" became more pressing as individuals' trust in traditional institutions (religious or otherwise) decreased, and an emergent "spiritual marketplace" presented an overwhelming number of choices with regard to one's beliefs and practices. In this context, various "techniques of the self," including drug experimentation, meditation, prayer, and various self-help programs came to characterize quest culture. An important pitfall of this ethos is an over-emphasis on the self, relativism, and aversion to hierarchy, that is, a kind of prideful narcissism one author describes as "Boomeritis" (Wilber 2002).

A "Web" of Metaphors: The 1990s

Faith in technology led to a shift in political alliances as counter-culture leaders and economic conservatives both came to regard market-born technologies as natural and inevitable (Turner 2006, p. 224). By the mid-1990s, counter-culture elites allied themselves with "free-market ideologues" like Newt Gingrich, former U.S. Representative from Georgia and 50th Speaker of the House of Representatives from 1995 to 1999, who played a key role in crafting pro-business legislation (McChesney 2013, p. 105). Echoing the shift toward commercialization in radio broadcasting earlier in the century, politicians and industry leaders had quietly privatized the infrastructure of the Internet before crafting legislation that solidified the power of Silicon Valley entrepreneurs (McChesney 2013, p. 104). Even Google founders Larry Page and Sergey Brin, who had once denounced advertising-based search engines as "inherently biased toward the advertisers," soon developed the most successful ad-placement model in the industry (McChesney 2013, p. 102).

A few years after Tim Berners-Lee engineered the protocols underlying what we now call "the Web," the U.S. Congress passed what was and still is "arguably one of the most important pieces of U.S. legislation" due to its sweeping effect on all forms of electronic media (McChesney 2004, p. 51). Driven by an alliance of technology elites and economic conservatives, the Telecommunications Act of 1996 (the Telecom Act) represents the culmination of an ideology according to which cyberspace is an extension of Earth's natural systems and "life is in fact a computer" (Frank 2001, p. 356). Indeed, economic conservatives had long understood markets as "natural" in the sense of "inevitable and right" (Turner 2006, p. 224). Today, computer networks are said to improve market efficiency by mimicking biological systems. As one scholar explains, "the Net modeled an ideal social, biological, political, and economic sphere; computers were the latest stage in the evolution of those spheres" (Turner 2006, p. 226).

The foundation of the Telecom Act had been laid out in a manifesto called "A Magna Carta for the Knowledge Age" (Dyson et al. 1994). It argues essentially that to obstruct the development of digital technologies would be "to resist the forces of history, nature, technology, and American destiny all at once" (Turner 2006, p. 230). With the support of pro-market technology elites like Esther Dyson behind him, Newt Gingrich incorporated these arguments into legislative initiatives, arguing for a new era in which "technology would do away with the need for bureaucratic oversight" and "deregulation would free markets to become the engines of political and social change they were meant to be" (Turner 2006, p. 215). With typical flair,

Gingrich told *Wired* magazine that such policies were part of a divinely inspired "mission" (quoted in Turner 2006, p. 231). Thus, while the Telecom Act "enshrined in law the notions that undergirded the 'Magna Carta'" (Turner 2006, p. 230), it also announced a religiously imbued economic vision that one onlooker described wryly as 'One Market under God'" (Frank 2001).

In the Telecom Act, the Californian ideology of libertarian techno-utopianism, fused with religious conservatism, became the law of the land (Barbrook and Cameron 1998). It encapsulated in policy form a powerful "computational metaphor" that had driven technologists since Norbert Weiner's cybernetic research decades before (Turner 2006, p. 230). This view understands human life in terms of computer and information systems. In conjunction with the "market populism" of the 1990s, the computational metaphor precipitated an ethos of unbridled technical development on the premise that "the 'New Economy,' the way of the microchip, is writ into the very DNA of existence" (Frank 2001, p. 356). The effects of the legislation include unprecedented industry consolidation and a diminution of long-held public interest values. But the "spectacular mix of hubris and hyperbole" (Turner 2006, p. 230) espoused in the Magna Carta has hardly abated, continuing in the aggressive initiatives of profit-seeking entrepreneurs who have come to shape Web 2.0.

Ray Kurzweil, known for his controversial ideas about artificial intelligence, argued concurrently with the passage of the Telecom Act that the ability to scan the "architecture" of the brain in sufficient detail was the only real obstacle to simulating human intelligence with computers (Carr 2010, p. 175). In a secular recapitulation of Judeo-Christian apocalyptic themes, Kurzweil takes the computational metaphor to its logical conclusion by suggesting that a rapidly approaching Singularity, or merger of human and computer intelligence, will yield a new era of unprecedented well-being and virtual immortality (Geraci 2010, pp. 8–9). Much like religious adherents who understand ecological degradation as a necessary element of the end-times narrative, Kurzweil's rapturous vision encourages ideological blindness to the ill effects of technological growth. The Singularity narrative lends legitimacy to unrestrained technical development, suggesting that any process that can be outsourced to an algorithm or transformed into a computational format should be, without delay. In essence, the computational *metaphor* becomes a computational *imperative*.

There are grave consequences to understanding human beings in terms of the technologies they create. New technologies reshape our understanding of human physiology, psychology, and communication with unpredictable results. Efforts at developing artificial intelligence hinge on the view that the human brain is essentially an information processor. While neuroscientists dispute Kurzweil's view of the brain, the metaphor persists partly because of the hope it engenders. Kurzweil and others believe that the much anticipated Singularity will generate super-intelligent computers that will out-perform humans in all important respects, including the ability to solve our most pressing social problems.

Despite the scientific and philosophical criticisms of Kurzweil's ideas (Myers 2010; Searle 2008), Google co-founders Larry Page and Sergey Brin have embraced the computational metaphor. In 2012, Google hired Kurzweil to further its vision of artificially intelligent systems that might, in the words of co-founder Sergey Brin, "be like the Mind of God" (quoted in Vaidhyanathan 2011b). Google's belief that software engineering can transcend the moral trappings of human judgment has yielded aggressive campaigns that defy cautionary pronouncements from legal authorities and consumer groups (Vaidhyanathan 2011a, p. 77). Over the past decade, technology elites have amassed enormous power by articulating a quasi-religious ideology that justifies uninhibited commercial development. They have capitalized on the religious trappings of Silicon Valley culture and assumed the role of new medieval churchmen. We live in an era where "innovations in digital technologies, including the virtual spaces of the Internet, are accorded near-mystical qualities" (Mansell 2012, pp. 1–2; McChesney 2013, p. 5). As Google hired Kurzweil to expand its quest for artificial intelligence, tech leaders flocked to conferences like Wisdom 2.0, where tech gurus extend and contemporize the market catechism through subtle appropriations of Buddhist philosophy and practices.

Black-Nosed Buddhas: Silicon Valley's Market-Friendly Mindfulness

In defense of Facebook's controversial privacy policy changes in 2011, Mark Zuckerberg insisted that the company would not be "trapped" by convention but instead would "always keep a beginner's mind" with regard to its business practices (quoted in Matyszczyk 2010). His use of the phrase "beginner's mind" reflects a deep-rooted commingling of Zen Buddhism and American corporate culture (Grieve 2015, pp. 104–6). His use of the phrase is ironic. The point of maintaining a "beginner's mind" is to recognize and uproot habitual patterns of thought, regardless of their nature. But in a corporate context, the phrase carries an implicit restriction: effective leaders cultivate a beginner's mind only with regard to conventions that limit growth and productivity and never with regard to market ideology itself. Zuckerberg's off-the-cuff remark is symbolic of a broader appropriation of east-Asian philosophies by Silicon Valley elites. Such statements add rhetorical flair, an air of authentic counter-culture legitimacy, to an otherwise conventional political-economic status quo—one which exacerbates existing economic inequality and treats human suffering as a market externality.

Just as market-friendly forms of Christianity succeeded in the twentieth century, east-Asian philosophy and practices find a home in Silicon Valley when they are compatible with free-market ideology. At one time idealistic, counter-culture leaders largely abandoned the anti-commercial ethos of early Internet culture. As ideas derived from Buddhism permeated tech culture, thought leaders selected approaches consonant with American-style consumerist individualism.

This trend was present in Apple CEO Steve Jobs's early experimentation, in which Zen meditation in its Americanized form served as a route to "cathartic euphoria" rather than a catalyst for compassion (Brazier 2002, p. 162). Jobs claimed to prefer Zen's lack of "religious structure" and its emphasis on "experience, intuition, and self-fulfillment through inner consciousness" (quoted in Robinson

2013, p. 86). Although he traveled to India and studied Zen meditation in Los Altos, Jobs ultimately decided that "Edison did more to influence the human race than Buddha," according to his friend and fellow cyber-enthusiast Timothy Leary (quoted in Dery 1997, p. 28).

Biographer Walter Isaacson claims that while Jobs had once cited his Zen teacher Kobun Chino in arguing against materialist attachment to consumer products, "in the end Jobs's pride in the objects he made overcame his sensibility that people should eschew being attached to such possessions" (2011, p. 262). Such pride also precipitated Jobs's temperamental rants against both products and "shithead" employees (Isaacson 2011, p. 561). Noting his treatment of employees as well as the labor conditions in Apple's Chinese factories, one critic highlighted "the core tenet of Buddhism that Jobs seems to have bypassed: the importance of treating everyone around you, even perceived enemies, with basic respect and loving kindness" (Silberman 2015). This same critic suggests wryly that "a more skillful practitioner" of *zazen* meditation might have "tried to find ways to bring out the genius in his employees without humiliating them—and certainly would have found ways of manufacturing products that didn't cause so much suffering for impoverished workers in other countries" (Silberman 2015).

Jobs's version of east-Asian philosophy is reminiscent of an old Buddhist morality tale. According to this story, a nun created her own figure of Buddha, covering it with gold leaf. For years, she took it wherever she went; until finally she settled in a temple where she found many Buddhas, each with its own shrine. Once there, "The nun wished to burn incense before her golden Buddha. Not liking the idea of the perfume straying to others, she devised a funnel through which the smoke would ascend only to her statue. This blackened the nose of the golden Buddha, making it especially ugly" (Reps and Senzaki 1998, p. 64). The black-nosed Buddha, of course, is a metaphor for selfishness. It symbolizes a spiritual philosophy lacking in integrity: a self-centered practice where the practitioner has lost sight of what really matters.

Silicon Valley is enthralled with meditation and yoga but only to the extent that it increases productivity. Even Chade-Meng Tan, Google's in-house mindfulness guru, admits that his Search Inside Yourself program succeeds in reducing personal stress but falls short in terms of generating compassion (Healey 2014a).

Collectively, the black-nosed Buddha represents a morally tarnished economy where elites reap the benefits of mindfulness practice, even as they market products designed to distract users and that are manufactured in unjust labor conditions. In fairness, many executives begin as wide-eyed idealists. Google's executives, for example, initially rejected the idea that advertising would support their search engine. Over time, the logic of capitalism "whipped them into shape. Any qualms about privacy, commercialism, avoiding taxes, or paying low wages to Third World factory workers were quickly forgotten." From a Buddhist standpoint, "the system has attained not only a life of its own but its own *cetanā* volitions [i.e., mental or mind-like intentionality], quite apart from the motivations of the individuals who work for it and who will be replaced if they do not serve that institutional motivation"

(Loy 2013, p. 419). "Our economic system," as such, "promotes structural *dukkha* [suffering] by institutionalizing greed" (Loy 2013, p. 417).

Business leaders may be sincere in their practice but unwittingly tend to neglect the teachings of "greater scope" in favor of "a teaching of lesser scope," the latter of which "has a substantial element of selfishness about it" (Brazier 2002, p. 198).[1] In the networked era, in other words, the pipe that funnels smoke to the black-nosed Buddha is patented and armed for its own protection (Healey 2014b, 2015).

Conclusion: Brave Little Tailors and the Erasure of History

We cannot understate how deeply embedded the "mythos of the communication revolution" became in American religious history during the electronic era, or how it overshadowed all subsequent developments (Carey 1989, pp. 113–41). And what the telegraph did for the American West, the Internet is supposedly doing for the world, but frequently the rhetoric is equally histrionic. There is a perceived "transcendent" quality of digital communication technologies that continues to be seen as "the motive force of desired social change, the key to the recreation of a humane community, the means for returning to a cherished naturalistic bliss" for human beings worldwide (Carey 1989, p. 115).

Camping's end-times, date-setting mishap, and Kurzweil's promised "Singularity" remind us that predicting the future of anything—in this case, religious events or technological developments—must be rooted in a humble understanding of particular historical contexts and how such historical pasts connect to the future. Yet in a bittersweet taste of technological irony, as communication theorist and cultural critic Neil Postman observed in his now classic and highly prescient *Technopoly: The Surrender of Culture to Technology* (1992), technological society's most insidious accomplishment was to convince people that the future does not need any connection to the past. Not surprisingly, then, we see how Silicon Valley's moral catechism falsely equates information with virtues like wisdom, promotes individuality over community, and cuts off people from the past, including tradition.

By "tradition" we do not mean a set of outdated, finger-wagging rules that serve to prop up the powers-that-be. Rather, we see tradition in terms of "accumulated wisdom," including rituals and customs that remember and honor voices from our collective past (Schultze 2002, p. 75; see also Chesterton 1990, p. 48). In this sense, tradition is not merely blind adherence to old rules, but an active process of personal responsibility whereby we interpret and apply established insights, preserving and curating them for the next generation.

More than two decades after Postman's proclamation, mainstream and religious critics can agree on at least one thing: the religion of technological optimism embraces the enticing idea that self, and not others, defines our past, present, and future. It therefore denies adherence to any tradition that calls individuals to reflect on the past and to cultivate memory. Quite simply, a collective memory announcing that we are accountable to others for how we treat others—not just how we treat ourselves—works against the ascension of self-interest and immediate gratification at the heart of Silicon Valley's moral catechism. Noting the religious overtones of its hopeful expectations, author and tech critic Jaron Lanier derides the Singularity as "rapture for nerds" and warns of its implications:

> If you believe the Rapture is imminent, fixing the problems of this life might not be your greatest priority. You might even be eager to embrace wars and tolerate poverty and disease in others to bring about the conditions that could prod the Rapture into being. In the same way, if you believe the Singularity is coming soon, you might cease to design technology to serve humans, and prepare instead for the grand events it will bring.
>
> (Lanier 2011, p. 25)

As we reflect on concerns like these of Lanier and others highlighted throughout this chapter, we are reminded of a folk tale called "The Brave Little Tailor" from *Grimm's Household Tales,* in which the protagonist amazes giants and kings with apparently miraculous acts (Grimm and Grimm 1906). In one scene, a giant literally squeezes water from a boulder. The tailor, wielding a round of cheese that resembles a stone, appears to do the same and renders the giant speechless. Again and again, the tailor fools his opponents, climbing a social ladder into seats of great power through various slights of hand.

Today, in what are really the baby stages of the digital age, we consumers and citizens are often fooled as the giants were. We believe all too readily that the tailors of clean code and slick design can produce water from stones, when in fact they are performing a slight of hand. The tools held up before us in the latest much-anticipated Apple release event, or in a dazzling Verizon phone commercial, are said not just to solve simple day-to-day problems but to provide unprecedented access to the highest human virtues.

To equate technological development with the achievement of human virtue in this way is to suggest that one can squeeze water from a stone. However, in contrast to the Grimm brothers' fairy tale where deception is understood as such by the deceiver, the brave little tailors of Silicon Valley marry the manipulative appeal of brand marketing to a sincerely held belief in the liberating power of software engineering and information networks. What makes today's technologists unique is their impassioned belief that digital products will transform and ultimately redeem the world as evolving super-intelligent networks surpass mere human understanding. Today's tech evangelists offer belabored apologetics for the social ills of mass advertising and market capitalism on the premise that its eventual fruits will satiate the universal human appetite for peace and happiness.

Silicon Valley's moral catechism represents precisely the type of fanaticism and hubris that the Founders had sought to avoid in their arguments on behalf of religious disestablishment, religious liberty, and freedom of the press. Just as the pre-Revolutionary preacher George Whitefield had appropriated the tools of the marketplace to "ply a religious trade in the open air of the marketplace," today's techno-utopians act as secular evangelicals on behalf of "the Gospel of 'Singularity,'" where human beings and computer systems converge (Clements 2011). Just as

Whitefield succumbed to the vices of egregious self-promotion and cynical manipulation of the press, today's tech elite leverage cutting-edge neuro-marketing techniques to cultivate public acquiescence to their ever-increasing status as moral and technical gatekeepers. In Brueggemann's terms, "God is now 'on call,' and access to him is controlled by the royal court. ... No marginal person may approach this God except on the king's terms" (Brueggemann 2001, p. 35).

What precisely are those terms? They are, of course, the core assumptions that drive the catechism of Silicon Valley, with its naïve equation of human virtue and technical prowess. Those assumptions constitute the focus of the next several chapters, which beg for an alternative consciousness devoted not just to critiquing and dismantling the status quo but also to helping us imagine a hopeful, and more hope-filled, technological future.

Note

1 We do not mean to posit a simplistic dichotomy between an allegedly "authentic" Buddhism and Western-style Buddhism, where the former is morally upright and the latter is bankrupt. For a discussion of this issue, see Healey (2015).

References

Armstrong, Ben. *The Electric Church.* Nashville, TN: Thomas Nelson, 1979.

Barbrook, Richard, and Andy Cameron. "The Californian Ideology." Alamut. September 18, 1998. http://www.hrc.wmin.ac.uk/hrc/theory/californianideo/main/t.4.2.html.

Benhabib, Seyla. *The Claims of Culture: Equality and Diversity in the Global Era.* Princeton, NJ: Princeton University Press, 2002.

Brazier, David. *The New Buddhism.* New York: Palgrave Macmillan, 2002.

Brueggemann, Walter. *The Prophetic Imagination.* 2nd ed. Minneapolis, MN: Fortress Press, 2001.

Carey, James, ed. *Communication as Culture: Essays on Media and Society.* Boston, MA: Unwin Hyman, 1989.

Carr, Nicholas. *The Shallows: What the Internet Is Doing to Our Brains.* New York: W. W. Norton, 2010.

Chesterton, G. K. *Orthodoxy: The Romance of Faith.* New York: Image Books, 1990.

Christians, Clifford G. "Jacques Ellul's Conversions and Protestant Theology." *Journal of Media and Religion* 5, no. 3 (2006):147–60.

———. "Redemptive Media as the Evangelical's Cultural Task." In *American Evangelicals and the Mass Media,* edited by Quentin J. Schultze, 331–56. Grand Rapids, MI: Zondervan Academie, 1990.

Clements, Warren. "Futuristic Documentary Is Both Exhilarating and Sad." *The Globe and Mail,* March 4, 2011. https://www.theglobeandmail.com/arts/futuristic-documentary-is-both-exhilarating-and-sad/article622834/.

Czitrom, Daniel. *Media and the American Mind from Morse to McLuhan.* Chapel Hill, NC: University of North Carolina Press, 1982.

Davis, Erik. *TechGnosis: Myth, Magic, and Mysticism in the Age of Information.* New York: Harmony Books, 1998.

Dayton, Donald. *Theological Roots of Pentecostalism.* Grand Rapids, MI: Baker Academic, 1987.

Dery, Mark. *Escape Velocity: Cyberculture at the End of the Century.* New York: Grove Press, 1997.

Dewey, John. *Individualism Old and New.* New York: Prometheus Books, 1999.

Dyson, Esther, George Gilder, George Keyworth, and Alvin Toffler. "Cyberspace and the American Dream: A Magna Carta for the Knowledge Age." Original release August 22, 1994. *Information Society* 12, no. 3 (1996): 295–308.

Ellul, Jacques. *Presence of the Kingdom.* 1948. Reprint ed., New York: Seabury, 1967.

———. *Propaganda: The Formation of Men's Attitudes.* New York: Knopf, 1971.

———. "Symbolic Function, Technology and Society." *Journal of Social and Biological Structures* 1 (1978): 207–18.

Ewen, Stewart. *PR! A Social History of Spin.* New York: Basic Books, 1996.

Fleischacker, Samuel. "Adam Smith's Reception among the American Founders, 1776–1790." *The William and Mary Quarterly* 59, no. 4 (October 2002): 897–924.

Frank, Thomas. *One Market under God: Extreme Capitalism, Market Populism, and the End of Economic Democracy.* New York: Anchor, 2001.

Geraci, Robert M. *Apocalyptic AI.* New York: Oxford University Press, 2010.

Gomery, Douglas. "Nickelodeons to Movie Palaces." In *Communication in History: Technology, Culture, Society*, edited by David Crowley and Paul Heyer, 201–6. 2nd ed. White Plains, NY: Longman, 1995.

Graham, Billy. "The Future of TV Evangelism." *TV Guide* 31, no. 10 (1983): 8.

Grieve, Gregory Price. "A Virtual Bodhi Tree: Untangling the Cultural Context and Historical Genealogy of Digital Buddhism." In *Buddhism, the Internet, and Digital Media: The Pixel in the Lotus*, edited by Gregory Price Grieve and Daniel Veidlinger, 93–113. New York: Routledge, 2015.

Grimm, Jacob, and Wilhelm Grimm. *Grimm's Household Tales*, edited by E. Norris. New York: Educational Publishing, 1906.

Hagerty, Barbara Bradley. "Divining Doomsday: An Old Practice with New Tricks." All Things Considered, National Public Radio. May 12, 2011. http://www.npr.org/2011/05/12/136239062/divining-doomsday-an-old-practice-with-new-tricks.

Hatch, Nathan O. *The Democratization of American Christianity.* New Haven, CT: Yale University Press, 1989.

Healey, Kevin. "Coercion, Consent, and the Struggle for Social Media." *Explorations in Media Ecology* 13 (2014a): 195–212.

———. "Solitude and Presence: Photo Reflections on Natural and Digital Ecologies." *Nomos Journal.* February 27, 2014b. http://nomosjournal.org/2014/02/solitude-and-presence/.

———. "Disrupting Wisdom 2.0: The Quest for 'Mindfulness' in Silicon Valley and Beyond." *Journal of Religion, Media and Digital Culture* 4, no. 1 (2015): 67–95.

———. "Information Is Not Wisdom, Convergence Is Not Integrity: Proverbs for an Era of Digital Humanism." *Explorations in Media Ecology* 15, nos. 3–4 (2017): 355–72.

Healey, Kevin, and Robert Woods Jr. "Processing Is Not Judgment, Storage Is Not Memory: A Critique of Silicon Valley's Moral Catechism." *Journal of Media Ethics* 32, no. 1 (2017): 2–15.

Isaacson, Walter. *Steve Jobs.* New York: Simon & Schuster, 2011.

Krueger, Alan B. "The Many Faces of Adam Smith: Rediscovering *The Wealth of Nations.*" *New York Times*, August 16, 2001.

Kruse, Kevin M. *One Nation under God: How Corporate America Invented Christian America.* New York: Basic Books, 2015.

Lambert, Frank. *The Founding Fathers and the Place of Religion in America.* Princeton, NJ: Princeton University Press, 2006.

Lanier, Jaron. *You Are Not a Gadget: A Manifesto.* New York: Vintage Books, 2011.

Loy, David R. "Why Buddhism and the West Need Each Other: On the Interdependence of Personal and Social Transformation." *Journal of Buddhist Ethics* 20 (2013): 401–21.

McChesney, Robert W. *The Problem of the Media: U.S. Communication Politics in the 21st Century.* New York: Monthly Review, 2004.

———. *Digital Disconnect: How Capitalism Is Turning the Internet against Democracy.* New York: The New Press, 2013.

Mansell, Robin. *Imagining the Internet: Communication, Innovation, and Governance.* Oxford: Oxford University Press, 2012.

Martin, William. *With God on Our Side: The Rise of the Religious Right in America.* New York: Broadway Books, 1996.

Marvin, Carolyn. *When Old Technologies Were New: Thinking about Electric Communications in the Late Nineteenth Century.* New York: Oxford University Press, 1987.

Marsden, George M. *Fundamentalism and American Culture: The Shaping of Twentieth-Century Evangelicalism 1870–1925.* New York: Oxford University Press, 1980.

Maslin, Janet. "Will the Future Be a Trillion Times Better?" *New York Times,* October 3, 2005. http://www.nytimes.com/2005/10/03/books/03masl.html.

Matyszczyk, Chris. "Zuckerberg: I Know That People Don't Want Privacy." CNET. January 10, 2010. https://www.cnet.com/news/zuckerberg-i-know-that-people-dont-want-privacy/.

Miller, Vincent J. *Consuming Religion: Christian Faith and Practice in a Consumer Culture.* New York: Continuum, 2004.

Moore, R. Lawrence. *Selling God: American Religion in the Marketplace of Culture.* New York: Oxford University Press, 1994.

Myers, Kenneth A. *All God's Children and Blue Suede Shoes: Christians and Popular Culture.* Westchester, IL: Crossway Books, 1989.

Myers, Paul Z. "Ray Kurzweil Does Not Understand the Brain." Pharyngula Science Blog. August 17, 2010. http://scienceblogs.com/pharyngula/2010/08/17/ray-kurzweil-does-not-understa/.

Postman, Neil. *Amusing Ourselves to Death.* New York: Penguin, 1985.

———. *Technopoly: The Surrender of Culture to Technology.* New York: Knopf, 1992.

Postone, Moishe. "Review of *The Theory of Communicative Action: Vol. 2: Lifeworld and System: A Critique of Functionalist Reason,* by Jurgen Habermas." *Contemporary Sociology* 19, no. 2 (March 1990): 170–6.

Robeck, Cecil M., Jr. *The Azusa Street Mission and Revival: The Birth of the Global Pentecostal Movement.* Nashville, TN: Emanate Books, 2006.

Robinson, Brett T. *Appletopia: Media Technology and the Religious Imagination of Steve Jobs.* Waco, TX: Baylor University Press, 2013.

Roof, Wade Clark. *Spiritual Marketplace: Baby Boomers and the Remaking of American Religion.* Princeton, NJ: Princeton University Press, 1999.

Reps, Paul, and Nyogen Senzaki, eds. *Zen Flesh, Zen Bones: A Collection of Zen and Pre-Zen Writings.* Boston: Tuttle Publishing, 1998.

Sawhney, Harmeet. "Universal Service: Prosaic Motives and Great Ideals." *Journal of Broadcasting and Electronic Media* 38, no. 4 (1994): 375–95.

Schultze, Quentin J. "The Mythos of the Electronic Church." *Critical Studies in Mass Communication* 4, no. 3 (September 1987): 245–61.

———. *Redeeming TV: How TV Changes Christians: How Christians Can Change TV.* Downer's Grove, IL: InterVarsity Press, 1992.

———. *Habits of the High Tech Heart: Living Virtuously in the Information Age.* Grand Rapids, MI: Baker Books, 2002.

————. *Christianity and the Mass Media in America: Toward a Democratic Accommodation.* East Lansing, MI: Michigan State University Press, 2003.

Searle, John R. *Philosophy in a New Century: Selected Essays.* New York: Cambridge University Press, 2008.

Silberman, Steve. "What Kind of Buddhist Was Steve Jobs, Really?" PLOS Blogs Network. October 25, 2015. https://blogs.plos.org/blog/2015/10/25/what-kind-of-buddhist-was-steve-jobs-really/.

Silk, Mark. *Unsecular Media: Making News of Religion in America.* Champaign, IL: University of Illinois Press, 1995.

Smith, Adam. *An Inquiry into the Nature and Causes of the Wealth of Nations*, edited by Edwin Cannan. Chicago, IL: University of Chicago Press, 1977.

Standage, Tom. *The Victorian Internet: The Remarkable Story of the Telegraph and the Nineteenth Century's Online Pioneers.* New York: Walker & Company, 1998.

Stevens, Elizabeth Lesly. "The Promise of Rapture for the High-Tech Elite." *New York Times*, April 23, 2011. http://www.nytimes.com/2011/04/24/us/24bcstevens.html.

Swaggart, Jimmy. "Divine Imperatives for Broadcast Ministry." *Religious Broadcasting.* November 1984, 14.

Turner, Fred. *From Counterculture to Cyberculture: Stewart Brand, the Whole Earth Network, and the Rise of Digital Utopianism.* Chicago, IL: University of Chicago Press, 2006.

Vaidhyanathan, Siva. *The Googlization of Everything (And Why We Should Worry).* Berkeley: University of California Press, 2011a.

————. "The Googlization of Everything." Berkman Klein Center. March 7, 2011b. https://cyber.harvard.edu/events/2011/02/vaidhyanathan.

Ward, Mark, Sr. *Air of Salvation: The Story of Christian Broadcasting.* Ada, MI: Baker Books, 1994.

Weber, Max. *The Protestant Ethic and the Spirit of Capitalism: And Other Writings*, edited by Peter Baehr. Trans. Gordon C. Wells. 1905. Reprint ed., New York: Penguin Classics, 2002.

Wilber, Ken. *Boomeritis: A Novel That Will Set You Free.* Boston, MA: Shambala Publications, 2002.

Woods, Robert H., Jr., and Kevin Healey. *Prophetic Critique and Popular Media: Theoretical Foundations and Practical Applications.* New York: Peter Lang, 2013.

Wuthnow, Robert. *After Heaven: Spirituality in America Since the 1950s.* Berkeley, CA: University of California Press, 1998.

Zukowski, Angela Ann. "Evangelization as Communication." In *The Church and Communication*, edited by Patrick Granfield, 158–78. Kansas City, MO: Sheed and Ward, 1994.

PART II

3

INFORMATION IS NOT WISDOM

On the morning of February 15, 2014, Amanda Ream zipped up a bag containing a protest banner emblazoned with the words "Eviction Free San Francisco." Over the previous several months, similar banners had appeared at events organized by this self-described "direct action group whose mission is to help stop the wave of evictions in San Francisco" (Eviction Free San Francisco 2019). With fellow activists in tow, Ream headed for the fifth yearly installment of the Wisdom 2.0 conference, where Silicon Valley leaders discuss the benefits of mindfulness, meditation, and yoga. As a member of Oakland's East Bay Meditation Center, Ream aimed to expose the irony of discussing "corporate mindfulness" amid the tech industry's gentrification of local neighborhoods.

With fabricated badges in hand, the protestors sat amid unknowing attendees before taking the conference stage during a panel titled "3 Steps to Build Corporate Mindfulness the Google Way" (Caring-Lobel 2014). As fellow activists held up the banner, Ream handed out flyers that read, "Thank you for your practice. We invite you to consider the truth behind Google and the tech industry's impact on San Francisco." Meanwhile Erin McElroy, self-described as "an anarchist, an anti-capitalist" and member of the Heart of the City activist collective, chanted through a bullhorn, "Wisdom means stop displacement! Wisdom means stop surveillance!" (Eaton 2014; Bowles 2014). The crowd initially applauded, thinking they were the first to experience some new kind of Google performance art. They soon figured out what was going on. Not long after, a feisty tug-of-war for the banner broke out on stage between protestors and Google security officers. As they were ushered off the stage, the protestors managed to wrestle the banner from the hands of a rather persistent security officer (Caring-Lobel 2014).

Disrupting Wisdom 2.0

The literal tug-of-war between information and wisdom at Wisdom 2.0 raises fundamental questions about the role of technology and tech companies in society: Are tech companies uniquely positioned to cultivate wisdom, individually and collectively? Does wisdom consist merely of the accumulation and dissemination of information? On both counts, the answer from these protestors is clearly "No." In fact, all politics aside, in highlighting the role of tech companies in the ongoing gentrification of San Francisco, Ream and her colleagues explicitly accuse tech companies like Google of lacking wisdom if we understand it in terms of collective well-being and happiness.

Information, knowledge, and wisdom are not synonymous. Information and knowledge are certainly related, but they are not sufficient criteria for wisdom. Wisdom is a "higher-type of knowledge" that involves an aptitude for understanding and using information "for the benefit of oneself and society" (Elliott and Spence 2018, p. 183). Wisdom is never selfish or self-centered. It catalyzes the common good. It recognizes "what is intrinsically good and right, what is worth knowing and remembering, and how to use it wisely, if at all" (Schultze 2002, p. 53). Wisdom helps us to answers questions like: How do we live well together? How do we pursue happiness as a community, a nation, a species? In answering such questions, information and technology are important resources, to be sure. But their contribution to the common good depends on the presence and exercise of prudence.

By contrast, tech companies insist on a simple equation between information and wisdom. Instead of considering the wisdom of the past, they turn to technological prophecy in the form of artificial intelligence or Ray Kurzweil's famed human-machine merger called the "Singularity." Google, in particular, expresses an almost singular emphasis on information as the vehicle for technological and social progress. Although Google's information-driven mission sounds good in theory, it translates quickly into moral hubris.

But if information is wisdom as Silicon Valley supposes, then technical development is both inevitable and inherently progressive. This perspective locates the capacity for ethical behavior not in human judgment but in the emergent intelligence of abstract technological systems. Google's mission encapsulates the religion of "informationism," that is, a "faith in the collection and dissemination of information as a route to social progress and personal happiness" (Schultze 2002, p. 21). It represents "the growing notion that one company—Google—could or would solve some of the greatest and most complex human problems simply by applying the principles of engineering" (Vaidhyanathan 2011a, p. xiii).

Beyond the localized protests in San Francisco like those involving Amanda Ream and "Eviction Free San Francisco," Google's global initiatives have raised serious concerns among citizens, consumer groups, and government watchdog agencies. Google's efforts to collect and retain user data, for example, have placed privacy at the top of the list. Google's practices have resulted in a number of Federal Trade Commission investigations and Federal Communication Commission fines.

The company's move to consolidate privacy policies across its many assets (including search, YouTube, Gmail, Google Maps, and Google Calendar) drew opposition from consumer groups and three U.S. Attorneys General, plus legal warnings from Japan and the European Union (Angwin and Valentino-Devries 2012). And while the evidence of harm from tech companies' arrogance is plentiful, most consumers and users have neither the time nor the interest to understand the nuances of their favorite platform's privacy policies, never mind a company's broader strategic goals. Despite the noble posture of attendees at Wisdom 2.0, the combined arrogance of elites and users' "blind faith in Google" are a recipe not for wisdom but for mindlessness.

This chapter examines several specific consequences of Silicon Valley's misguided notion that information is equivalent to wisdom, what we call "faux wisdom." We argue that advances in messaging power without a corresponding awakening of moral sensibilities leave us drowning in information abundance, acting more like machines than humans and confused about the purpose of life. The sheer magnitude of our information accessibility undermines our very ability to determine how good or incisive the information really is, and what it means for the quality of our lives and our communities. Over time, such indiscriminate information intake can lead to "informational promiscuity" or "impersonal relationships based on feigned intimacies and lacking moral integrity" (Schultze 2002, p. 35). In response, we chart a course for understanding how to "inform wisely" and avoid informational incoherence. We conclude this chapter by sharing examples of individuals and organizations who have developed "resistance thinking" in the form of practices and initiatives that harness the power of information in service of wisdom.

The Catechism: Information Is Wisdom

When asked in an interview what the perfect search engine would be like, Google co-founder Sergey Brin replied, "It would be like the Mind of God" (quoted in Vaidhyanathan 2011b). Though striking, the comment was a logical extension of views held by both Brin and his partner, Larry Page. From the very beginning, Page "viewed Google as an embryonic form of artificial intelligence" (Carr 2010, p. 172). As early as 2000, Page suggested that "artificial intelligence would be the ultimate version of Google" (Carr 2010, p. 172). In a speech at Stanford two years later, he hinted at the implications of this perspective, suggesting that "the ultimate search engine is something as smart as people—or smarter" (Carr 2010, p. 172). In fact, Page has indicated a broader belief that the Internet itself will eventually come to life—an event that some technologists believe has already happened (Lanier 2011, p. 49). In this scenario, software engineers play the role of midwives, birthing super-intelligent beings equipped to solve a vast range of human problems. In its embrace of engineering, Google's corporate culture recapitulates the "belief that intelligence is the output of a mechanical process, a series of discrete steps that can be isolated, measured, and optimized" (Carr 2010, p. 173). No wonder that from its inception Google has re-envisioned traditional models of corporate organization, placing engineers at the helm rather than designers, managers, and marketing experts (Auletta 2010, p. 20).

Formed in 1998 in a Menlo Park garage, Google was notable enough by 2001 to draw a visit from vice president Al Gore (Auletta 2010, p. 58). A decade later, it was "not just the largest Internet company in the world; it was one of the largest media companies, taking in more than $22 billion in sales a year, almost all of it from advertising, and turning a profit of about $8 billion" (Carr 2010, pp. 155–6). Despite its short history and relatively small workforce, Google's revenues have been impressive enough to spark debates among technology experts about whether Google will soon surpass its competitors. Its financial success is matched by its growing influence in legal and policy matters.

In pursuit of its mission of organizing the world's information, the company has embarked on ambitious projects that reach deeply into popular culture, government, and libraries throughout the world. Google's data-collection initiatives, for example, have legal repercussions that extend from the United States to China, an international phenomenon called "the Googlization of everything" (Vaidhyanathan 2011a). Yet the company's brand image of benign simplicity, epitomized by its official motto, "Don't be evil," has helped the Internet giant to fend off scrutiny about its projects and business practices.

This Is Your Brain on Google

Decades ago lay Catholic theologian and French sociologist Jacques Ellul warned that "excessive data do not enlighten the reader or the listener; they drown him" (Ellul 1973, p. 87). Today the problem is compounded through vast networks of shared data. The Internet, by design, fosters or cultivates the unfettered and indiscriminate dissemination of information in ways that are "capricious and unpredictable" (Elliot and Spence 2018, p. 183). Before information can become knowledge, it must be subjected to scrutiny: Is it truthful? Is it accurate? Wisdom lies a step beyond that. If we understand wisdom as "being able to see and appreciate the deepest significance of whatever occurs," we must understand not just the details, but the ultimate meaning of whatever knowledge we have accumulated (Emmons 1999, p. 154). While the judicious cultivation of information may yield real benefits, blind trust in the unfettered collection and aggregation of data "derails any quest for moral wisdom" (Schultze 2002, p. 21).

With habitual use, Internet technologies may actually inhibit critical thinking skills: the very capacities essential for envisioning long-term social change. Companies like Google benefit by having users interact with information not just more frequently but more quickly. This way, they can serve more ads and collect more information about users. Making one's way around this environment requires specific cognitive skills. Over time, due to its neuroplasticity the user's brain re-shapes itself to handle these new cognitive tasks.

Search engines and social media networks treat online content as a means to an end, namely, the collection of personal data that can be used to serve targeted advertisements. Especially in the context of marketers' efforts to "design for inter-ruption" (Alistair 2012), this process cultivates patterns of thought quite distinct from silent reading of traditional printed texts. Research on neuroplasticity—or the brain's ability to reshape itself through habit—indicates that searching and reading online shift our cognitive attention to a moment-by-moment discernment of relevance and importance (Carr 2010, p. 122). We must decide what to pay attention to and what to ignore, or when and what to click. While such skills are often useful, these habits interfere with the process of meaningfully interpreting information and integrating it into existing cognitive schemas.

In laboratory settings, subjects who are asked to multi-task experience difficulty in interpreting the meaning of their experience. In everyday settings like school, work, or recreation, these cognitive patterns undermine "deep reading" (Carr 2010, pp. 122–33) and lead us instead to act as hunters and gatherers of information with little patience for nuance. Though such behavior is antithetical to the achievement of wisdom, it is consistent with marketers' goal of encouraging consumers to "act on impulse and fantasy instead of reason" (Sachs 2011, p. 144). Moreover, deep reading generates fewer of the clicks, mouse-overs, and searches that constitute the raw data that sites package and sell to advertisers. Stillness of thought in the long stretch toward wisdom is revenue lost in the marketing game.

Let us be clear: we are not arguing that Google, or the Internet at large, makes us stupid, as popularly quipped. But it does encourage certain types of cognitive skills more than others. It channels our intelligence along certain paths while neglecting others. Developmental psychologists argue that while we may gain "new strengths in visual-spatial intelligence," we may lose our capacity for the type of "deep process-ing" required for "mindful knowledge acquisition, inductive analysis, critical think-ing, imagination, and reflection" (Carr 2010, p. 141). As we spend more time online, we become "more likely to rely on conventional ideas and solutions rather than challenging them with original lines of thought" (Carr 2010, p. 140). In the process, the human capacity for prophetic imagination is rendered fragile as well, including users' ability and willingness to challenge the ideology that drives the architecture of their favorite digital platforms.

The "University of Google"

Online personalization and targeted advertising also apply downward pressure to the quality of content as traditional sources scramble to recover lost revenue. The commercialization of the Internet has disrupted individual and institutional judgment by displacing traditional gatekeeping functions between editors and readers, doctors, and patients. Celebratory accounts such as Clay Shirky's (2008) *Here Comes Everybody*, which describe the fruits of crowd-sourcing and partici-patory culture, overlook the subtle ways that advertising-driven business models undermine the noble aspirations of corporate mission statements. While search rankings are optimized for shopping and consumption, they do not always enhance democratic debate or facilitate the process of learning. Investigative reporting and long-form journalism lose out to armchair critics, bloggers, and content farms who mass-produce articles and videos to match the latest search term trends. Touted as guarantors of relevance, such personalization strategies exacerbate users' tendency to seek out self-affirmation, regardless of the veracity of one's views.

Such patterns can have troubling results when it comes to online health information, which is among the most sought-after online material (Rosen 2012, p. 143). Based partly on articles discovered through what she called "the University of Google," actress Jenny McCarthy argued publicly that autism is linked to childhood vaccinations, a notion based on research that has since been retracted and denounced as "an elaborate fraud" by the *British Medical Journal* (Godlee et al. 2011, p. 78).

Similarly, online doctors' ratings tend to prioritize bedside manner and patient satisfaction over accuracy in diagnosis (Hensley 2014). One Stanford University medical researcher details the story of a young patient named Ashley who claimed to suffer from depression. Ashley reluctantly agreed to a consultation with the researcher, who diagnosed her as anorexic. She had apparently been seeking anti-depression medication for its effectiveness as an appetite suppressant, having gleaned such information from online "pro-anorexia" groups. The psychologist running the young woman's group session soon asked her to leave, citing her "constant defiance and the distorted, partial knowledge clearly gleaned online that Ashley would use to refute every fact the group leader was trying to communicate" (Aboujaoude 2011, p. 201). In combination with the selective use of online pharmaceutical information, patients in such scenarios often rely on ratings websites to find a doctor willing to prescribe a desired medication, regardless of whether it is appropriate or not.

Such problems are not necessarily resolved through the aggregation of vast amounts of information, or Big Data. The common assumption that it does amounts to "Big Data fundamentalism," that is, "the idea with larger data sets, we get closer to objective truth" (Hardy 2013). Such data sets can certainly serve as important tools for tracking political discourse, or for predicting and managing disease outbreaks and weather emergencies. As shown in the 2012 case of hurricane Sandy, however, it is clear that aggregate data can also be prejudicial and misleading. Kate Crawford, a researcher at Microsoft Research, describes the twenty million Twitter posts about the hurricane as "very privileged urban stories," since the relatively small percentage of Americans who use Twitter are young and wealthy compared to the general population (Hardy 2013). The locations most desperate for assistance during hurricane Sandy yielded few tweets. As in the case of medical diagnoses, proper response efforts in weather emergencies require not simply access to information but coordination between researchers, journalists, and governments to provide necessary context and informed judgment.

Social media also facilitates widespread belief in a range of politically consequential rumors such as the belief that Barack Obama is Muslim or that scientists have not reached a consensus on the issue of climate change (Sunstein 2012, pp. 91–106). This problem reached its apex during the 2016 U.S. presidential election when false stories planted by foreign governments proliferated on Facebook. Sincerity and truthfulness are no longer commonly held norms for political discourse in what news reporters often call the "post-truth" era.

As became clear during Mark Zuckerberg's congressional testimony in April 2018, software engineers design algorithms to please and reward users and not to inform with accuracy or steer users from propaganda. We refer to this problem as the *personalization of truth*. While users do bear responsibility in these cases, we must also recognize the role of tech companies' efforts to generate trust among users. The perception that Google's search results, or Facebook's News Feed algorithm, are intelligent and objective tends to increase users' trust, thereby reducing their willingness and capacity to discern truth from fiction or to care about that distinction in the first place. Blind faith in tech undermines our better judgment about the truthfulness of information we encounter.

Challenging the Catechism: Information Is Not Wisdom

While we reject the catechism that information is inherently good, we likewise reject the notion that information and its digitization is inherently bad. But that does not mean it is morally neutral. The proliferation of data fundamentally alters our culture's moral ecology. If it makes some decisions easier, it makes others more complicated and pressing. It raises the stakes for everyone. The question is how to harness the power of information *in service of* wisdom from the individual to the collective.

Wisdom involves the capacity to translate new information *from* the world outside into knowledge *about* that world, in a way that facilitates prudent judgment in our engagement *with* the world. To be wise is to have at one's disposal not just a sophisticated map of oneself and the world in which one lives but also the capacity and the willingness to redraw one's map continually. That capacity is difficult to achieve because it means we must continually relinquish our assumptions about what we think we know, and even who we think we are, to realize a deeper truth about ourselves and the world around us. Wisdom requires not just judgment but courage, humility, tenacity, persistence, and grit.

In a message on the 48th World Communications Day, Pope Francis argued that since "the speed with which information is communicated exceeds our capacity for reflection and judgment," we need to cultivate "more balanced and proper forms of expression," including especially "the ability to be silent and to listen" (Pope Francis 2014). There is plenty of noise in the digital age; so much noise that we can barely hear ourselves think. But are we listening? To listen fully, we first need the capacity to withstand silence; to stand, or sit, in a silent space; to be alone in the space of one's own thoughts; to be still. But since stillness and silence usually fail to produce data, listening in this meaningful way is anathema to Silicon Valley's moral catechism. Listening is inefficient. Yet listening has a power much like Martin Luther King Jr.'s non-violent social activism. Though the latter initially appears to lack any substantive action, it can actually rejuvenate us and help promote social justice. Listening opens up space for us to reconsider who we are, who we should trust, and how we should act.

Perhaps this is why, in part, many of us find it difficult to appreciate the benefits of reading printed material. We skim text online, but we are not avid, cover-to-cover readers of books. A book made of pulp, fiber, and ink does not personalize itself on the spot, nor does it record and share your experience of reading for others to comment upon. Reading requires self-discipline: the ability to maintain focus and attention and to keep re-committing oneself to the task at hand. In an important sense, reading has become a form of resistance, a counter-practice that defies the economic logic and cognitive demands of the digital landscape. The act, and art, of reading printed books is experiencing a renaissance of sorts among younger people. This renewed interest in print, we suggest, represents a crack in the catechism and an opportunity to move beyond the predominant narrative that information is tantamount to wisdom.

Reading as Resistance

It is likely that we read more today than we did decades ago. But it is a different type of reading, and behind it resides a different type of thinking. In the digital age, our thinking has become somewhat hyper-textual as we struggle to pay attention to longer forms of writing, or longer forms of anything for that matter. Thought-life takes on a choppy quality that mirrors the way we quickly scan multiple online sources. Our minds expect to consume information in the same way the Web sends it out: in a fast, mercurial-moving stream of bits and bytes. "Once I was a scuba diver in the sea of words," explains Nicholas Carr, award-winning author of *The Shallows*. "Now I zip along the surface like a guy on a Jet Ski" (Carr 2010, p. 7).

On December 31, 2012, *Newsweek* ended its 80-year print run and transitioned to an online-only format. At the time, it was "the most widely-read magazine yet to give up on print media" (Daniel and Hagey 2012). Three years later, the National Education Association reported that only a third of fourth and eighth graders were reading at grade level (Johnson 2016). These trends are related. The demise of print and the transition to digital have not only changed how and why we read but have also negatively impacted our ability to comprehend and understand the content we read.

But we need not indulge in moral panic about the death of print, or the loss of reading as a foundational skill. Despite important shifts in the production and consumption of written content, interest in reading, including printed books, is enjoying a renaissance of sorts even among college-aged people. On one hand, this renaissance is symptomatic in a way that is concerning: it reflects an implicit, perhaps unconscious response to the stresses of information overload. On the other hand, it offers a ray of hope: despite the presence of these stressors, people young and old are finding ways to resist the imperatives of the digital economy—the constant pressures to move and think faster, to glean information rather than to reflect and interpret, to find and generate meaning.

Initial upward trends in the e-book market were misleading. Sales of e-books spiked by a whopping 1,260 percent from 2008 to 2010 (Alter 2015). And yet, despite the increasing dominance of Amazon and big box stores like Walmart, independent bookstores are experiencing a resurgence. In 2015, the American Booksellers Association reported significant increases in the number of its members' stores and the span of their locations (Alter 2015).

Meanwhile, many elementary and high schools have implemented programs to increase frequency and interest in reading among students. Such programs go by numerous acronyms including Drop Everything and Read (DEAR), Free Uninterrupted Reading (FUR), or simply Silent Sustained Reading (SSR).

As an undergraduate student at University of New Hampshire (UNH) in 2017, Patrick Niland focused his senior capstone project on his love of reading printed books. Recalling the SSR program from his high school experience, Patrick wrote, "this practice became something we would do every day. We would carve out twenty minutes and the class would read silently. This was met with some resistance by the students. But I always enjoyed it" (Niland 2017). During his final semester at UNH, Patrick decided to read three novels in addition to his assigned class readings: Haruki Murakami's *Kafka on the Shore*, John Steinbeck's *Of Mice and Men*, and Robert Palmer's *Deep Blues*. He later reported the following:

> I personally find myself happiest when I'm supplementing my day to day life with a book. While the most stressful parts of the semester might be in front of me, I've found comfort in disconnecting from my phone and reading for an extended period of time. ... I was able to use reading as a powerful tool for re-centering my life. In doing so I was able to turn several of my closest friends on to reading literature.
>
> (Niland 2017)

As part of the service component of his project, Patrick returned to his elementary school to read to a first-grade class. He visited the classroom of his own first-grade teacher, Ms. Allman. "I'm truly touched to be able to gain this experience," Patrick wrote, adding, "Reading to children is something of great importance. It helps with their development."

During the following fall semester at UNH, then-senior Justin Rogers completed a similar capstone project focused on what Daniel P. Barbezat and Mirabai Bush (2014, p. 115) call "contemplative reading," or what Justin prefers to call "mindful reading." Over the course of the semester, Justin set goals for himself and kept track of his achievements. In his final paper, he reported his progress:

> By not having a screen in front of my face in the hour or two before bed, my circadian rhythm could reach some sense of normality, and I found that I was able to fall asleep easier on nights I had done reading before bed. This also had the effect of being able to wake up more easily and retain the information the next morning.
>
> (Rogers 2018)

Justin was especially interested in the cognitive differences between reading print material versus online text. Drawing from recent cognitive research, he argued that literature is a kind of simulation that runs on the software of the mind, and that print material is better at facilitating this imaginative capacity, while digital reading platforms impose distracting cognitive barriers (Oatley 1999). "This capacity to run the simulation in your mind is [a form of] practice," Justin writes, "and it builds the skills necessary for wisdom" (Rogers 2018). Like Patrick, Justin's project upends the stereotype of "digital natives" as being averse to, and even contemptuous of, analog media.

Furthermore, research demonstrates that when we screen-read, we are less likely to take part in "metacognitive learning regulation," which includes strategies such as setting specific goals, rereading difficult portions, or checking our understanding as we go. In one research study, students took multiple-choice exams about expository texts either on computers or paper. Half the students were limited to seven minutes of study time; the other half could review the text for as long as they liked. When pressured to read quickly, screen readers and paper readers performed equally well. But when managing study time, paper readers scored 10 percentage points higher. Paper readers presumably approached the exam with a more studious mindset than screen-readers and more effectively directed their attention and working memory (Ackerman and Goldsmith 2011).

Karolyn Kinane, Associate Director of Faculty Engagement and Pedagogy at the University of Virginia's Contemplative Sciences Center, has spent over a dozen years developing contemplative approaches to reading. Her work underscores the insights reported by students like Patrick and Justin. Kinane understands reading not merely as a passive activity of information gathering but also as a spiritual practice of meaning-making that strengthens one's ethical commitments and ties to one's community and the broader world. This framework makes sense given the history of religious believers in leveraging reflective reading as a path to wisdom. Judaism, for example, describes four distinct aspects of the practice of reading: *lectio*, or reading and understanding a text; *meditatio*, which involves reflection and contextualizing a text; *oratio*, or listening within and living the meaning of a text; and *contemplatio*, which means being still and meeting God in a text (Barbezat and Bush 2014, p. 111). As a professor of English literature, Kinane aims to cultivate in students similarly reflective dispositions toward works like *Beowulf*, the legends of King Arthur, or Christopher Marlowe's *The Tragical History of Doctor Faustus*.

We spoke to Professor Kinane about her approach to reading and its relation to contemporary issues of information-overwhelm. For reading to be more than information gathering, she notes, it must fulfill the definition of a practice, that is, something that has a clear intentionality to it. As suggested by Patrick's and Justin's projects, reading becomes a reflective practice when it occurs within a bounded time and place; in other words, when we relate to reading as a sacred activity deserving of our exclusive attention. Theoretically speaking, it is possible to engage texts in this way when we read essays or articles on the Internet. However, as Kinane (2018) notes, "the medium might not lend itself to that kind of intentionality."

FIGURE 3.1   Prof. Karolyn Kinane (center), Associate Director of Faculty Engagement and Pedagogy at the University of Virginia's Contemplative Sciences Center, at the 38th Annual Medieval and Renaissance Forum. Students presented contemplative approaches to medieval and Renaissance texts. Pictured left to right: John Rodgers, Rachael Ferranti, Karolyn Kinane, Lindsey DeRoche, and Jessica Eldridge.

What does such focused attention and set-aside time provide for readers? Here again, Kinane's approach reflects the religious traditions in which contemplative practices are rooted. Most education is focused on delivery of content and acquisition of skills. We often read to retain information just long enough to pass a quiz. But when we conceive of reading as a form of practice, she argues, this framework "leads us to think about our classes and homework in devotional terms." We begin to examine our own foundational values; the people and things we care about most deeply. We begin to ask ourselves, "What am I devoted to?" The classroom then becomes a context in which we do more than acquire information, knowledge, or skills. We develop the capacity to recognize, understand, and even change our habitual dispositions toward the texts we read and the characters within them. We can approach a text that is centuries old, and arguably outdated, and approach it with curiosity and humility. We can approach any text with what Kinane describes as "faith," a kind of proactive trust that the texts we read can have meaning for us if we are willing to discover and generate it together with our fellow students and, importantly, our teachers.

This capacity to examine our own dispositions, and to have faith in the ultimate meaningfulness of even the most dated, strange, or offensive text, is applicable in almost every area of life. Consider the context of political partisanship in the United States at the time of this writing and imagine if politicians and citizens alike had the capacity to apply Kinane's techniques of contemplative reading. Kinane tells us, "Imagine that this text was true, good, beautiful, or interesting to someone. How could you empathize with someone who finds it true, good, or beautiful?" Such willingness to approach strange texts with a disposition of humility, or even what Kinane calls "enchantment," is directly applicable to issues of public reasoning and public discourse, as for instance when we hear a political speech or read an op-ed in the newspaper. "How can we take the insights we gain from engaging these texts through these reading practices," Kinane asks, "and apply them right here, right now, in our own relationships?"

Religious Tradition as Resistance

Kinane's approach highlights how listening to a religious tradition can serve as a form of resistance thinking. Traditions offer a spiritual journey through the distraction of digital culture into conversations about enduring heart-and-mind habits that cut across time and culture. As Kinane demonstrates, listening to religious tradition helps to cultivate moral wisdom and other non-technical virtues that confront Silicon Valley's confusion about the relationship between information and wisdom.

We use "religion" not to refer to a particular religious faith or institution but more broadly to the ultimate meaning and purpose of life, along with complementary practices, habits, or customs that support ultimate meaning and purpose. Religion comes from the root word *religio*, which means "to rebind" (Greenleaf 2002, p. 231). Religion's purpose is to "reveal to people how they can be reconciled to each other, to themselves, and to the physical world" (Schultze 2002, p. 72). To act religiously in the world, then, is to "rebind" the brokenness we experience in our relationships with other beings present in the cosmos and the environment itself.

Environmental activist and cultural critic Wendell Berry suggests that religion answers a crucially important question: *What Are People For?* (Berry 1990). We must answer that question first before we can ask wisely what information technologies are for, and how we should use them. Technologies are made for human beings; in other words, human beings are not made for technology. As the primary carriers of non-instrumental wisdom, religious traditions confront the "secular-rational logic of informationism" and remind us to keep "first things first" (Schultze 2002, p. 74).

The record of a tradition gathered in sacred texts, writings, and practices suggests a starting place in our search for "first things." We do not mean tradition as "outdated rules, meaningless habits, or petty moralisms" that sustain oppressive power structures, but tradition as the "accumulated wisdom and the resulting disciplines, customs, and beliefs that a people carries from person to person through generational time—all of it nurtured as a living dialogue that includes the remembered 'voices' of the past" (Schultze 2002, p. 75).

When viewed this way, tradition involves personal responsibility. Community members are responsible for seriously engaging what is passed down: for interpreting it, applying it to the present moment, and preserving it for the next generation. As information technologies substitute newer information for wisdom, religious traditions make available proven "rebinding" agents.

English philosopher and Catholic lay theologian G. K. Chesterton calls tradition a "democracy of the dead" that "refuses to submit to that arrogant oligarchy who merely happen to be walking around" (Chesterton 1990, p. 48). Following a religious tradition, then, does not mean we return to a dead culture but instead embrace a way of remembering time-tested wisdom in ever-changing cultural contexts. A tradition must be flexible enough to address unpredictable challenges, to seize unexpected cultural opportunities, and to overcome its own shortcomings. Although traditions are not completely static, they do seek to preserve what is good and right in human culture by giving us the ethical "oughts" that digital culture finds inefficient and irrelevant (Schultze 2002, p. 75).

Reconnecting with Tradition

Traditional counter-voices today can help to keep alive religious tradition as a frame of moral reference. One example is The Institute of Buddhist Studies and their Public Theologies of Technology and Presence (PTTP) program, funded by the Henry Luce Foundation. Scholars across several disciplines draw on the study and practice of many different religions including Buddhism, Judaism, Hinduism, Catholicism, and Africana religions to address "the ways in which technologies reshape human relationships and alter how people are or are not 'present' with each other" (Public Theologies 2019). (As mentioned in our Acknowledgments, PTTP is a direct sponsor of this book project.) The International Institute for the Study of Technology and Christianity (IISTC) is a non-profit organization dedicated to studying similar issues from a Judeo-Christian tradition. Through its blog and journal *Second Nature*, IISTC draws readers from several religions into critical conversations about the relationship between new media and human flourishing. Wisdom chasers such as those mentioned above challenge Silicon Valley's moral catechism by offering stimulating insights into the way technology affects self-identity, interpersonal relationships, and moral commitments across the public sphere.

Tradition-based counter-voices may also exist in more traditional communal media institutions, such as religious publications or presses. For example, *Tikkun* describes itself as "the Prophetic Jewish, Interfaith & Secular Voice to Heal and Transform the World" (https://www.tikkun.org/). *Commonweal, U.S. Catholic, Christianity Today*, and *Christian Century* tackle Silicon Valley's hypocrisy and technological hubris that elevate human achievement over human dignity and social justice. Wisdom Publications publishes books, podcasts, and online courses that advance critical scholarship on classic and contemporary Buddhism and help individuals locate "teachings and practices for a wise and compassionate life" (Wisdom Publications https://www.wisdompubs.org/about-wisdom). Paulist Press and InterVarsity Press provide Catholic and Protestant critical scholarship, respectively, that demonstrate how we have grown comfortably numb to the narcotic-like effects of digital drug 2.0, which impedes our personal growth, spiritual formation, and service to others.

Instead of delivering trendy content in an effort to attract new audiences, such publications and presses foster "communion and discernment that help the tribe to locate itself at the intersection of tribal tradition and the public interest" (Schultze 2003, p. 92). Over the long run, these efforts will strengthen tradition interdependence, but also serve a prophetic role for their readers by helping them to see mainstream culture and their own tribe critically through the lens of their own religious tradition. For without "a shared religious language and common core labels, tribal media cannot sustain significant prophetic conversation" (Schultze 2003, p. 99). They will lose their own special perspective on the world around them.

In short, the customs and practices found in religious traditions can cultivate non-instrumental virtues that challenge Silicon Valley's moral catechism, protect human freedom, and help democracy flourish. People following religious tradition were primary movers and shakers for some of the most significant social advances in history, including the abolition of the slave trade, Civil Rights in the United States, and the overthrow of apartheid in South Africa. Nineteenth-century French diplomat and political scientist Alexis de Tocqueville, best known for his work *Democracy in America*, observed that such values mainly arise not from participation in civil affairs but from voluntary commitments to religious traditions (de Tocqueville 2000, pp. 278–79). A transformative society relies on religious traditions' roots that give us a sense of responsibility for things greater than our self-interests.

Conclusion

As the tug-of-war for Eviction Free San Francisco's banner concluded, one Google senior manager tried to calm the now-stunned crowd by instructing onlookers to "check in with your body" and "feel what it's like to be in conflict with people with heartfelt ideas." The Wisdom 2.0 team issued a rapid response, praising its corporate sponsor for its "kindness and compassion. Of course, only in a country where corporations are legally people could a corporation be mindful, too" (Caring-Lobel 2014). Good advice. But something is a bit off.

On the website of the Buddhist Peace Fellowship, Katie Loncke, who had attended the first Wisdom 2.0 conference in 2010, took issue with the senior manager's handling of the protest. "What about the mindfulness, happiness, and wellbeing of the people mining coltan in the DRC, or the people assembling iPhones at the infamous Foxconn sweatshops? I mean, if we exclude them from the picture, then yes, we can calmly check in with our bodies. … But such deep exclusion invites deep delusion" (Loncke 2014). Fellow protestor Amanda Ream likewise described the senior manager's response as "a case study in spiritual bypassing," since "no one addressed the issues we were raising, not then or later on in the conference" (Ream 2014).

To be sure, the path to wisdom includes a judicious embrace of digital media and information processing. Search engines and social media provide access to valuable information which may contribute to the accumulation of knowledge and, in turn, wisdom if users can become adept at "seeking true beliefs and weeding out false ones" (Taylor 2016, p. 603). But as Professor Kinane cautions, we are not, collectively speaking, even adept at this initial skill, as exemplified by the influence of "fake news" and foreign propaganda on U.S. elections. The path to wisdom still begins, and is sustained by, the flesh-and-blood work we do with each other in traditionally analog spaces—Patrick's library, Professor Kinane's classroom, or traditional religious spaces, for example. The resurgence of interest in reading printed books is therefore reassuring, but it cannot solve the broader systemic issues outlined here. We will return to broader policy solutions in Chapter 9.

We certainly can and should continue to harness the informational power that Web 2.0 technologies provide. But using that power wisely is a complex proposition. As American astronomer and best-selling author Clifford Stoll explains, the assumption that information and power are co-equal and inherently good is a distortion of Francis Bacon's famous saying "knowledge is power." Most likely, Bacon was referring to Proverbs 24:5: "A wise man has great power, and a man of knowledge increases strength" (Stoll 1999, p. 143). Understood in this sense, power ought to be moderated by moral wisdom. The two are not synonymous. Whatever level of technological achievement we experience, its ultimate value to human beings will depend on our ability to listen wisely to non-instrumental counter-voices.

References

Aboujaoude, Elias. *Virtually You: The Dangerous Powers of the e-Personality*. New York: W. W. Norton, 2011.

Ackerman, Rakefeet, and Morris Goldsmith. "Metacognitive Regulation of Text Learning: On Screen versus on Paper." *Journal of Experimental Psychology: Applied* 17, no. 1 (2011): 18–32.

Alter, Alexandra. "The Plot Twist: E-Book Sales Slip, and Print Is Far from Dead." *The New York Times*, September 22, 2015. https://www.nytimes.com/2015/09/23/business/media/the-plot-twist-e-book-sales-slip-and-print-is-far-from-dead.html.

Angwin, Julia, and Valentino-Devries, Jennifer. "Google's iPhone Tracking." *The Wall Street Journal*, February 17, 2012. http://online.wsj.com/article/SB10001424052970204880404577225380456599176.html.

Auletta, Ken. *Googled: The End of the World as We Know It*. New York: Penguin, 2010.

Barbezat, Daniel P., and Mirabai Bush. *Contemplative Practices in Higher Education: Powerful Methods to Transform Teaching and Learning*. San Francisco, CA: Jossey-Boss, 2014.

Berry, Wendell. *What Are People For?* New York: North Point Press, 1990.

Bowles, Nellie. "Coffee with an Anarchist: Memes and Motives behind Blocking Google Buses." Vox. April 22, 2014. https://www.vox.com/2014/4/22/11625908/coffee-with-an-anarchist-memes-and-motives-behind-blocking-google.

Caring-Lobel, Alex. "Protesters Crash Google Talk on Corporate Mindfulness at Wisdom 2.0 Conference." Tricycle. February 17, 2014. https://tricycle.org/trikedaily/protesters-crash-google-talk-corporate-mindfulness-wisdom-20-conference/.

Carr, Nicholas. *The Shallows: What the Internet Is Doing to Our Brains*. New York: W. W Norton, 2010.

Chesterton, G. K. *Orthodoxy: The Romance of Faith*. New York: Image Books, 1990.

Christian Century Magazine. https://www.christiancentury.org/.

Christianity Today Magazine. https://www.christianitytoday.com/.

Commonweal. https://www.commonwealmagazine.org/.

Croll, Alistair. "Design for Interruption." Solve for Interesting. November 6, 2012. http://solveforinteresting.com/design-for-interruption/.

de Tocqueville, Alexis. *Democracy in America,* edited and translated by Harvey C. Mansfield and Delba Winthrop. Chicago, IL: University of Chicago Press, 2000.

Daniel, Robert, and Keach Hagey. "Turning a Page: *Newsweek* Ends Print Run." *The Wall Street Journal,* December 26, 2012. https://www.wsj.com/articles/SB10001424127887324660404578201432812202750.

Eaton, Joshua. "Gentrifying the Dharma: How the 1 Percent is Hijacking Mindfulness." Salon. March 5, 2014. https://www.salon.com/2014/03/05/gentrifying_the_dharma_how_the_1_is_hijacking_mindfulness/.

Elliott, Deni, and Edward H. Spence. *Ethics for a Digital Era.* Hoboken, NJ: John Wiley & Sons, 2017.

Ellul, Jacques. *Propaganda: The Formation of Men's Attitudes,* translated by Konrad Kellen and Jean Lerner. New York: Vintage Books, 1973.

Emmons, Robert A. *The Psychology of Ultimate Concerns: Motivation and Spirituality in Personality.* New York: Guilford Press, 1999.

Eviction Free San Francisco. 2019. https://evictionfreesf.org/about/.

Godlee, Fiona, Jane Smith, and Harvey Marcovitch. "Wakefield's Article Linking MMR Vaccine and Autism Was Fraudulent." *British Medical Journal,* January 5, 2011. https://www.bmj.com/content/342/bmj.c7452.

Google. "Mission Statement." https://about.google/.

Greenleaf, Robert K. *Servant Leadership: A Journey into the Nature of Legitimate Power and Greatness,* edited by Larry C. Spears. 25th Anniversary Edition. Mahwah, NJ: Paulist Press, 2002.

Hardy, Quentin. "Why Big Data Is Not Truth." *The New York Times,* June 1, 2013. http://bits.blogs.nytimes.com/2013/06/01/why-big-data-is-not-truth/.

Hensley, Scott. "Online Doctor Ratings as Useful as Those for Restaurants." Shots: Health News from NPR. February 20, 2014. http://www.npr.org/blogs/health/2014/02/20/279628686/online-doctor-ratings-about-as-useful-as-those-for-restaurants.

The International Institute for the Study of Technology and Christianity. https://iistc.org/.

Johnson, Chandra. "The Digital Age Is Changing Literacy Education." WRAL. October 24, 2016. https://www.wral.com/the-digital-age-is-changing-literacy-education/16154674/.

Kinane, Karolyn. Interview by Kevin Healey. Personal interview. Concord, NH, December 12, 2018.

Lanier, Jaron. *You Are Not a Gadget: A Manifesto.* New York: Vintage Books, 2011.

Loncke, Katie. "Why Google Protesters Were Right to Disrupt Wisdom 2.0." Buddhist Peace Fellowship. February 17, 2014. http://www.buddhistpeacefellowship.org/why-google-protesters-were-right-to-disrupt-wisdom-2-0/.

Niland, Patrick. Personal conversation with Kevin Healey. University of New Hampshire, Durham, NH, April 20, 2017.

Oatley, Keith. "Meetings of Minds: Dialogue, Sympathy, and Identification, in Reading Fiction." *Poetics* 26, nos. 5–6 (August 1999): 439–54.

Pope Francis. "Message of Pope Francis for the 48th World Communications Day." June 1, 2014. https://w2.vatican.va/content/francesco/en/messages/communications/documents/papa-francesco_20140124_messaggio-comunicazioni-sociali.html.

Public Theologies of Technology and Presence Program. Institute of Buddhist Studies. http://www.shin-ibs.edu/luce/.

Ream, Amanda. "Why I Disrupted the Wisdom 2.0 Conference." Tricycle. February 19, 2014. https://tricycle.org/trikedaily/why-i-disrupted-wisdom-20-conference/.

Rogers, Justin. Personal conversation with Kevin Healey. University of New Hampshire, Durham, NH, September 5, 2018.

Rosen, Larry D. *iDisorder: Understanding Our Obsession with Technology and Overcoming Its Hold on Us.* New York: Palgrave Macmillan, 2012.

Sachs, Jeffrey D. *The Price of Civilization: Reawakening American Virtue and Prosperity.* New York: Random House, 2011.

Schultze, Quentin J. *Habits of the High-Tech Heart: Living Virtuously in the Information Age.* Grand Rapids, MI: Baker Academic, 2002.

———. *Christianity and the Mass Media in America: Toward a Democratic Accommodation.* East Lansing: Michigan State University Press, 2003.

Shirky, Clay. *Here Comes Everybody: The Power of Organizing without Organizations.* New York: Penguin Press, 2008.

Stoll, Clifford. *High Tech Heretic: Reflections of a Computer Contrarian.* New York: Anchor Books, 1999.

Sunstein, Cass. "Believing False Rumors." In *The Offensive Internet: Speech, Privacy, and Reputation,* edited by Saul Levmore and Martha C. Nussbaum, 91–106. Cambridge, MA: Harvard University Press, 2012.

Taylor, Rebecca M. "Open-Mindedness: An Intellectual Virtue in the Pursuit of Knowledge and Understanding." *Educational Theory* 66, no. 5 (2016): 599–618.

Tikkun Magazine. https://www.tikkun.org/.

U.S. Catholic. http://www.uscatholic.org/.

Vaidhyanathan, Siva. *The Googlization of Everything (and Why We Should Worry).* Berkeley, CA: University of California Press, 2011a.

———. "The Googlization of Everything." Berkman Klein Center. March 7, 2011b. https://cyber.harvard.edu/events/2011/02/vaidhyanathan.

Wisdom Publications. https://www.wisdompubs.org/about-wisdom.

4

TRANSPARENCY IS NOT AUTHENTICITY

In the winter of 2014, Sarah Slocum walked into Molotov's Bar in San Francisco. There, she claims, she was a victim of "a hate crime": one directed not against her gender or racial identity but against her status as an unapologetic tech enthusiast. Slocum had been promoting Google's latest product, Glass, which at the time was an unprecedented innovation in wearable tech. Glass looks similar to an ordinary pair of eyeglasses, but it connects via Bluetooth to the Internet. Users can record images and video or view online information from within their own field of vision. Google's promotional website painted participants in heroic terms: "From chefs to cyclists, Glass Explorers are the first to make, move, and marvel through Glass. They're bold and inspiring and they're helping shape the future of Glass" (Healey and Stephens 2017, p. 377).

Despite its slick design, Glass is conspicuous enough that some creeped-out bystanders described it as a "dystopian skull accessory" (Matham 2014). The creepy factor was apparently too much for the patrons at Molotov's bar that evening. After a brief, profanity-laden exchange in which Slocum bemoaned the "white trash" who had confronted her, another patron ripped the smart glasses from Slocum's face (Alexander 2014). And while Slocum claimed that "Glass haters" had "instigated the fight" with their abusive taunts (Pachal 2014), the *Los Angeles Times* reported that the encounter only became violent when one of Slocum's friends "threw a punch at one of the hecklers" (Guynn 2014). Portions of the incident, caught on video by Slocum herself, quickly went viral. Bold, indeed.

Living with Glassholes

The attacks on Glass users came at a time when anti-tech activism had already garnered headlines, for example, in organized protests against "Google buses" that carried tech employees of Google, Apple, and Facebook from San Francisco to Silicon

Valley. Some news reports framed Glass as "a symbol of privilege and its perceived infringement on people's privacy" (Castañeda 2014) and further as "a presumed symbol of the tech industry as a whole" (Gross 2014). There was a strong sense that the product had become a problem rather than a solution. Less than a year after it had begun, the company announced that it would suspend the Explorers program and cease production of Glass.

It was Slocum's video of the incident that ultimately brought her so much negative attention. Her rationale for doing so is noteworthy, since it gets to the heart of this chapter. According to one reporter, Slocum willingly uploaded the video "because she wanted to be transparent" (Alexander 2014). In other words, she wanted the world to know what really happened. She had nothing to hide. If only there were more video, more audio, more data, then we could know the truth. The more we record and share of even the most intimate or embarrassing moments in our lives, the closer we get to living an authentic life. So says the catechism.

Slocum's attitude echoes the promotional rhetoric of Google's marketing campaign for Glass. With a wink, nod, or swipe of the finger, users could purportedly remain "in the here and now" by accessing the web within their field of vision or seamlessly recording events for later viewing (Healey and Stephens 2017, p. 377). Google and its Glass Explorers view the device as a catalyst for living life more fully. If problems arise like the one Slocum encountered, then tech companies and their enthusiastic supporters deploy self-serving rationales that downplay their responsibility or absolve them entirely.

While there are surely benefits to wearable tech like Glass, such unbridled enthusiasm blinds us to the challenges they pose. Glass could certainly increase market value for established commercial industries including the oil, airline, hotel, and museum industries, which saw opportunities for improved workplace efficiency and customer service. Hospitals, medical professionals, and employees in the public sector and military could also benefit. Yet the concerns in the face of such benefits are plentiful. Doctors and clinics would face legal difficulties in drafting new privacy codes. The potentially fatal distraction posed by Glass prompted U.S. and British authorities to seek restrictions for motorists. Owners and patrons wondered whether users might photograph or film others without consent. Some casinos and bars banned the device outright. The threat of copyright piracy led industry leaders to push for bans in movie theaters. Consumer advocates framed Glass as a method for Google to amass and commodify user information. European watchdog agencies sought to compel Google's compliance with established data-collection regulations (Healey and Stephens 2017, p. 377). Developer and Glass owner Ben Nelson acknowledged that opinions differ about whether Glass is appropriate but insisted that "within the next 10 years it's going to become commonplace either way" (Wood 2013). *Business Insider* reported in September 2015 that Google would resuscitate its much-maligned Glass project under the new name Project Aura (D'Onfro 2015).

In this chapter, we explore the ways that digital messaging and the latest innovations, like Glass, disconnect us from the world in significant ways. One of the most significant ways is how it confuses the non-instrumental virtue of authenticity: it confuses "saying what we mean and meaning what we say" (Schultze 2002, p. 131) with transparency. Authenticity is not just about expressing to others what is inside one's mind. It is also about being "true" to something beyond one's ego cravings. It is about being true to ideas that transcend one's ego altogether, and to which all individuals are committed. Rather than supporting such standards, digital culture chokes authenticity by providing "unbridled freedom to be all things to all people to give ourselves over to the highest bidder or to the most persuasive master" (Schultze 2002, p. 131). It supports bombastic, self-obsessed individualistic personas that are unrooted in a sense of shared responsibilities and common purpose. In response, we consider ways that authentic communicators and storytellers can help us to challenge Silicon Valley's religion of technological optimism by discovering truth, fostering empathy, and promoting integrity—core values upon which authenticity depends.

The Catechism: Transparency Is Authenticity

Given the concerns outlined above, the term "Glasshole" warrants much wider application than it has recently enjoyed. In this broader, metaphorical sense, a Glasshole is someone who demonstrates a sense of entitlement to the power afforded by privileged access to digital media technologies and information networks. Glassholes further rationalize the privileged use of such technologies, and the disruptions they cause, by appealing to myths of technological neutrality, objectivity, inevitability, or utopianism. Consequently, they treat the concerns and demands of those impacted by disruptive technologies with dismissiveness, contempt, or disdain.

Of course, Glass is merely a symbol of the catechism. It goes beyond one device or platform. It represents a pervasive view that equates full exposure, rampant sharing, with a life authentically lived. We will explore the many forms this argument takes. As a matter of shorthand, however, the simple equation of transparency with authenticity creates a nation of Glassholes. There are a few key groups who qualify for this ignoble title and further illustrate the catechism's confusion between transparency and authenticity.

First Group: Silicon Valley Executives

Technology executives have a flair for rationalizing their exploitation of user data and treating users' concerns with contempt. In 1999, Sun Microsystems' CEO Scott McNealy stated flatly, "You have zero privacy anyway. ... Get over it" (Sprenger 1999). Ten years later, little had changed. Google CEO Eric Schmidt suggested, "If you have something that you don't want anyone to know, maybe you shouldn't be doing it in the first place" (Streitfeld 2013).

In perhaps the most egregious example of self-serving rhetoric Craig Brittain, a rogue entrepreneur in the revenge porn industry, justified his non-consensual release of explicit images without consent by former romantic partners. He rationalized his solicitation and distribution of such images by framing it as part of a "progressive cause" in which public information including nude photos of every person would soon become "a normal thing" and thereafter would "no longer be associated with stigma or shame or humiliation" (Garfield 2012). Victims disagree and have urged passage of legislation outlawing such behavior.

Such an understanding of social ethics burdens political and social minorities with the assumption that existing social norms are uniformly just rather than discriminatory. Social media companies rarely consider the privacy needs of undocumented immigrants, victims of domestic abuse, or sexual minorities (Hasinoff 2015). Default settings mostly impact unskilled users, who tend to have lower incomes and therefore less access to legal protection. Minorities placed into "zero mobility" marketing categories become targets for predatory financial instruments (Fung 2014). As one critic argues, "the 'public by default' environment … isn't always the great democratizer; for many, it's exactly the opposite" (Boyd 2010). Meanwhile, Mark Zuckerberg spent over $30 million to protect his own privacy, purchasing four homes in his neighborhood to stave off developers who hoped to use his proximity to develop a marketing strategy (Shontell 2013). As privacy becomes a privilege, so too does authenticity.

More recently, privileged access to user data sparked a backlash against OkCupid and Facebook. Christian Rudder faced criticism after revelations that OkCupid, an American-based, internationally operating online dating site, had conducted real-time experiments on users. He voiced no regrets. In a message addressed to his website's users, Rudder included an image of a guinea pig on which he had scrawled the word "You." "Guess what, everybody," he pronounced, "That's how websites work" (Bell 2014). Mark Zuckerberg's similar disdain for user concerns is widely known, including his description of early Facebook users as "dumb fucks" for their willingness to share personal information (Vargas 2010).

Though official company statements and promotional materials are usually more polished, they nevertheless tend to serve the interests of owners and engineers rather than users (Hoffmann et al. 2016; Zimmer 2010). Mark Zuckerberg's idiosyncratic use of the term "sharing," for example, "not only situates Facebook in society, but also situates society for Facebook" (Hoffmann et al. 2016, p. 16). While it is helpful to analyze the use of specific terms, often we need to read between the lines. Taken as a whole his statements in interviews and in his own Facebook posts show "how Zuckerberg's language reinforces and normalizes only specific kinds of user identity as 'authentic'" (Hoffmann et al. 2016, p. 16).

In his pronouncements, Zuckerberg blurs any meaningful distinction between a user's online profile and what he calls the "real self." He says that people have a "core desire to express who they are" (Rose 2011). Facebook's architecture assumes that this core desire can, and should, be realized online. Facebook COO Sheryl Sandberg has insisted that "[t]he social web can't exist until you are your real self online" (Rose 2011). For Zuckerberg, as Facebook creates "opportunities for people to share more things," such sharing "leads to this kind of broader social change where I think now there's more transparency" (Computer History Museum 2010). Yet the notion that informational transparency is the necessary and sufficient grounds for an authentic life is both inaccurate and ethically fraught. It is inaccurate because, against the grain of contemporary social psychology, it falsely posits the authentic self as a static and unchanging entity. It is ethically fraught because it posits "sharing" as an unqualified social good and fails to recognize how technology fosters a "collaborative self" based primarily on the digitally constructed perceptions and approvals of others.

Author and MIT professor Sherry Turkle asserts that the social-mediated "collaborative self" is pulling participants away from the non-digital personal encounter by social media's ability to lessen the risk of verbal and non-verbal initiatives. Tweets can be contoured; conversations on Gchat can avoid the vulnerability of being "too emotional" (Turkle 2015, p. 34). The second screen provides an intriguing opportunity to "make yourself a me," or write yourself into the person you want to be or that others in your social world would approve of. At the moment, you begin to have a thought or feeling you can test it out and have it immediately validated by others. Positive responses are then collected, refined, and eventually woven into an other-directed, idealized (not real) self in an effort to curry popularity, status, and, by extension, self-esteem. Once established, you feel compelled to market this collaborative identity through as many social media platforms as possible, further blurring the lines between private person and public persona. Self-awareness and self-expression ultimately give way to impression management and self-promotion. "Know thyself" in the social media universe is replaced with "share, show, and maintain thyself."

Truthfulness, whether in the presentation of one's self online or in political discourse, is a key sign of authenticity. Working against truthfulness is the catechism's religion of informationism that reduces truth to the most recent facts and findings with "no deeper sense of revealed truth" (Schultze 2002, p. 132). Truth-telling, explains media scholar Quentin J. Schultze, "obligates us to far more than simply creating versions of reality that are in tune with our own interests or with those of our employer or client." Pursuing truth means that "we try to embody truth in our lives, to be carriers of reality rather than fabricators of virtual reality." In digital culture, then, truth-telling is "one means of orienting ourselves to 'authentic being'" (Schultze 2002, p. 130).

Second Group: Opportunists, Political or Otherwise

Paradoxically, and against all evidence, the catechism would have us believe that privacy is best achieved through massive exposure, or so-called transparency in all things in front of and behind closed doors. One critic summarizes this argument as follows: "Perhaps there would be more of a sense of privacy in big numbers. At some point no one would care anymore if a congressman tweeted a picture of his penis. Yawn. When people do not care enough to look, then privacy will be restored. This is a common hope in the 'transparency' movement" (Lanier 2013, p. 316).

The "yawn" factor is typically an exercise in privilege, as epitomized by the now-infamous tweet from Dharun Ravi, roommate of former Rutgers University student Tyler Clementi: "Roommate asked for the room until midnight. I went into molly's [*sic*] room and turned on my webcam. I saw him making out with a dude. Yay" (Schweber 2012). Other tweets from Ravi ensued, and Clementi obsessed about them before committing suicide two days later by jumping off the George Washington Bridge. A passing amusement for Ravi and his friends became a source of humiliation for a young gay man. The incident was an extreme invasion of privacy, a type uniquely afforded by networked digital cameras, wearable, or otherwise. With due respect to Sarah Slocum, it was a hate crime more worthy of the name. Such, at least, was the verdict from a jury of Ravi's peers (Trumbull 2012). It matters little that he wielded a different type of camera: Dharun Ravi, like Craig Brittain, acted like a Glasshole.

Reflecting on the tragedy, psychologist Elias Aboujaoude (2010) notes that the control of one's reputation and image are central to human development. "Psychological autonomy means being able to keep your personhood to yourself and dole out the pieces as you see fit, sharing yourself with people you think are worthy and with whom you want to form a special bond," he explains. While authenticity may be an expression of one's true self, "you don't truly possess your 'self' if you don't have custody of the facts of your life." As a psychological resource, therefore, privacy "gives individuals the freedom necessary for an undistorted reflection on the true self and for authentic behavior and self-presentation" (Trepte and Reinecke 2011, p. 67).

Similarities between Glass and police body cameras are striking. Although some body cameras are clipped to an officer's uniform, others are mounted on the side of eyeglasses. The debates, however, are decidedly different. While the Glass program was driven in top-down fashion by technology elites, the embrace of police body cameras emerged in response to a grassroots movement in the wake of police killings of young black men, most notably Michael Brown in Ferguson, Missouri, in 2014. Furthermore, whereas the discussion of Glass highlighted the gaps between the privileged and the marginalized in the information society, in the debates about police violence, body-camera technology appeared as a point of near-consensus. In the discussion of Glass, wearable cameras appeared as a solution in search of a problem. In the discussion of police body cameras, wearable technology appears as a solution to the problem of racially charged police tactics for activists and to the problem of false citizen complaints for law enforcement. Thus, while it was difficult to pinpoint tangible results of the social movement that emerged in the wake of Brown's death, a year afterward, one journalist suggested that "the embrace of body cameras" was the "one concrete verifiable change" it had precipitated (Kaste 2015).

Political officials and activist groups both embraced body-camera technology on the premise that it would increase transparency and accountability. The San Francisco Public Defender and the President of the National Association for the Advancement of Colored People (NAACP) both called for widespread implementation body cameras. President Obama requested funding for training programs and 50,000 body cameras. Unsurprisingly, reporters consulted law enforcement, political officials, and academic experts far more often than activists. Public officials were generally enthusiastic about body cameras. Before Brown's death, law enforcement had already begun evaluation research. A year-long study begun in 2012 and co-authored by Tony Farrar, Chief of Police in Rialto, California, concluded that body cameras reduce use-of-force incidents by about 60 percent and citizen complaints by about 90 percent (Ariel et al. 2015, pp. 523–24). Coverage suggested a widespread perception that wearable cameras would benefit everyone. A California police chief argued, "When we believe we're being watched by some authority figure, we behave better" (Berman 2015). An activist group from Ohio claimed that they aimed "to protect citizens and police alike, by arming our citizens with knowledge, and our officers with body cameras" (Sigov 2014). Wearable cameras thus appeared as tools to be harnessed to build community and strengthen a democratic polity.

Two important assumptions have driven debates about body cameras. First, there is a clear discourse of truth surrounding body cameras. Farrar, who conducted the Rialto study, argues that "Video is very transparent," adding that "It's the whole enchilada" (Stross 2013). In his campaign to implement body cameras, South Carolina Representative Wendell Gilliard likewise argued, "Cameras don't lie" (Guo 2015). Senator Tim Scott argued that if the officers involved in Freddie Gray's death had been wearing body cameras, "we would know exactly what happened" (Diamond 2015). Support for body cameras was premised on the notion that police officers and citizens would behave more appropriately in their presence, and that they would provide the undivided truth of police-citizen interactions.

Second, there is a clear discourse of inevitability from activists and law enforcement officials. Mayors, chiefs of police, officers, and journalists repeatedly referred to body cameras as "the future of policing" or "the wave of the future." With regard to adaption by most, if not all, agencies, one South Dakota Police Chief remarked, "It seems inevitable" (Mueller 2015). An Ohio Police Chief remarked, "I don't think they're a phase. I think communities are going to demand that level of accountability from police" (Seitz 2015). In stark contrast to the Glass Explorers program, which shut down after significant public backlash, by the fall of 2015 the American Civil Liberties Union (ACLU) predicted that "in 10 years, you will see police body cameras as regularly as you see police dash cams," and the Connecticut NAACP's criminal justice committee called their adoption a "foregone conclusion" (Hladky 2015).

The embrace of body cameras is a reminder that while wearable technologies might enable more effective governance, the relative ease of applying such technological solutions may yield standardized, packaged interventions that pay little attention to the culture of policing and the needs of communities. As a result, power may accrue to an emergent set of gatekeepers, namely, engineers and operators of increasingly opaque data-collection systems. The technologically mediated gaze thus renders the population transparent to elites, while the operations of Big Data remain opaque to the population.

Wearable police cameras, by contrast, have been embraced not only by law enforcement and public officials but also by activists who aim to resist racial privilege and its abuses. Activist support for body cameras is both an effort to empower citizens, as well as a demand that white citizens recognize the injustice faced by racial minorities. Body cameras represent the possibility of a transparent democratic society, serving the public interest by holding both officials and citizens accountable. Yet the realization of this goal depends on what one scholar calls the "organization of observability," that is, the ways in which people's actions are made available to each other for assessment or judgment (Kidwell 2005, p. 421). Without thoughtful development and policymaking, it is unlikely that new technologies will enable an organization of observability that serves the public interest. Instead, such technologies are likely to augment already existing patterns.

Third Group: Overzealous Hacktivists

No longer just a hobby, hacking has become a political ideology. Though often anti-corporate and contemptuous of commercial media, hacktivism echoes Silicon Valley's catechism by elevating informational and data transparency as an end in itself. Vigilante hacktivists regularly dig up video, audio, and personal data against perceived offenders. Depending on their political views, the public often experiences a gut-level satisfaction in, for example, seeing the Church of Scientology or the Westboro Baptist Church get doxxed or otherwise hacked (Olson 2012). It is the same type of rush many felt on seeing the video of Iraqi journalist Muntadhar al-Zaidi throwing his shoes at George W. Bush during a 2008 Baghdad press conference (Associated Press 2008). We sympathize, and cheer, when someone who has been wronged lashes out.

But when the urge to lash out usurps the virtues of prudence and judgment, our actions can backfire. As impatience grew in the wake of Michael Brown's death in Ferguson, Missouri, hacktivists circulated two police officers' names, both of which were incorrect (Kushner 2014). In that case, it is possible that hacktivists had been nudged by federal agents in an attempt to discredit them. But in other cases, it is clear that hacktivists sometimes act with malicious intent, releasing personal e-mails of CEOs or harassing and threatening critics and their families.

Hacktivists from the activist group Anonymous appear as trickster figures, playing malicious jokes in a spirited attempt to nudge a slacking culture toward action or understanding. But the trickster's moral position is precarious. As more experienced hacktivists acknowledge, risky tactics can backfire and undermine a group's more noble goals. It is easy to backslide on that slippery slope from vigilante savior to vengeful prankster. The hacktivists most worthy of praise are those who resist the urge to act like a Glasshole.

Consider the case of WikiLeaks and its self-appointed leader, Julian Assange. As the Obama administration continued and expanded many of the previous administration's policies in Iraq and Afghanistan, Assange emerged as another ideological proponent of transparency, framing digital networks as a potential bludgeon that might beat the corporate state into conformity to its own espoused principles through massive exposure of corruption, malfeasance, and criminality. WikiLeaks espouses a belief that transparency, when demanded of elites by activists, can restore democratic principles that have been lost. Taken to its extreme, this approach mimics Silicon Valley's reductive assumption that technology is uniquely capable of solving social issues that traditional political and social institutions have failed to address.

In 2016, WikiLeaks' efforts resulted in the release of a treasure trove of documents from the Democratic National Committee including the passport and social security numbers of private citizens. The Sunlight Foundation's John Wonderlich argues that WikiLeaks is no longer a trusted organization advocating on behalf of government transparency. "It's not striving for objectivity. It's more careless," Wonderlich said, adding that WikiLeaks is now motivated by an ideologically fueled sense of vengeance and retribution (Vick 2016). Speaking anonymously to *Time* magazine, one activist explained that the group once acted "like publishers and journalists" but lamented that "they turned out not have any principles" (Vick 2016). Even American whistleblower Edward Snowden who revealed details about classified government surveillance programs described WikiLeaks' "hostility to even modest" redaction of documents "a mistake" (Meyer 2016).

WikiLeaks' tendency to err on the side of raw data collection and dissemination is "symptomatic of a brand of open-access ideology" in which "the crisis in investigative journalism is neither understood nor recognized" (Lovink and Riemens 2013, p. 248). Like the hacker group Anonymous that often supports its efforts, WikiLeaks' rhetoric of transparency is typically a mirror image of corporate and state surveillance efforts, defending the group's secrecy as a prerequisite for its goal of increasing transparency elsewhere. Yet the argument that WikiLeaks "needs to be completely opaque in order to force others to be totally transparent" leads to an ethical quandary in which "you beat the opposition, but in a way that makes you indistinguishable from it" (Lovink and Riemens 2013, p. 250). Like Facebook, through such contradictions WikiLeaks implicitly acknowledges that transparency is not tantamount to authenticity: a judicious measure of secrecy and privacy is necessary for the authentic development of persons, organizations, and nations.

In both commercial and political contexts, the transparency movement is typically spearheaded by highly skilled engineers and activists. Despite public rhetoric espousing the benefits of transparency, the implicit lesson of these organizations is that people with better computer skills are somehow more entitled to live an authentic life. While "the transparent world so desired by idealistic techies might tame old-fashioned governments on occasion," as long as such inequities remain unacknowledged "it will also empower new kinds of network power" (Lanier 2013, pp. 306–8). Author and legal scholar Stanley Fish explains it this way:

> Information, data and the unbounded flow of more and more speech can be politicized—it can, that is, be woven into a narrative that constricts rather than expands the area of free, rational choice. When that happens—and it will happen often—transparency and the unbounded flow of speech become instruments in the production of the very inequalities (economic, political, educational) that the gospel of openness promises to remove. And the more this gospel is preached and believed, the more that the answer to everything is assumed to be data uncorrupted by interests and motives, the easier it will be for interest and motives to operate under transparency's cover.
>
> (Fish 2018)

Security experts warn that in its quest for radical transparency, WikiLeaks has allowed itself to become "weaponized" by state actors whose strategic goals have little to do with the cultivation of robust democratic discourse (Howard and Wonderlich 2016). As such it had become a threat to, rather than a guardian of, public discourse.

Challenging the Catechism: Transparency Is Not Authenticity

Originally from an unknown author, Harley Davidson popularized a simple quote that effectively summarizes the virtue of authenticity: "When writing the story of your life, don't let anyone else hold the pen." Agency is the key to authenticity. If we simply live out the pre-written scripts or narratives of others, we may enjoy some creative latitude, but ultimately we do not express a vision that is uniquely our own (see Sheldon et al. 1997). Of course, to craft a vision requires the support of a community, and no one person is an island. Paradoxically, an authentic life is one lived in relation to, and in service of, others.

The "weaponization" of information noted above violates this understanding of authenticity through a willful, strategic, and aggressive manipulation of others' access to and understanding of data. To weaponize information is to grab the pen from others and write a plausible but intentionally incomplete story that serves one group's interest over another's. It is an appropriation of agency through deception and manipulation. To employ more scholarly language, the weaponization of information violates norms associated with "information as action" (Elliott and Spence 2017, p. 185). This includes a clear respect for others' right to freedom and well-being.

But there are far more mundane variations on this problem. Who holds the pen, so to speak, when you are writing your latest Facebook post or tweet? Surely you are, right? Maybe. Without being deterministic, we need to understand how software engineers, especially for "free" platforms like Facebook, are specifically in the business of coercing user attention and soliciting voluntarily authored and shared content.

One definition of authenticity is that it is a matter of "choosing to choose" or "making one's choices one's own and so being 'answerable' or 'responsible' (*verantwortlich*) for one's life" (Guignon 2002, p. 71). Online and off, we are challenged by environments (supermarkets, News Feeds, and so forth) which greet us with carefully crafted instances of what marketers call "choice architecture." Our environments are designed by marketers and engineers to nudge us toward certain behaviors, even if they cannot determine it completely. To the extent that these manipulations are invisible, obscure, or otherwise opaque to us, our ability to think and act authentically is challenged. This is the impetus for a range of initiatives, from media literacy programs in elementary schools to increased clarity and, indeed, increased transparency in user-end agreements for online platforms. (As we will discuss in Chapter 8, we are not arguing against transparency but for a nuanced understanding of what genuine or authentic transparency might look like, which is consensual and reciprocal rather than strategic, instrumental, and coercive.)

Social media platforms are designed to make certain kinds of behavior, and even certain kinds of feelings, more likely. Facebook conducted research specifically aimed at manipulating users' emotions by tweaking its News Feed algorithm. Its researchers analyzed whether seeing more happy posts might make users likely to write happier posts themselves (Kramer et al. 2014). Happy users are engaged users who return to the platform frequently. As noted earlier in this chapter, in interviews and public statements Facebook executives repeatedly argue that what people post on their platform provides a window into, in fact constitutes, the user's authentic self. Facebook's architecture assumes that this core desire can, and should, be realized online. Zuckerberg described user profiles as "where you have everything about you" and where "millions of people" go to tell "the story of their life" (F8 2011). An individual's personal history, he says, is "all there and you can get to it all if you wanted. It's your whole life" (F8 2011).

While such understandings of the self are helpful in justifying Facebook's business model, they are a far cry from contemporary social-psychological understandings of the self and its authentic expression. As one author put it, "you don't actually have a solid, unchanging, authentic self" that can be uncovered, revealed, and expressed fully formed (Rogers 2016, p. 135). Authenticity is not a matter of uncovering one's hidden self but of exemplifying one's aspirational social roles and the social virtues they require. In this sense, authenticity means "to bridge the gap between is and ought" by embodying the reality one articulates as one's stated moral and ethical commitment (Ferrara 2009, pp. 22–23). While emotions surely play an important role in such an achievement, their indulgence is not an end in itself. As one observer rightly perceives, "authenticity has nothing to do with getting in touch with your inner feelings. Instead, authenticity is a matter of living in such a way that your life has cumulativeness and purposiveness as a whole" (Guignon 2000, p. 72). Consider this explanation: "In the authentic way of living, I take responsibility for the character I am forming through my actions, and I assume my identity by being answerable for the kind of person I am. To be authentic, in this view, is to satisfy the old injunction: 'Become what you are'" (p. 73).

The task of achieving authenticity is never complete. We are always in the process of becoming who we are. At least the path of becoming authentic is always available to us, if we choose to follow it. The key is not merely a willingness to share loudly one's gut reactions or unfiltered thoughts. Authenticity instead consists of being able to develop an awareness and understanding of one's emotions, and to have the capacity for unbiased processing of them (Kernis and Goldman 2006). We are more than our gut reaction. Yet platforms like Twitter and Facebook cater not to the democratic value of sustained and nuanced deliberation, but instead to impulsive, self-congratulatory behavior that dumbs down and tribalizes political discourse (Vaidhyanathan 2018, pp. 163–66).

Moreover, voters' concern for honesty and authenticity has become, ironically, an opportunity for strategic political exploitation, a kind of spiral of insincerity and inauthenticity (Healey 2010, p. 544). Research on reality television suggests that audiences are often complicit in the success of these campaigns, since viewers tend to prefer a "contrived authenticity" or "hyper-authenticity" that is self-conscious of external manipulations (Rose and Wood 2005, pp. 294–95). As one journalist perceptively noted, authenticity in the era of mass media often means little more than becoming "the master of your own artificiality." Today, "fake authenticity" becomes attractive, even desirable, as throngs of would-be celebrities and politicians clamor for adulation, notoriety, or simply power (Adatto 2008, p. 54).

Beyond making the weaponization of information more likely, this has led to a state of political discourse where instead of simply taking information out of context, politicians and their spokespersons are now willing to invent "alternative facts." As one observer explains, "when there are no guidelines, monitors, gatekeepers or filters," what you have are "the perfect conditions for the unchecked proliferation of what has come to be called 'fake news'" (Fish 2018).

Holding the Pen, Literally

Thomas Jefferson (1899) once remarked, "When angry, count ten, before you speak; if very angry, a hundred" (pp. 74–75). Jefferson knew that authenticity is not just a matter of jettisoning the mental filters that keep offensive comments from slipping out. Your authentic self is not found merely in your gut reaction. It is found in the quiet space that opens up when you pause; when you see your anger but it does not use or control you; when you acknowledge your gut response, pause, and allow your higher self to emerge and respond. Judeo-Christian tradition refers to this as self-control: "Everyone should be quick to listen, slow to speak and slow to become angry" (James 1:19b). So, take a breath before you tweet! Your authentic self is not something you are, but something you become within the reflective space where you integrate your gut's intuition, your heart's compassion, and your mind's reason.

Not coincidentally, the last few years have seen an uptick of interest in practices that re-introduce that essential moment between reaction and response, where we pause long enough to develop a holistic, integrated vision of what is happening around us, and what to say and do about it. Consider, for example, Lakshmi Pratury's (2008) TED talk on "The Lost Art of Letter Writing." A business and social entrepreneur with deep roots in Silicon Valley's tech culture, Pratury has long been at the forefront of technical innovation in service of the public good. Yet she understands the importance of balance and of tech design rooted in human values. Pratury explains that when he died, her father left a notebook filled with his handwriting. She realized after his death that "no one ever writes to me anymore." She asks, "Why can't we have letter-writing *and* e-mail exchange in our lives?" When she needs a hug, she takes out his letters, "and the paper that touched his hands is in mine." If everyone were to write a letter to someone he or she loves, "We may actually start a revolution where our children go to penmanship classes!" (Pratury 2008).

Over ten years later, students at the University of New Hampshire took up the charge in a semester-long letter-writing exercise.[1] Students in a capstone-level seminar chose two would-be letter recipients from among their usual social media acquaintances. They carefully selected paper, pens, envelopes, and other materials to include with their letters. Perhaps most importantly, they found the navy-blue U.S. postal service letter box which they had often passed on their way to class but which

FIGURE 4.1 A student from Kevin's class places her letter in a U.S. Postal Service box. Many students had never composed a hand-written letter or dropped one into a box of this type.

none had ever used. As a class, the students brought the first of their hand-written letters to class and, one-by-one, placed them in the receptacle a few yards from their classroom.

In their blog entries reflecting on the letter-writing exercise, students consistently noted the material nature of this analog form of communication. Lindsey wrote, "There is something about letters that make them more valuable than quick typing on a keyboard to convey a message—an imperfectness that makes them perfect to hold fondly." Casey reported that "due to the physical act of holding the letter" and seeing the unique handwriting styles of her friend versus that of her father, she got "a much better feeling" for their personalities. "While reading, I could almost hear their voices in my head," she wrote. Michael noted that when he started writing to his two friends, he was "much more in tune with my surroundings because I felt like I needed to fill them in on what I was doing physically at that moment." He described the room where he sat, and the pen he held—things he rarely shares in a text.

Another common theme in students' blog entries speaks directly to the need to pause and reflect in our communication. "There's also the element of time," Lindsey writes. Along with "the slight giddiness one gets when anxiously awaiting arrival of a letter," as writers we also experience "the slight sense of confusion of not knowing" whether a concern will have passed, or a topic become outdated, by the time it arrives. By the same token, as Michael suggests, "With letters, it may be weeks or months before you get a response, so what you write in the letter is much more valuable." For that reason, he says, "I was being careful writing in ink on paper and not just typing something that I could delete shortly after if I didn't like the outcome or if I misspelled something. I took more time and I became more aware and more thoughtful." In other words, he slowed down. Casey similarly notes that "Sitting down and taking the time to create a conversation allowed me to discuss things that I was genuinely curious and interested about, and also allowed me to think more deeply about the conversation in the letter." Summing it up for the class, Yulin told her classmates that she had "a great and magic letter-writing experience." The process of delivering and waiting for the letters, she said, gave her a better understanding that "good things are a long time in coming."

The point of such exercises is not that letter writing is always better than texts or e-mails. But the revival of letter writing as a rewarding storytelling art form is revealing. A quick Google search for "the lost art of letter-writing" returns dozens and dozens of results. Digital communication is good for many things, but we cannot equate online sharing with authentic living. The flesh-and-blood nature of letter writing that students report speaks directly to the sense that digitization blurs the distinction between what is real and what is fake. As noted in one sociological study:

> Individuals celebrate authenticity in order to balance the extreme dislocation that characterizes life in the postmodern world, in which traditional concepts of self, community, and space have collapsed. This collapse has led to a widespread internalization of doubt and an obsession with distinguishing the real from the fake.
>
> (Lewin and Williams 2009, p. 66)

We naturally seek out and appreciate "real" connections that are "rooted in 'felt' reality as opposed to the passionless-ness of mass-production" (Lewin and Williams 2009, p. 69; see also Boyle 2004). Moreover, by connecting in a more physical way, we realize that our "true" self is not something we simply find within us and share. Authenticity is instead a process of becoming that depends upon, and is inextricable from, our relationship with others.

Contemplative scholar Karolyn Kinane notes that writing exercises, such as the one described above, enhance and complement critical thinking skills. In approaching communication this way, "we seek connection, communion, and understanding. We step into another person's shoes and perspectives to better understand them and ourselves" (Kinane 2018; see also Barbezat and Bush 2013, pp. 129–35). Such perspective-taking practices cultivate compassion and empathy. They "encourage us to explore our deeply held values, biases, and preferences so that we can move through and with them into compassionate engagement with the Other" (Kinane 2018). Empathy "requires us to forego our own rhetorical agendas at times for the sake of considering others' interest rather than our own" (Schultze 2002, p. 133). Living empathetically means "bearing the truth of life together, carrying each other's real joys and burdens." Yet Silicon Valley elites are often "too inclined to empathize only with their clients or their peers rather than with their broader communities" (p. 133).

More importantly, perhaps, such exercises are critical when it comes to confronting the catechism since at its core "authenticity embraces empathy" (Schultze 2002, p. 132), an increasingly precious commodity in the digital age. For instance, according to the University of Michigan's Institute for Social Research (ISR), there is an empathy paradox of increasing social disconnection in the age of increasing digital connectivity. The ISR analyzing data on empathy among 14,000 college students over the last thirty years found a 47 percent drop in their empathy index, much of it in the last decade (Douthat 2010). "A contradictory portrait it is," explains one critic: "high connectivity for the Wi-Fi generation and low connectivity in terms of emotional concern for others" (Christians 2013, p. 331).

Conclusion

The response from around the world to Sarah Slocum's viral video of her Molotov's Bar "hate crime" was, in a word, unsympathetic. Transparent? Yes. Authentic? Probably not. One of the many tweets that circulated widely read as follows:

> @SarahSlocum you really drive the whole "white privilege" thing home with the "hate crime" bit. Bravo, you really are a #glasshole.
>
> (Castañeda 2014)

On Facebook and Twitter, Slocum responded by celebrating the product and hinting that critics were anti-techies who would eventually change their minds about Glass. Slocum even asked Google to fly her to the South by Southwest Music Festival in Austin, Texas, to help inform individuals about the benefits of Glass. Slocum's authenticity was further called into question as her sketchy past surfaced, which included a restraining order filed against her for video-recording individuals in their home through an open window (Alexander 2014).

In a *Washington Post* column, one sympathizer compared the kind of anti-tech activism Slocum faced to the "anti-immigrant propaganda" suffered by his grandfather under the Chinese Exclusion Act (Lee 2014). Criticism of such arguments spread to cable television where shows like *The Daily Show* openly mocked the comparison between civil rights activists and Glass Explorers. For many, Google's new wearable gadget symbolized the pervasive surveillance that characterizes the digital economy as a whole. The term "Glasshole" became popular in online debates not just about Glass but also more broadly about the entrepreneurs who populate Silicon Valley.

On a personal level, being authentic means more than simply revealing our gut reactions and unfiltered thoughts, or in the case of Slocum, unfiltered thoughts and images. It takes courage because to become what we are we must give up a sense of certainty. We must become vulnerable. On the scale of socio-political systems, this means that the mere exposure of any and all information does not invariably reveal the truth, nor does it necessarily force organizations to hold themselves accountable to their own stated values. A genuine process of dialogue, deliberation, and understanding between communities, organizations, parties, and nations requires more than mere information. It, too, is a process, and only by slowing down long enough to engage thoughtfully can we, as a community of nations, become who we truly are.

Note

1 For a discussion of letter writing as a contemplative practice, we recommend Brenda Miller and Holly J. Hughes' *The Pen and the Bell: Mindful Writing in a Busy World* (2012).

References

Aboujaoude, Elias. "A Violin Requiem for Privacy." *The Chronicle of Higher Education*, October 7, 2010. https://www.chronicle.com/article/A-Violin-Requiem-for-Privacy/124849.

Adatto, Kiku. *Picture Perfect: Life in the Age of the Photo Op*. Princeton, NJ: Princeton University Press, 2008.

Alexander, Kurtis. "Sarah Slocum: The Infamous Face of Google Glass." SFGate. March 26, 2014. https://www.sfgate.com/news/article/Sarah-Slocum-the-infamous-face-of-Google-Glass-5348911.php.

Ariel, Barak, William A. Farrar, and Alex Sutherland. "The Effect of Police Body-Worn Cameras on Use of Force and Citizens' Complaints against the Police: A Randomized Controlled Trial." *Journal of Quantitative Criminology* 31 (2015): 509–35.

Associated Press. "Raw Video: Iraqi Journalist Throws Shoe at Bush." YouTube. December 14, 2008. https://www.youtube.com/watch?v=OM3Z_Kskl_U.

Barbezat, Daniel P., and Mirabai Bush. *Contemplative Practices in Higher Education: Powerful Methods to Transform Teaching and Learning*. Hoboken, NJ: John Wiley & Sons, 2013.

Bell, Karissa. "OkCupid Defends Human Experiments: 'That's How Websites Work.'" Mashable. July 28, 2014. https://mashable.com/2014/07/28/okcupid-human-experiments/#tmJE5GwvuskU.

Berman, John. "Do Body Cameras Help?" *This Hour with Berman and Michaela*. CNN. April 10, 2015. http://www.cnn.com/TRANSCRIPTS/1504/10/ath.01.html.

Boyd, Danah. "Making Sense of Privacy and Publicity." SXSW. Austin, TX, March 13, 2010.

Boyle, David. *Authenticity: Brands, Fakes, Spin and the Lust for Real Life*. London: Harper Perennial, 2004.

Castañeda, Carlos E. "Woman's Google Glass Attack in SF Bar Spurs Huge Social Media Backlash." CBS SF BayArea. February 26, 2014. http://sanfrancisco.cbslocal.com/2014/02/26/google-glass-attack-againstsocial-media-consultant-spurs-huge-backlash/.

Christians, Clifford G. "Evangelical Perspectives on Technology." In *Evangelical Christians and Popular Culture: Pop Goes the Gospel*, edited by Robert H. Woods Jr., vol. 1, 323–40. Santa Barbara, CA: Praeger, 2013.

Computer History Museum. "The Facebook Effect (Interview with Zuckerberg and Kirkpatrick)." Paper 30. *Zuckerberg Transcripts*. July 25, 2010. http://dc.uwm.edu/zuckerberg_files_transcripts/30.

D'Onfro, Jillian. "Google Has Hired a Bunch of Engineers from Amazon's Lab126 for a New Wearable Tech Initiative Called 'Project Aura.'" *Business Insider*, September 16, 2015. https://www.businessinsider.com/google-project-aura-revealed-2015-9.

Diamond, Jeremy. "Scott: 'We Would Know Exactly What Happened' to Freddie Gray with Police Cameras." CNN. April 29, 2015. https://www.cnn.com/2015/04/29/politics/tim-scott-body-cameras-baltimore/index.html.

Douthat, Ross. "The Culture of Narcissism." *New York Times*, June 2, 2010. https://douthat.blogs.nytimes.com/2010/06/02/the-culture-of-narcissism/.

Elliott, Deni, and Edward H. Spence. *Ethics for a Digital Era*. Hoboken, NJ: John Wiley & Sons, 2017.

F8 2011. "F8 2011 Keynote." *Zuckerberg Transcripts*. Paper 40. September 24, 2011. http://dc.uwm.edu/zuckerberg_files_transcripts/40.

Ferrara, Alessandro. "Authenticity without a True Self." In *Authenticity in Culture, Self, and Society*, edited by Phillip Vannini and J. Patrick Williams, 21–35. Burlington, VT: Ashgate, 2009.

Fish, Stanley. "Transparency Is the Mother of Fake News." *New York Times*, May 7, 2018.

Fung, Brian. "Why Civil Rights Groups Are Warning against 'Big Data.'" *The Washington Post*, February 27, 2014. http://www.washingtonpost.com/blogs/the-switch/wp/2014/02/27/why-civil-rights-groups-are-warning-against-big-data/.

Garfield, Bob. "Is Anybody Down?" On the Media. November 16, 2012. https://www.wnycstudios.org/story/251306-is-anybody-down.

Gross, Doug. "Google Glass Targeted as Symbol by Anti-tech Crowd." CNN Business. April 15, 2014. https://www.cnn.com/2014/04/14/tech/mobile/google-glass-attack/index.html.

Guignon, Charles. "Authenticity and Integrity: A Heideggerian Perspective." In *The Psychology of Mature Spirituality: Integrity, Wisdom, Transcendence*, edited by Polly Young-Eisendrath and Melvin E. Miller, 62–74. Philadelphia: Routledge, 2000.

Guo, Jeff. "Police Don't Always Tell the Truth: Where Are South Carolina's Body Cameras?" *Washington Post*, April 8, 2015. https://www.washingtonpost.com/blogs/govbeat/wp/2015/04/08/police-dont-always-tell-the-truth-where-are-south-carolinas-body-cameras/.

Guynn, Jessica. "Woman Saying She Was Attacked in Bar Won't Stop Wearing Google Glass." *Los Angeles Times*, February 25, 2014. http://www.latimes.com/business/technology/la-fi-tn-woman-attacked-says-she-wont-stop-wearing-google-glass-20140225-story.html.

Hasinoff, Amy Adele. *Sexting Panic: Rethinking Criminalization, Privacy, and Consent*. Urbana, IL: University of Illinois Press, 2015.

Healey, Kevin. "The Pastor in the Basement: Discourses of Authenticity in the Networked Public Sphere." *Symbolic Interaction* 33, no. 4 (Fall 2010): 527–52.

Healey, Kevin, and Niall Stephens. "Augmenting Justice: The Politics of Wearable Technology from Silicon Valley to Ferguson." *Journal of Information, Communication and Ethics in Society* 15, no. 4 (2017): 370–84.

Hladky, Gregory B. "General Assembly Sends Mixed Signals on Police Body Cameras." The *Hartford Courant*, May 3, 2015. http://www.courant.com/politics/hc-police-body-camera-legislation-20150503-story.html.

Hoffmann, Anna Lauren, Nicholas Proferes, and Michael Zimmer. "'Making the World More Open and Connected': Mark Zuckerberg and the Discursive Construction of Facebook and Its Users." *New Media & Society* 20, no. 1 (July 2016): 1–20.

Howard, Alex, and John Wonderlich. "On Weaponized Transparency." Sunlight Foundation. July 28, 2016. https://sunlightfoundation.com/2016/07/28/on-weaponized-transparency/.

Jefferson, Thomas. *The Writings of Thomas Jefferson, Volume 10*. New York: G. P. Putnam's Sons, 1899.

Kaste, Martin. "After Tumultuous Year for Police and African-Americans, What's Changed?" NPR. August 7, 2015. https://www.npr.org/2015/08/07/430221577/after-tumultuous-year-for-police-and-african-americans-whats-changed.

Kernis, Michael H., and Brian M. Goldman. "A Multicomponent Conceptualization of Authenticity: Theory and Research." In *Advances in Experimental Social Psychology, Volume 38*, edited by Mark P. Zana, 283–357. San Diego, CA: Elsevier Academic Press, 2006.

Kidwell, Mardi. "Gaze as Social Control: How Very Young Children Differentiate 'the Look' from a 'Mere Look' by Their Adult Caregivers." *Research on Language and Social Interaction* 38, no. 4 (2005): 417–49.

Kinane, Karolyn. "Contemplative Reading: Some Definitions and Examples." College Contemplative [academic blog]. April 8, 2018. https://collegecontemplative.wordpress.com/2018/04/08/contemplative-reading-some-definitions-and-examples/.

Kramer, Adam D. I., Jamie E. Guillory, and Jeffrey T. Hancock. "Experimental Evidence of Massive-Scale Emotional Contagion through Social Networks." *Proceedings of the National Academy of Sciences of the United States of America* 111, no. 24 (June 17, 2014): 8788–90.

Kushner, David. "What Anonymous Got Wrong in Ferguson." *New Yorker*, September 5, 2014. https://www.newyorker.com/tech/annals-of-technology/anonymous-got-wrong-ferguson.

Lanier, Jaron. *Who Owns the Future?* New York: Simon & Schuster, 2013.

Lee, James. "People Say Tech Is Invading San Francisco. They Said the Same about My Immigrant Grandfather." *Washington Post*, July 30, 2014. http://www.washingtonpost.com/posteverything/wp/2014/07/30/i-grew-up-in-san-francisco-now-im-one-of-the-techies-displacing-local-residents/.

Lewin, Philip, and J. Patrick Williams. "The Ideology and Practice of Authenticity in Punk Subculture." In *Authenticity in Culture, Self, and Society*, edited by Phillip Vannini and J. Patrick Williams, 65–83. Burlington, VT: Ashgate, 2009.

Lovink, Geert, and Patrice Riemens. "Twelve Theses on WikiLeaks." In *Beyond WikiLeaks: Implications for the Future of Communications, Journalism and Society*, edited by Benedetta Brevini, Arne Hintz, and Patrick McCurdy, 245–53. New York: Palgrave Macmillan, 2013.

Matham, Adarsh. "Blurred Vision." *New Indian Express*. May 18, 2014. http://www.newindianexpress.com/lifestyle/tech/2014/may/18/Blurred-Vision-614094.html.

Meyer, David. "Edward Snowden Is Not Down with WikiLeaks' Methods." *Fortune*, July 29, 2016. http://fortune.com/2016/07/29/snowden-criticizes-wikileaks-clinton/.

Miller, Brenda, and Holly J. Hughes. *The Pen and the Bell: Mindful Writing in a Busy World*. Boston: Skinner House Books, 2012.

Mueller, Chris. "The Long Lens of the Law: Body Cams 'Future of Law Enforcement.'" *The Daily Republic* [Mitchell, SD], January 11, 2015. https://www.mitchellrepublic.com/news/3653080-long-lens-law-body-cams-future-law-enforcement.

Olson, Parmy. "Anonymous Targets Westboro Baptist (Again) over Threat to Picket Newtown." *Forbes*, December 18, 2012. https://www.forbes.com/sites/parmyolson/2012/12/17/anonymous-targets-westboro-baptist-again-over-threat-to-picket-newtown/#10d11339d9ba.

Pachal, Pete. "Woman Robbed, Assaulted for Wearing Google Glass in a Bar." Mashable. February 26, 2014. http://mashable.com/2014/02/26/google-glass-assault/#58sVIs_BD5qS.

Pratury, Lakshmi. "The Lost Art of Letter-Writing." TED Talks. January 9, 2008. https://www.youtube.com/watch?v=rG6xlKzFFrI.

Rogers, Holly B. *The Mindful Twenty-Something: Life Skills to Handle Stress … and Everything Else*. Oakland, CA: New Harbinger Publications, 2016.

Rose, Charlie. "Charlie Rose—Exclusive Interview with Facebook Leadership: Mark Zuckerberg/Sheryl Sandberg." *Zuckerberg Transcripts*. Paper 45. 2011. https://dc.uwm.edu/zuckerberg_files_videos/239.

Rose, Randall L., and Stacy L. Wood. "Paradox and the Consumption of Authenticity through Reality Television." *Journal of Consumer Research* 32, no. 2 (September 2005): 284–96.

Schultze, Quentin J. *Habits of the High-Tech Heart: Living Virtuously in the Information Age.* Grand Rapids, MI: Baker Academic, 2002.

Schweber, Nate. "Rutgers Student Saw Twitter Posts by Roommate about Spying." *New York Times*, March 6, 2012. https://www.nytimes.com/2012/03/07/nyregion/tyler-clementi-monitored-dharun-ravis-twitter-posts-about-him.html.

Seitz, Amanda. "Miami U Spends $16k for Police Body Cameras." *Dayton Daily News*, February 13, 2015. www.daytondailynews.com/news/news/miami-u-spends-16k-for-police-body-cameras/nkBDR/.

Sheldon Kenyon M., Richard M. Ryan, Laird J. Rawsthorne, and Barbara Ilardi. "Trait Self and True Self: Cross-Role Variation in the Big-Five Personality Traits and Its Relations with Psychological Authenticity and Subjective Well-Being." *Journal of Personality and Social Psychology* 73, no. 6 (1997): 1380–93.

Shontell, Alyson. "Mark Zuckerberg Just Spent More Than $30 Million Buying 4 Neighboring Houses for Privacy." *Business Insider*, October 11, 2013. http://www.businessinsider.com/mark-zuckerberg-buys-4-homes-for-privacy-2013-10.

Sigov, Mike. "Rally Urges Police Body Camera Use." *Toledo Blade* [Ohio], October 29, 2014. http://www.toledoblade.com/Police-Fire/2014/10/29/Rally-urges-police-body-camera-use.html.

Sprenger, Polly. "Sun on Privacy: 'Get Over it.'" *Wired*, January 26, 1999. http://www.wired.com/politics/law/news/1999/01/17538.

Streitfeld, David. "Google Glass Picks Up Early Signal: Keep Out." *New York Times*, May 6, 2013. http://mobile.nytimes.com/2013/05/07/technology/personaltech/google-glass-picks-up-early-signal-keep-out.html.

Stross, Randall. "Wearing a Badge, and a Video Camera." *New York Times*, April 6, 2013. https://www.nytimes.com/2013/04/07/business/wearable-video-cameras-for-police-officers.html.

Trepte, Sabine, and Leonard Reinecke. 'The Social Web as a Shelter for Privacy and Authentic Living." In *Privacy Online: Perspectives on Privacy and Self-disclosure in the Social Web*, edited by Sabine Trepte and Leonard Reinecke, 61–73. New York: Springer, 2011.

Trumbull, Mark. "Dharun Ravi Guilty of Anti-Gay Hate Crime in Rutgers Spycam Case." *Christian Science Monitor*, March 16, 2012. https://www.csmonitor.com/USA/Justice/2012/0316/Dharun-Ravi-guilty-of-anti-gay-hate-crime-in-Rutgers-spycam-case.

Turkle, Sherry. *Reclaiming Conversation: The Power of Talk in a Digital Age.* New York: Penguin Press, 2015.

Wood, Colin. "Will Everyone Wear Google Glass Someday?" *Government Technology*. December 5, 2013. http://www.govtech.com/products/Someday-Everyone-Will-Wear-Google-Glass.html.

Vaidhyanathan, Siva. *Anti-Social Media: How Facebook Disconnects Us and Undermines Democracy.* New York: Oxford University Press, 2018.

Vargas, Jose Antonio. "The Face of Facebook." *New Yorker*, September 13, 2010. https://www.newyorker.com/magazine/2010/09/20/the-face-of-facebook.

Vick, Karl. "WikiLeaks Is Getting Scarier Than the NSA." *Time*, August 12, 2016. http://time.com/4450282/wikileaks-julian-assange-dnc-hack-criticism/.

Zimmer, Michael. "Facebook's Zuckerberg: 'Having Two Identities for Yourself Is an Example of a Lack of Integrity.'" Michael Zimmer. May 14, 2010. http://www.michaelzimmer.org/2010/05/14/facebooks-zuckerberg-having-two-identities-for-yourself-is-an-example-of-a-lack-of-integrity/.

5

CONVERGENCE IS NOT INTEGRITY

In the fall of 2013, singer-songwriter Sinéad O'Connor penned an open letter to Miley Cyrus. The younger pop star, who had spent years transforming herself from Disney's family-friendly Hannah Montana to a transgressive sex symbol, had claimed O'Connor's iconic "Nothing Compares 2 U" music video as inspiration for her provocative "Wrecking Ball" video. In that video Cyrus appears brightly lipsticked, licking a sledgehammer and, in a climactic scene, fully nude while swinging on a wrecking ball. O'Connor, who had famously shaved her head to ensure that fans and critics would focus on her music rather than her appearance, expressed her dismay: "You have enough talent that you don't need to let the music business make a prostitute of you," she wrote, adding that she expressed this sentiment "in the spirit of motherliness and with love" (O'Connor 2013).

O'Connor's motherly advice offers the wisdom of her experience on two related virtues: authentic self-expression and artistic integrity. In Chapter 4, we covered the virtue of authenticity, and we can see how that plays out here. Both artists express an understanding of authenticity best summarized by an old saying of unknown origin that we also introduced in Chapter 4: "When writing the story of your life, don't let anyone else hold the pen." No longer would Cyrus let Disney hold the pen. But O'Connor wonders if the young singer had simply handed that pen to someone else, in this case, industry elites hell-bent on sexual exploitation. Both scripts serve the industry first and foremost.

If authenticity means holding the pen while writing your life's story, then a key characteristic of *integrity* means writing a story that holds up over time by skillfully integrating the different aspects of who you are. To live with integrity is to have at one's disposal "an overall organizational framework that unites separate goal strivings into a coherent structure" (Emmons 1999, p. 113). Commercial pressures often force artists to make a difficult either/or choice: either I am a successful sex symbol, or I am a creative innovator without a fan base. Artistic integrity is a matter of refusing the simple choices presented to us. Ideally, it is a matter of insisting on saying "yes" to all aspects of ourselves: I am both this and that; I can and will be a whole person, and I will bring my whole self to the story I write or the songs I sing.

"Wrecking Ball" was eventually nominated as Video of the Year. Rather than giving an acceptance speech, Cyrus turned the microphone over to a mystery date named Jesse, who used the opportunity to speak about homelessness among children and teens. *Billboard* magazine described it as "a selfless, totally unexpected move from Cyrus," one which ran counter to the script she had been expected to play out (Lynch 2014). While some of her behavior is self-indulgent, Cyrus is politically engaged. She has worked to raise awareness of HIV and AIDS and to end poverty among disadvantaged lesbian, gay, bisexual, transgender, and queer (LGBTQ) youth through her Happy Hippie Foundation. Speaking to *Out* magazine after her 2014 VMA performance, Cyrus recalled, "I just thought, it's such this opportunity. ... If I'm going to have all that attention, what do I actually want to say? What do people need to hear?" (Krochmal 2015).

A Movement toward Integrity

As the O'Connor/Cyrus incident illustrates, the different aspects of our identity should fit together into a coherent whole, even if some aspects are more important than others. Our most deeply held values should carry through even when it is inconvenient, or when an easier path is available. One way of putting it is that integrity is what you do when you think no one is looking, or, importantly, when you think you can get away with something even if others are looking. As Cyrus insisted, she is both a sex-positive, spotlight-loving woman and a thoughtful, politically engaged citizen. Cyrus took a risk, regardless of whether one agrees with her personal artistic or lifestyle choices. Clearly, she might have to sacrifice commercial success in favor of more deeply held commitments.

Importantly, Cyrus felt a moral obligation to use her platform for the benefit of others who might succumb to the pressures of an exploitative industry within an unjust economic system. This points to another characteristic of integrity: concern for others. Living with integrity means not just writing a coherent story that holds up across time and diverse social contexts but also one that resonates with the stories others are writing (or are trying to write). Integrity seeks not just internal coherence within oneself, but also coherence across and within the various political-economic and social systems in which one lives. Integrity is not an individual achievement. Instead, integrity involves "a willing sensitivity to the needs of the whole" (Beebe 2000, p. 12). We cannot forge a coherent narrative of our own lives without caring for others and working toward justice in the world. Hope and love are essential virtues as we struggle against the downward pull of cynicism and disgust.

Notice, though, that coherence is not the same as uniformity or monotony. Integrity is not a matter of making all things the same but of bringing together or integrating elements that are each unique. Each organ in one's body is unique in its own right, but the integrity of one's body consists in the coherence of many different organs and systems. Some autoimmune diseases are caused by the body's attack on its own systems. In this sense, healthiness is a delicate balance of unity and difference. The same principle applies to what we call the body politic when political or organizational leaders talk about "unity through diversity."

Neither is integrity simply a matter of treating all aspects of oneself with equal importance. Recall our discussion of Karolyn Kinane's contemplative approach to reading English literature in Chapter 3. Kinane (2018) notes that in the legends of King Arthur, the chivalric conflicts of Camelot, Lancelot, and Gawain represent "moments of value and action" where our different commitments collide. We cannot always be everything to everyone. "There comes a time in your life," Kinane tells us, "when you have to make a choice." For example, the late Senator John McCain is regarded by many as an exemplar of integrity because during his time of capture in Vietnam he was willing to sacrifice physical safety and being safe at home with his family for his commitment to his fellow prisoners. He chose moral integrity over bodily integrity.

We may not all be famous artists like Miley Cyrus or war heroes like John McCain, but similar questions of personal and collective integrity arise for everyone, even in the most mundane contexts. We all want to lead lives that make us feel like a whole person. And we all live within structures that tend to fragment and force us to make tough choices as individuals and communities. However, these structures are increasingly engineered by software programmers and driven by data. These structures are progressively convergent, meaning that technologies that were once separate are now virtually inseparable. Convergence happens in both devices and systems. A smartphone is a computer, a telephone, a radio, and a television all at once. Perhaps and more importantly, these devices, and the apps that run on them, collect and aggregate data about their users. Data convergence and hardware convergence go hand in hand.

While these issues are clearly complex, in this chapter we explore how the catechism of Silicon Valley frames integrity as a matter of simple, consumer-friendly choices we make in an increasingly convergent media marketplace. Consumers often acquiesce to changes in personal devices and even in the digital economy writ large; however, sometimes users do voice concerns, and even resist, such changes. Since the catechism conflates technology and human virtue, seeing information and devices as at least morally neutral and perhaps even morally infallible, tech leaders see users' resistance as evidence of laziness, irrational fear, or moral ineptitude. It is not the technology that is flawed, they say, or the commercial industries that profit from it; it is the lack of moral virtue among users that is causing problems. When social or economic problems arise in the digital economy, the catechism locates the source of moral failure in users, not in gadgets or corporate business practices. This is why, as we discuss later in this chapter, Mark Zuckerberg insists that Facebook users' resistance to the "real identity" policy is evidence of a "lack of integrity" among users (Kirkpatrick 2010, p. 199). It has nothing to do with Facebook, his argument implies.

Again and again, Silicon Valley refuses to acknowledge how its products and services are implicated in emergent issues of political fragmentation and economic inequality. Often implicitly, but sometimes in strikingly explicit language, companies like Facebook and Google accuse users of moral failure, even as their own products and services undermine the integrity of the systems they depend upon for their success. In the process, they amplify propaganda, exacerbate economic exploitation, and facilitate hate speech and tribal partisanship. Regardless of how sincere and well-meaning they may be in their views, many tech leaders' understanding of human psychology and moral development is deeply flawed, and we are beginning to see the consequences that arise when such flawed views are encoded into the platforms we use every day. With regard to the virtue of integrity, it should be clear that while we all strive for coherence and wholeness, it cannot be imposed upon us by decree, either through user-end policies or platform designs. We need room for messiness, contradiction, and playfulness in the process of our own struggles for integrity. We need tech to be a bit more humble, to hear the voices of users with clarity, and to attend to their concerns with respect.

The Catechism: Convergence Is Integrity

Since the mid-nineties, technical convergence has tended to exacerbate problems of social fragmentation, even as industry elites have touted its personal and social benefits. Data aggregation by social networking platforms, employers, and other third parties "is morally troubling because it threatens to disrupt the delicate web of relationships that constitute the context of social life, injecting into workplace and business contexts information of the wrong type, under inappropriate transmission principles" (Nissenbaum 2010, p. 228).

In the day-to-day routines most of us experience, integrity might mean that a parent achieves a sense of balance between work and family life, that career aspirations and commitments resonate rather than conflict with family obligations. Advertisements and advice columns often suggest that convergent media technologies enhance this sense of integrity. As once-separate devices like the telephone, camera, and computer come together in the form of the tablet or smartphone, so too can our work and family lives. Some business consultants even claim that we should renounce efforts to "balance" work and home life altogether and instead "blend" them into a uniform mixture (Ashkenas 2012). Smartphones supposedly make this possible. Marketing and branding expert Abby Euler (2013) reassures her readers, "my responsibilities at work and at home do not have to be at odds with each other. I physically leave the office, but my computer and iPhone go with me."

Thus, technologies are marketed as a solution to a perceived lack of coherence in our professional and personal lives. But as some critics suggest, rather than achieving harmonious balance or blending, convergent media often "scrambles" different parts of our lives until we feel disoriented (Vaidhyanathan 2018, pp. 19–20). While some top-ranking executives say blending our multiple social roles is "simple" (Tobak 2012), many workers in high-stress, high-salary jobs report difficulty integrating work and family life (Smith 2012, p. 16). Research indicates that smartphones and other technologies have increased unpaid overtime work, with half of surveyed employees reporting that they "feel they have no choice" but to sacrifice time with family (McChesney 2013, p. 218). Those who primarily use their smartphone for Internet access report difficulty in focusing on one task or giving undivided attention to other people (Smith 2012). One study suggests that cell phone use is correlated with decreased willingness to volunteer for community service and a general lack of interest other people's lives (Abraham et al. 2011). For some users, it appears, digital media tend to exacerbate the problems of work-life balance rather than ameliorate them.

One problem in this discussion is that key decisions about work-life balance are made in top-down fashion, so they reflect the perceptions and interests of executives rather than employees. For example, Yahoo CEO Marissa Mayer caused an uproar by banning telecommuting altogether. Her goal was to preserve the integrity of both work life and family life by keeping them separate. But her employees included many working mothers for whom this top-down decree made it nearly impossible to fulfill their parenting duties. So even when organizational leaders acknowledge issues of personal and institutional integrity, they err on the side of propping up the latter at the expense of the former. As networked devices have increased pressure to work longer hours, many companies have streamlined office productivity by monitoring employees' online shopping and other non-work activities (Madden and Jones 2008, p. 35). When corporate elites dismiss efforts to separate work and family life as "an exercise in futility," it appears that their preference for "blending" refers to a one-way process: one that allows work to enter more deeply into family life but not vice versa (Euler 2013). In the United States especially, such rhetoric also neglects broader political-economic issues, such as the fact that many workers simply cannot afford smartphones due to the steep prices arising from the near-duopoly status of AT&T and Verizon or to the fact that the family protections afforded to employees, including paid parental leave, lag significantly behind those of their European counterparts (McChesney 2013, p. 112).

We noted earlier in this chapter that not everyone is a famous artist like Miley Cyrus, and surely it goes without saying that neither is everyone a high-paid CEO with abundant resources to balance or blend work and family to one's personal satisfaction. In the context of our digital economy, most people's concerns boil down to a few apparently simple demands that are difficult to achieve: let me find satisfaction in both work and family life; do not blend or scramble them all up into one, but do not arbitrarily separate them either; let me decide how to negotiate that balance, and give me the opportunity and the resources to make such decisions. With so much to gain financially by controlling the narrative around the convergence of devices and data, Silicon Valley executives have little incentive to understand, much less attend wholeheartedly to, such demands from users.

The Privilege of Integrity

Let us return for a moment to the metaphor of health and well-being in one's body and in the body politic from earlier in this chapter. Traditionally, people have turned to pastors, physicians, and psychotherapists when dealing with crises of integrity. For the last few decades, people have increasingly turned to tech experts. Unsurprisingly, technologists are all too happy to play the part.

As noted in Chapter 1, in interviews and public statements Facebook founder Mark Zuckerberg often describes himself as if he were a psychoanalyst in relation to his users. While he may be sincere, critics argue that such corporate rhetoric "rework[s] familiar concepts in ways that serve Facebook's interests" (Hoffmann et al. 2016, p. 4). Facebook not only offers a rhetorical framework for understanding human psychology, it also encodes that psychological framework into its platform architectures in ways that both enable and restrain user engagement. Facebook's understanding of human psychology, as evidenced by its platform architecture, its policy decisions, and simply the way Zuckerberg talks about his users, comprise an ethically fraught instance of psychoanalysis conducted outside of the traditional confines of the clinic (Healey and Potter 2018).

Facebook's "real identity" policy, which prohibits pseudonymous profiles, exemplifies the merger of human virtue and market values by refusing any meaningful distinction between online profiles and what Zuckerberg calls the "real self." As we explained in Chapter 4, this policy embodies the problematic notion that informational transparency is equivalent to authenticity, an assumption that is both inaccurate and ethically fraught. Nevertheless, it forms the foundation of Zuckerberg's self-styled role as part-engineer, part-psychoanalyst. Public backlash erupted when the Facebook CEO offered a defense of the "real identity" policy in which he moralistically denounced users' use of multiple profiles: "You have one identity. The days of you having a different image for your work friends or co-workers and for the other people you know are probably coming to an end pretty quickly. Having two identities for yourself is an example of a lack of integrity" (Kirkpatrick 2010, p. 199).

Facebook's "real identity" policy sparked resistance from domestic abuse victims, political activists, and other marginalized groups (Barmann 2014a; Hoffmann 2016). While he later acknowledged that "there are lots of services that are good with pseudonyms," he insisted that Facebook's approach was still superior "if you're talking about mapping out a *real* community" (Y Combinator 2013, emphasis added). Importantly, Zuckerberg's perspective is undercut by contemporary psychoanalytic theory, which rejects "fantasies of perfect integrity and wholeness" (Frosh 2010, p. 163), insisting instead that individuals construct multiple identity positions which "may be quite fluid and even mutually contradictory" (Frosh 2010, p. 99).

The integrity issue flared up again late in 2014, when Facebook "launched a new crackdown on people using stage names, adopted nicknames, or drag names as their primary profile names" (Barmann 2014a). Critics lambasted Zuckerberg's naive understanding of integrity. One reporter described it as "ridiculously short-sighted and anti-intellectual" (Barmann 2014b). Another observer remarked, "Zuckerberg must have skipped that class [at Harvard] where Jung and Goffman were discussed" (Zimmer 2010). Those theorists, for instance, understood the self as multifaceted, with no single perspective or presentation accounting for the entirety of an individual. The various facets of one's self do not always cohere logically but often contradict each other. The self "isn't a thing or an entity; it's a process." The self consists of a "potential for growth that will naturally unfold under the right circumstances, and that can be damaged or hidden in a hostile environment" (Frosh 2010, p. 113).

The analytical error embedded in Facebook's real identity policy can pose real risks. Enforcement of the policy burdens the user-patient with "a demand for a certain mode of narrative integrity that is simply not possible without doing violence to the actuality of the fragmented psyche" (Frosh 2010, p. 146; see also Butler 2005, p. 42). The LGBTQ community clearly perceived this danger, and the real identity policy sparked particularly intense outrage among drag queen users (Barmann 2014a, 2014b), many of whom saw their alternate "drag" profiles disappear. Transgender users also protested, as in Anna Lauren Hoffmann's (2016) argument that transgender folks "use fake names to manage their own conflicting audiences by making themselves visible to those who may offer love and support, but invisible to those who may wish them harm." In this sense, Facebook's real identity policy bolsters the company's bottom line "at the expense of the wellbeing of its most vulnerable members" (Hoffmann 2016). Zuckerberg's dismissal of such concerns exemplifies how normalizing discourses "remove the other's otherness" through processes where "as soon as the other claims a right to maintain its difference, it is regarded as hostile" (Frosh 2010, p. 131).

Zuckerberg's presumptuous statement about identity and integrity is both naïve and revealing. Corporate notions of personal virtue are "underpinned by an immense privilege" since those who boast of having nothing to hide rarely identify as racial, political, or sexual minorities (Lennard 2013). In 2014, Facebook issued a formal apology in response to the backlash from LGBTQ users. But the unintended problems associated with Facebook's algorithms have only become more glaring. Zuckerberg's naïve yet passionate understanding of his users' "personal, emotional, and spiritual needs" has led him to double-down on his company's mission of creating a more connected and open world by expanding the company's global reach, even by reaching out to authoritarian leaders like Filipino president Rodrigo Duterte (Melber 2017). In Egypt and Myanmar as much as in the United States, Facebook has undermined the integrity of social and political systems by exacerbating corruption. Those in positions of power have learned to game the system, so to speak, leveraging social media to sow discord, rally support for authoritarianism, and demonize those less powerful, thereby leaving economic and social minorities vulnerable to psychological and physical violence.

The Challenge of Institutional Integrity

If integrity is a state of being in which "no part of the self is split off in the unconscious so that it is inaccessible" (Beebe 2000, p. 13), it may be incompatible with the dynamics of market capitalism, an economic system that concentrates wealth and power into relatively few hands while externalizing risk. Silicon Valley tends to generate "integrity bubbles," or limited contexts of work and family life in which a small but satisfied group enjoys an experience of harmony unavailable to others (Healey 2013). In the sense of compatibility between one's professional and personal life, integrity may be available mostly to the privileged few. Perhaps it is not surprising that, in a tech-centered economy, the same companies that are highly rated for work-life balance (including Facebook and Google) produce the very products and services that many people blame for causing difficulty in negotiating multiple commitments. Ironically, many employees of Silicon Valley companies chose to send their children to the relatively expensive Waldorf schools, where technology is prohibited (Richtel 2011), while public schools forego hiring new staff or raising teacher pay in favor of million-dollar contracts to bring Apple's iPads into the classroom (Gilbert 2013). But integrity for some, and not others, is arguably not integrity at all.

Emphasizing the democratizing potential of convergent technologies, self-described "critical utopian" scholars like Henry Jenkins downplay these broader institutional issues. Just as Facebook was getting off the ground, Jenkins (2006) wrote the book *Convergence Culture*, arguing that convergence represents a "cultural shift" with promising new relationships between audiences, producers, and content (pp. 3–12). Although his analysis is couched in numerous disclaimers and caveats, his central argument is that convergence creates an opportunity to restore a balance of power between the corporate state and the citizen consumer, bringing greater integrity to democratic life.

Jenkins argues that as fans of *American Idol* or *Harry Potter* force the broadcast and film industries to respond to their concerns, and as fans of *The Sims* run for political office in virtual elections, consumer, and political empowerment converge. No longer do we "watch television in our underwear" and "dress up to vote," creating an artificial separation between our consumptive and civic lives. Instead we "vote naked" as our living rooms become networked epicenters of collective political action (Jenkins 2006, p. 233). He continues this line of thought in his book *Spreadable Media* (2013), tracking the interplay between popular "trans-media" narratives and grassroots movements like Occupy Wall Street. While such arguments might be accurate with regard to micro-markets and grassroots media, here again it is a limited range of social actors who tend to benefit, namely, those who have the time and means to participate and who are attractive to advertisers (Meehan 2007). User-produced trans-media stories may be good at catalyzing targeted branding and marketing strategies but ultimately "do not add up to a grand narrative about the democratic potential of converging media" (Verstraete 2011, p. 545).

In the context of commercial markets, convergence tends toward the concentration of power rather than its dissolution. In addition to the continued dominance of advertising and marketing industries, key elements of the digital economy such as search engines and social networking platforms are especially prone to monopoly control as widespread use of a single service or platform tends to increase its efficiency and user-friendliness, a phenomenon known as network effects. Many monopoly-status firms are geographically concentrated as well, leading to a magnification of the widespread class inequalities of the digital era.

Nowhere is this process more evident than in the San Francisco bay area, where tensions between blue-collar residents and upwardly mobile tech employees have sharpened in recent years. Tech companies' online process of evaluating and sorting users according to socio-economic status is paralleled in real-world real estate and architectural strategies that displace local businesses and impinge on community space (Arieff 2013). One tech leader even proposed dividing California into six different states, with unique laws for residents of the new state of Silicon Valley (Rouse 2013). Rather than increasing collective intelligence through integration, the digital economy tends to sharpen class divisions, funneling attention toward consumer groups that marketers term "American Royalty" while neglecting concerns of the less powerful (Fung 2013). If we conceive of the body politic as a collective self, then the current state of affairs in the United States runs counter to our above-noted definition of integrity as including sensitivity to the needs of the whole, responsibility toward others, and genuine dialogue with those outside of one's immediate community.

Fear and anxiety, furthermore, are reliable drivers of commercial media. Social media amplifies this inflation of negativity, as seen in the spread of hyper-partisan "fake news" on Facebook during the 2016 U.S. presidential election (Bell 2016). Twitter similarly contributes indirectly to political polarization, with conservatives being more likely to use the platform to retreat into ideological echo chambers (Barberá et al. 2015). Consequently we retreat into filter bubbles, or safe cocoons of media content, that we find reassuring and validating with regard to our preconceived notion of ourselves and the world. We chat or post comments about others but rarely engage with others outside our limited social media circles. We become trapped in the moral swamp of fanaticism catalyzed by state-sponsored propaganda from home or abroad. The strong sense of belonging we feel often amounts to tribalism at the expense of civility between different social groups. The crisis of integrity is both personal and political.

The Paradox of Corporate Mindfulness

With the proliferation of training courses espousing the benefits of yoga and meditation, critics have coined the term "McMindfulness" to describe a cottage industry whose profit motives appear to contradict the ethical foundations of the practices it appropriates (Purser and Loy 2013). From a Buddhist standpoint, mindfulness is not a mere stress-reduction technique: it is a "distinct quality of attention" with transformative social potential.

Paradoxically, mindfulness programs are commonplace in companies that depend on advertising, an industry that manipulates attention to enhance revenues, often at the expense of economic justice (Purser and Loy 2013). Digital technologies enable more efficient techniques, and experts even encourage marketers to "design for interruption" (Croll 2012). Facebook, iPhones, and Google Glass exemplify such strategies. As one passionate onlooker (2008) argues, "Google is, quite literally, in the business of distraction" (Carr 2008). The paradox of corporate mindfulness is an outgrowth of the process of externalization in market capitalism: Silicon Valley employees reap the benefits of mindfulness, while externalizing the problems of fragmentation and distraction to users. In this section, we use the paradox of corporate mindfulness to illustrate the concept of systemic integrity; that is, integrity at the level of institutions and even entire societies.

Chade-Meng Tan spent eight years as a systems designer at Google before developing the company's Search Inside Yourself leadership training program. With a book of the same title, the Search Inside Yourself brand of business-friendly mindfulness has garnered praise from employees and even the Dalai Lama himself. Now "semi-retired," Tan fills the role of jocular corporate guru (Fasman 2012). Describing his current role at Google, Tan says, "A good analogy is Yoda, the old man who mostly says wise things, is ungrammatical, and shows you how to use the force" (Fasman 2012). The comparison is not without complications: the famous *Star Wars* character appeared on-screen in 1980 as an exile in the swampy caves of a lonely planet, subsisting on a goop that his young apprentice, Luke Skywalker, could barely tolerate. By contrast, as *The New York Times* notes, Mr. Tan "became rich—albeit not nearly as rich as the founders—after Google went public in 2004" (Kelly 2012). And unlike the young Luke, while reaping the benefits of Tan's in-house training, employees enjoy the benefit of free lunches in the Googleplex cafeteria.

For Tan and many other corporate leaders, mindfulness and profit go hand in hand. One does not have to "pick between being moral and successful," Tan explains, because "compassion is so pure I don't think there is any way to taint it" (Fasman 2012). Tan geared his programs to "the rich, corporate world" as part of a strategy for achieving world peace (Kelly 2012). "If I can turn the most powerful part of the world into a land of wisdom and compassion," he argues, "it's going to change the rest of the world" (Fasman 2012).

Scholars likewise chastise Google for the way its faith in the beneficence of software engineering encourages "hubris," from its deliberate thwarting of iPhone privacy settings (Angwin and Valentino-DeVries [2012] 2019) to its obstruction of the FCC's investigation of Street View (Shaer 2012). Apple and Facebook, both of which also promote mindfulness programs, have faced charges of tax avoidance and deception in user privacy practices. This paradox of "corporate mindfulness" is further compounded by the fact that these companies' products have ushered in an era of compulsive distraction. Some critics argue that the public's growing interest in yoga and meditation may be a direct measure of frustration with digital devices, while others have called for mindfulness programs in public schools to protect against the cognitive threats of mass advertising and digital distraction.

Corporate mindfulness programs address the stress of individual executives and employees without attending to the root causes of such stress. In the hands of proponents like Google's Chade-Meng Tan, such programs assume that global-economic problems may be solved by infusing an ethical sensibility at the top while leaving the structures of corporate capital intact. Moreover, they treat workplace stress as impediments to productivity rather than as symptoms of inequitable labor conditions. Paraphrasing one Google engineer, *The New York Times* describes mindfulness programs as "sort of an organizational WD-40, a necessary lubricant between driven, ambitious employees and Google's demanding corporate culture" (Kelly 2012).

In some cases, the employees targeted by these programs are not those climbing the ladder but those forced out through layoffs. This scenario unfolded at a session of Janice Marturano's Mindful Leadership program at General Mills. "General Mills had recently announced its first round of mass layoffs in decades," the *Financial Times* reports, and the session began with "some tears" (Gelles 2012). Some attendees "were having to fire members of their team, while others were losing their jobs." Marturano reportedly betrayed no sense of being "troubled by any apparent contradiction around using compassion to breed better capitalists" and insisted she is "very careful to retain the integrity of mindfulness itself" (Gelles 2012). But many critics cry foul, saying that corporate-friendly versions of meditation appropriate the "transformative power" of traditional spiritual practices (Carrette and King 2005, pp. 22–23). Instead of self-sacrifice and the cultivation of community, for example, "we find productivity, work-efficiency and the accumulation of profit put forward as the new goals" (Carrette and King 2005, p. 23).

We might describe this paradox as Silicon Valley's Faustian bargain. Karolyn Kinane, the contemplative scholar we introduced in Chapter 3, describes issues of personal and systemic integrity through the lens of Dr. Faustus, the legendary character who made a deal with the Devil in Christopher Marlow's *The Tragical History of Doctor Faustus*. She gave us a simple example. "I love songbirds," she explains, "but if I buy cheap sneakers made in environmentally unsustainable ways—ways that contribute to the death of the songbird—that's my Faustian bargain" (Kinane 2018). If tech leaders tout the stress-reduction benefits of mindfulness while producing the very devices that are the source of our distraction, we may rightly ask whether Silicon Valley has made such a Faustian bargain. But the metaphor applies to users as well. Too often, the digital economy turns us all into cyborg versions of Dr. Faustus. We want to connect with family and friends, so we use Facebook despite its role in propping up authoritarian governments and undermining democracy at home. We need to search for information, products, and services online, so we use Google despite its record of ignoring privacy concerns. We make such Faustian bargains because the digital economy tends toward monopoly control by a handful of powerful organizations.

In this chapter's opening discussion of Miley Cyrus, we noted that the struggle for integrity usually involves risk and sacrifice. Lynne McFall describes it this way:

> A person of integrity is willing to bear the consequences of her convictions, even when this is difficult. … A person whose only principle is "Seek my own pleasure" is not a candidate for integrity because there is no possibility of conflict—between pleasure and principle—in which integrity could be lost. Where there is no possibility of its loss, integrity cannot exist.
>
> (McFall 1987, pp. 9–10)

Systemic issues cannot be addressed through stress-reduction programs that assume the beneficence of unregulated markets. But engineers and executives often cannot see, or simply refuse to see, the unfortunate consequences of disruptive technology. As mentioned above, Google's Chade-Meng Tan refuses to acknowledge any contradiction between commercial profit and his efforts to "democratize enlightenment" through corporate mindfulness programs (Tan 2014). This response, we suggest, reflects a combination of willful blindness and naïve ignorance. If tech leaders perceive no troublesome consequences to their work or do not themselves experience such consequences, what need is there to change course?

Comfort and complacency for some means risk-taking and sacrifice for others. The crises of integrity, or the chivalric challenges described at the outset of this chapter, are not equitably distributed among the wealthy and the poor, majority and minority. Sometimes enhancing system integrity requires breaking from the system itself, a process with ethical and legal implications. Consider the case of Edward Snowden, the whistleblower who leaked classified information from the National Security Administration (NSA), exposing apparent coordination between the surveillance activities of the U.S. security apparatus and companies like Google. Snowden's actions caused deep divisions among citizens and government officials in the United States and abroad. In the United States, a bipartisan array of political officials denounced his actions for endangering American troops and undermining ongoing intelligence efforts. But he received support from others, including, for example, surveillance watchdog groups and United Nations representatives, for demonstrating an ethical sensibility often lacking in tech and government leaders. Snowden himself invoked the rhetoric of personal integrity, suggesting that he searched inside himself, so to speak, before taking drastic action, leaving the bubble of a self-described "paradise" for the sake of the public interest (Poitras and Greenwald 2013).

Arguably, the goal of such whistleblowing efforts is to promote mindfulness as a civic virtue, by subjecting data-collection programs to careful evaluation by legislators and the general public. As one observer explains, whistleblowers are "defending us from epistemic attack" by helping to "lift the hood that is periodically pulled over our eyes to blind us from the truth" (Ludlow 2013). If integrity is what one does when no one is looking, whistleblowers play an important role by calling attention to neglected or hidden issues.

On the weekend the surveillance leaks emerged, Tan tweeted cheerfully, "Yes, I'm in the movie *Internship*" and announced that the Chinese edition of *Search Inside Yourself* had launched. In the meantime, Snowden moved to an undisclosed location in Hong Kong. His passport was later revoked, forcing him to remain in limbo in the transit area of a Moscow airport while petitioning for asylum. Though Tan compares his wit and wisdom to that of Yoda, it seems that Snowden's fate more closely resembles that of the famed *Star Wars* character: the latter, realizing the odds against defeating the Empire, went into hiding in the dank caves of the planet Dagobah where he trained the young Luke Skywalker. Some of Snowden's supporters speak of him as a sort of Jedi hacker in exile, voicing hope that Snowden will inspire "comparable civil courage" (Ellsberg 2013). As consumer and government surveillance converge, activists have voiced ongoing support for Snowden's insistence upon "informed consent" as the basis for genuine democracy (Kelly and Tsvetkova 2013). For Snowden's efforts, in October 2013 the group Adams Associates for Integrity in Intelligence presented him with the Integrity in Intelligence Award. Though the legal questions here are beyond the purview of our expertise, it is clear that public debates surrounding the NSA and Snowden's leaks hinged largely on questions of both professional and institutional integrity, throwing the Faustian bargain of the digital economy into sharp relief.

Challenging the Catechism: Convergence Is Not Integrity

In this chapter, we began with a discussion of artistic integrity, followed by an extended discussion of systemic or institutional integrity. We are dealing with a complex topic here, because the virtue of integrity has both personal and collective dimensions. To conclude, let us return to the simplicity of our day-to-day interactions with technology, and see how these complex tensions show up in even the most mundane places. We will begin with an anecdote.

In early 2018, Amy Snow took her daughter Carson to the Los Angeles Type-In, a retro-tech event where "typewriter enthusiasts" of all stripes can play around on each other's machines and maybe "type a love letter just before Valentine's Day." Amy and Carson stopped to talk to special guests Haiku Guys + Gals who, of course, typed out a personalized poem for each.

Amy's read as follows:

> *When you are tempered*
> *By flames and transmutation*
> *No winds will break you*

Carson's haiku was about movies. "Mine," Amy posted via Instagram, was "about resilience." Describing the poems as "Our Truths," Amy followed her Instagram post with the hashtag#FreeHaiku.

It was a rare moment when, rather than colliding clumsily, the analogue and digital came together in a graceful embrace: the analogue poet led the dance, tapping out verse in 5–7–5 rhythm; meanwhile the digital photo announced it, with a hashtag spreading the message far and wide. Paradoxically, Instagram inspired others to set down their phones and reconnect with the aesthetics of the analogue.

Amy is no Luddite. As a high-powered branding and marketing guru, she has conducted one-on-one sessions with Uber executives and can describe the inside of the Googleplex as well as anyone. While embracing the digital, she aims to integrate time-tested humanistic values in the emerging digital economy. When Amy gave a guest lecture in one of our Media and Ethics seminars a few years ago, two pivotal concepts formed the basis of discussion: authenticity and integrity. These concepts, we suggest, are what is driving the revival of the typewriter.

For the sake of argument, let us suppose Amy and Carson shared a warm bowl of soup during their visit to the Type-In. The key to a good, hearty soup is to combine ingredients in a way that respects the integrity of each flavor. The chef might take

FIGURE 5.1 The type-written haiku Amy Snow received when she visited the Haiku Guys + Gals in Los Angeles.

some portion out, but not all, and mix it in a blender. We want to see what is in there: carrots, celery, potato. If you blend everything together too thoroughly, you lose the distinctness that each ingredient has to offer. A hearty soup is one where your palate can discern one element among others, and each serves its role in balanced relation to the others.

Too often, convergent technologies over-mix, over-blend, until we are left with a soup that our palate cannot enjoy. The ingredients have been processed beyond recognition. Digital convergence, as an ideology, not just a process, presses further. It wants to blend your soup, and your toast, and your coffee, even your spoon and fork, into one all-encompassing mixture. It might sound good in theory, but it probably tastes terrible. You might even break a tooth. In the case of digital media, we are talking about your work life, your family life, and your friendships. Would you want to blend these together until they were all one soup with no distinction between them? What about your grocery store purchases, your browsing history, and your travel itinerary? Would you want companies like Facebook or Amazon to have access to all of those data points and be able to piece them together as they see fit? Your answer to these questions is likely nuanced. Sometimes you want to blend work and family. You might indeed trust a certain company to know different aspects of your financial life. Notice that the key element here is your own judgment.

Whether in the kitchen, the music studio, or the writer's retreat, you want to be the artist. Integrity involves the judicious, consensual creation and negotiation of boundaries. We keep some things separate even as we integrate them into a larger whole with its own boundary. Typewriter enthusiasts love their machines, treating them as nearly sacred objects, precisely because they are bounded machines. They do one thing: they demand and cultivate focused attention on the process of writing. Because they are not designed to multitask and are not connected to a network, they do not and in fact cannot undermine the writer's attention with crude attempts to blend other tasks into the mix.

Songwriter John Mayer explains that even simple intrusions like Microsoft's spellchecker can needlessly interrupt an artist's "mercurial" thought process. Writing well requires a contemplative focus. Even the most creative artists, Mayer says, "have to sit at [an] altar to produce something" (*California Typewriter* 2017). In the flow of the creative process, Mayer continues, "You have to keep your heart rate down, and focus, and stay in that trance."

It is precisely the limitations of the machine, its technical boundaries, that make a typewriter a preferred altar for many. For Ton Sison, editor of the blog "i dream lo-tech," the typewriter is "a speedbump that forces me to focus" (Awehali 2014). Doug Nichol, the filmmaker, notes that while digital technology makes our lives "easier, faster, and less effortful," we are wise to remember that, sometimes, "making an effort is what gives life satisfaction" (Awehali 2014). In response to friends who tell him a computer might help him write faster, playwright David McCullough says bluntly, "I don't want to go faster. If anything, I'd prefer to go slower" (*California Typewriter* 2017).

As artists, writers intuitively understand this nuanced vision of integrity. They isolate the creative process. They create rituals around it to set it apart from other, more mundane parts of their day. These rituals heighten their sense of physical presence: I am in this place, at this time, doing this thing. This is why typewriter enthusiasts praise the sensorial aspects of writing on an analog machine. The tactile sensation of one's fingers on the keys, the sound of the letter-arms snapping against the ribbon and paper, these are physical cues that keep our attention focused. Such sensations tie the typist to the machine, the body to the location, the flow of thought to a precise moment in time.

By contrast, through its aggressive splicing-together of once-separate tasks, digital convergence too often violates the integrity, or wholeness, of each. If my phone is also a camera, and my laptop is also a typewriter and a television, I may feel I am neither a good conversation partner nor a thoughtful photographer. More to the point: If my work e-mail follows me home against my will into the sacred space of my family, I may feel I am neither a good employee nor a good parent. In bringing too many things together, radically and imprudently, convergence has the ironic effect of making coherence difficult and the experience of disintegration more likely.

Interest in typewriters is about "people seeking out tools that are durable, independent, private, and that focus the mind instead of creating distractions" (Awehali 2014). No wonder, then, that the ultimate statement of typewriter fetishism comes in the form of the so-called Typewriter Insurgency Manifesto, a document that, while written on a whim, became a viral phenomenon around the globe. In a defiant tone, the Manifesto frames the embrace of the typewriter as a moral imperative. It makes implicit claims about technology and integrity: "We strike a blow for self-reliance, privacy, and coherence, against dependency, surveillance, and *disintegration*" (Awehali 2014, italics added). We want the various aspects of our lives to fit together coherently, but we want to savor each ingredient for its unique flavor. Integrity is a hearty soup.

The Typewriter Insurgency is part of a broader movement to recapture a sense of integrity in the emerging digital economy. Just blocks from the Los Angeles Type-In, you can walk into Pop Obscure Records and browse through hundreds of vinyl records under the gaze of vinyl-era music icons like Debbie Harry, Jim Morrison, and Johnny Rotten, whose poster images cover the walls. Like their typewriting counterparts, vinyl enthusiasts enjoy the physicality of playing a record. It, too, is a tactile experience. Writing for *Variety*, reporter Owen Gleiberman (2017) connects the dots: "Vinyl made a comeback, and so did slow food and long beards. Why not the typewriter?"

Of course, there is a subtle paradox in the central story of *California Typewriter*. As we watch the film, the Oakland-based typewriter repair shop (after which the film is named) appears destined for bankruptcy. The doors will surely close if the owners fail to drum up business. There are plenty of typewriter enthusiasts scattered around the country, but how can one small family-owned shop cater to them all? Social media, anyone?

By the end of the movie, *California Typewriter* (the repair shop) is thriving. What saved their business? A WordPress blog. A Twitter feed. E-mail. These are the same networks that allow vinyl enthusiasts to find each other, or fans of do-it-yourself butter-churning or micro-brewers. Through digital promotion, *California Typewriter* publicized a highly successful gathering in 2013 (Awehali 2014). While the film celebrates the analogue, it also celebrates prudent use of the digital to amplify analogue virtues. Integrity favors both/and above either/or thinking. We can leverage digital media to celebrate embodiment and call on others to share their own embodied rituals—to become artists or, in this case, to become "typewriters."

As we learn early in the film, the term "typewriter" originally referred not to the machine, but to its operator. Job ads for "typewriters" were common. (Hereafter we will use the hyphenated term type-writer to refer to human users.) Today, of course, being a type-writer means something different. As suggested by the Insurgency Manifesto, it is an act of defiance. A form of resistance. A political and moral statement.

Conclusion

Despite Sinéad O'Connor's best motherly intentions, Miley Cyrus did not take too kindly to her advice. Her letter resulted in a nasty twitter war that included Cyrus making fun of O'Connor's 2011 experience with mental health issues (Rouse 2013). O'Connor fired back. Cyrus again. And so on.

The possibility that O'Connor's offering might lead to broader conversations about issues presented in this chapter were quickly lost in a hailstorm of pugilistic headlines, emotional outbursts, and threats of lawsuits.

Within the catechism, sustained conversations about the confusion between convergence and integrity appears somewhat inefficient, even "old-fashioned and constricting," explains media scholar Quentin J. Schultze, "when contrasted with the sea of available information" and preference for "libertine messaging." Schultze continues:

> Where is the unifying center—the integrity—of cyberspace? Perhaps no question is more important for societies that are fabricated increasingly out of technique. Are we as human beings more than the sum of our skills and techniques? Is there not much more to life than creating and consuming information, as well as purchasing and using the equipment that enables us to expend time messaging? Is there a deeply binding purpose to our efforts and even to our very being? If not, perhaps we are nothing more than morally mercurial personas with an inexplicable talent for influencing one another and with an insatiable desire to make the creation fully subservient to our own interests. Where is the integrating principle that illuminates the value of all others?
>
> (2002, p. 135)

Of course, if we rest content in our careful zigzag dance between analog and digital in our personal lives, we run the risk of complacency with the broader, systemic injustice of the digital economy. Like the Silicon Valley executives whose corporate mindfulness programs reduce personal stress while externalizing the risks of digital media, we consumers also run the risk of complacency. Not everyone can afford to pair a slick, retro-cool typewriter with the latest iPhone, switching judiciously from one to the other. If we merely attend to our own stresses, our own productivity and peace of mind, we unwittingly contribute to the stress and suffering of others.

And so, while we can and should begin to resist their dominance through simple acts of resistance—becoming a type-writer, for example—that is not good enough. The policy level is where we address these broader issues of institutional integrity. We will return to those issues and strategies in Chapter 9.

References

Abraham, Ajay T., Anastasiya Pocheptsova, and Rosellina Ferraro. "The 'Cellph'-ish effects of 'Self'-phone Usage." Association for Consumer Research Conference, St. Louis, MO, October 2011.

Angwin, Julia, and Jennifer Valentino-DeVries. "Google's iPhone Tracking: Web Giant, Others Bypassed Apple Browser Settings for Guarding Privacy." *Wall Street Journal*, June 20, 2019. [Original article date February 17, 2012]. https://www.wsj.com/articles/SB10001 424052970204880404577225380456599176.

Arieff, Allison. "What Tech Hasn't Learned from Urban Planning." *New York Times*, December 13, 2013. http://www.nytimes.com/2013/12/14/opinion/what-tech-hasnt-learned-from-urban-planning.html.

Ashkenas, Ron. "Forget Work-Life Balance: It's Time for Work-Life Blend." *Forbes*, October 19, 2012. http://www.forbes.com/sites/ronashkenas/2012/10/19/forget-work-life-balance-its-time-for-work-life-blend/.

Awehali, Brian. "Slow Type." *East Bay Express*. May 7, 2014. https://www.eastbayexpress.com/oakland/slow-type/Content?oid=3913741.

Barberá, Pablo, John T. Jost, Jonathan Nagler, Joshua Tucker, and Richard Bonneau. "Tweeting from Left to Right: Is Online Political Communication More Than an Echo Chamber?" *Psychological Science* 26, no. 10 (August 2015):1531–42. doi:10.1177/0956797615594620.

Barmann, Jay. "Drag Queens, Other Performers Outraged as Facebook Forces Them to Use Their Real Names [Updated]." SFIST. September 11, 2014a. http://sfist.com/2014/09/11/drag_queens_other_performers_outrag.php.

———. "Zuckerberg Has Always Believed That We're Only Entitled to One Identity." SFIST. September 19, 2014b. https://sfist.com/2014/09/19/zuckerberg_has_always_believed_that/.

Beebe, John. "The Place of Integrity in Spirituality." In *The Psychology of Mature Spirituality: Integrity, Wisdom, Transcendence*, edited by Polly Young-Eisendrath and Melvin E. Miller, 11–20. Philadelphia: Routledge, 2000.

Bell, Emily. "Facebook Can No Longer Be 'I Didn't Do It' Boy of Global Media." *Columbia Journalism Review*, November 11, 2016. http://www.cjr.org/tow_center/facebook_zuckerberg_trump_election.php.

Butler, Judith. *Giving an Account of Oneself*. New York: Fordham University Press, 2005.

California Typewriter. Directed by Doug Nichol. American Buffalo Pictures, 2017. Film.

Carr, Nicholas. "Is Google Making Us Stupid?" *The Atlantic*, July/August 2008. https://www.theatlantic.com/magazine/archive/2008/07/is-google-making-us-stupid/306868/.

Carrette, Jeremy, and Richard King. *Selling Spirituality: The Silent Takeover of Religion*. New York: Routledge, 2005.

Croll, Alistair. "Design for Interruption." Solve for Interesting. November 6, 2012. http://solveforinteresting.com/design-for-interruption/.

Ellsberg, Daniel. "Edward Snowden: Saving Us from the United Stasi of America." *The Guardian*, June 10, 2013. https://www.theguardian.com/commentisfree/2013/jun/10/edward-snowden-united-stasi-america.

Emmons, Robert A. *The Psychology of Ultimate Concerns: Motivation and Spirituality in Personality*. New York: The Guilford Press, 1999.

Euler, Abby. "Working Parents Should Focus on Work/Life Blend, Not Balance." *Houston Chronicle*, May 14, 2013. https://www.chron.com/jobs/salary/article/Working-Parents-Should-Focus-on-Work-Life-Blend-4535040.php.

Fasman, Jon. "Cheerfulness Is Next to Peacefulness." *The Economist*, August 20, 2012. https://www.economist.com/prospero/2012/08/20/cheerfulness-is-next-to-peacefulness.

Frosh, Stephen. *Psychoanalysis Outside the Clinic: Interventions in Psychosocial Studies*. London: Palgrave Macmillan, 2010.

Fung, Brian. "'X-tra Needy' and 'American Royalty': The Stereotypes Credit Card Companies Use to Target Us All." *Washington Post*, December 19, 2013. http://www.washingtonpost.com/blogs/the-switch/wp/2013/12/19/x-tra-needy-and-american-royalty-the-stereotypes-credit-card-companies-use-to-target-us-all/.

Gelles, David. "The Mind Business." *Financial Times*, August 24, 2012. https://www.ft.com/content/d9cb7940-ebea-11e1-985a-00144feab49a.

Gilbert, Ben. "Apple Providing iPads to Los Angeles School District in $30 Million Contract." Engadget. June 19, 2013. http://www.engadget.com/2013/06/19/apple-ipads-los-angeles-schools/.

Gleiberman, Owen. "Film Review: 'California Typewriter.'" *Variety*, August 17, 2017. https://variety.com/2017/film/reviews/california-typewriter-review-tomhanks-1202531511/.

Healey, Kevin. "Searching for Integrity: The Politics of Mindfulness in the Digital Economy." *Nomos Journal*, August 5, 2013. http://nomosjournal.org/2013/08/searching-for-integrity/.

Healey, Kevin, and Richard Potter. "Coding the Privileged Self: Facebook and the Ethics of Psychoanalysis 'Outside the Clinic.'" *Journal of Television and New Media* 19, no. 7 (2018): 660–76. https://doi.org/10.1177/1527476417745152.

Hoffmann, Anna Lauren. "Facebook Is Worried about Users Sharing Less—But It Only Has Itself to Blame." *The Guardian*, April 19, 2016. https://www.theguardian.com/technology/2016/apr/19/facebook-users-sharing-less-personal-data-zuckerberg.

Hoffmann, Anna Lauren, Nicholas Proferes, and Michael Zimmer. "'Making the World More Open and Connected': Mark Zuckerberg and the Discursive Construction of Facebook and Its Users." *New Media & Society* 20, no. 1 (July 28, 2016): 1–20.

Jenkins, Henry. *Convergence Culture: Where Old and New Media Collide.* New York: New York University Press, 2006.

Jenkins, Henry, Sam Ford, and Joshua Green. *Spreadable Media: Creating Value and Meaning in a Networked Culture.* New York: New York University Press, 2013.

Kelly, Caitlin. "O.K., Google, Take a Deep Breath." *New York Times*, April 28, 2012. https://www.nytimes.com/2012/04/29/technology/google-course-asks-employees-to-take-a-deep-breath.html.

Kelly, Lidia, and Maria Tsvetkova. "Fugitive Snowden to Seek Temporary Asylum in Russia." Reuters, July 12, 2013. http://www.reuters.com/article/2013/07/12/us-usa-security-snowden-meeting-idUSBRE96B07320130712.

Kinane, Karolyn. Interview by Kevin Healey. Personal interview. Concord, New Hampshire, December 12, 2018.

Kirkpatrick, David. *The Facebook Effect: The Inside Story of the Company That Is Connecting the World.* New York: Simon & Schuster, 2010.

Krochmal, Shana Naomi. "Why Miley Cyrus Is 'Free to Be Everything.'" *Out*. May 8, 2015. http://www.out.com/interviews/2015/5/08/miley-cyrus-free-be-everything.

Lennard, Natasha. "The Dangerous Ethics behind Google's Transparency Claims." Salon. June 12, 2013. https://www.salon.com/control/2013/06/11/the_dangerous_ethics_behind_googles_transparency_claims/.

Ludlow, Peter. "The Real War on Reality." *New York Times*, June 14, 2013. https://opinionator.blogs.nytimes.com/2013/06/14/the-real-war-on-reality/.

Lynch, Joe. "Miley Cyrus Turns VMA Acceptance Speech into Pleas for Homeless Youth." Billboard. August 24, 2014. https://www.billboard.com/articles/events/vma/6229207/miley-vmas-speech-homeless-youth.

Madden, Mary, and Sydney Jones. "Networked Workers." Pew Research Center, September 24, 2008. http://www.pewinternet.org/2008/09/24/networked-workers/.

McChesney, Robert W. *Digital Disconnect: How Capitalism Is Turning the Internet against Democracy.* New York: The New Press, 2013.

McFall, Lynne. "Integrity." *Ethics* 98 (October 1987): 5–20.

Meehan, Eileen R. Review of *Convergence Culture: Where Old and New Media Collide* by Henry Jenkins. *Journal of Communication* 57, no. 3 (August 2007): 599–612.

Melber, Ari. "Zuckerberg under Fire for Facebook's Deal with Rodrigo Duterte." *The Beat with Ari Melber*. MSNBC. December 30, 2017. https://www.youtube.com/watch?v=xk_ns1ynSRo.

Nissenbaum, Helen. *Privacy in Context: Technology, Policy, and the Integrity of Social Life*. Stanford, CA: Stanford University Press, 2010.

O'Connor, Sinéad. "Sinéad O'Connor's Open Letter to Miley Cyrus." *The Guardian*, October 3, 2013. https://www.theguardian.com/music/2013/oct/03/sinead-o-connor-open-letter-miley-cyrus.

Poitras, Laura, and Glenn Greenwald. "PRISM Whistleblower—Edward Snowden in His Own Words." Freedom of the Press Foundation. June 9, 2013. https://www.youtube.com/watch?v=3P_0iaCgKLk.

Purser, Ron, and David Loy. "Beyond McMindfulness." *Huffington Post*, August 31, 2013. https://www.huffingtonpost.com/ron-purser/beyond-mcmindfulness_b_3519289.html.

Richtel, Matt. "A Silicon Valley School That Doesn't Compute." *New York Times*, October 22, 2011. http://www.nytimes.com/2011/10/23/technology/at-waldorf-school-in-silicon-valley-technology-can-wait.html.

Rouse, Wade. "Miley Cyrus vs. Sinéad O'Connor: The Feud Escalates." People. October 4, 2013, https://people.com/celebrity/miley-cyrus-sinead-oconnor-twitter-fight-continues/.

Schultze, Quentin J. *Habits of the High Tech Heart: Living Virtuously in the Information Age*. Grand Rapids, MI: Baker Books, 2002.

Shaer, Matthew. "Google Gets $25K Fine for 'Impeding'" FCC Probe into Street View." *Christian Science Monitor*, April 17, 2012. https://www.csmonitor.com/Technology/Horizons/2012/0417/Google-gets-25K-fine-for-impeding-FCC-probe-into-Street-View.

Smith, Aaron. "The Best (and Worst) of Mobile Connectivity." Pew Research Center. November 30, 2012. https://www.pewinternet.org/2012/11/30/the-best-and-worst-of-mobile-connectivity/.

Tan, Chade-Meng. Personal communication to Kevin Healey. International Symposium for Contemplative Research, Boston, MA, November 2, 2014.

Tobak, Steve. "Work-Life Balance: A Common Sense Approach." CBS News, Moneywatch. May 25, 2012. https://www.cbsnews.com/news/work-life-balance-a-common-sense-approach/.

Vaidhyanathan, Siva. *Anti-Social Media: How Facebook Disconnects Us and Undermines Democracy*. New York: Oxford University Press, 2018.

Verstraete, Ginette. "The Politics of Convergence: On the Role of the Mobile Object." *Cultural Studies* 25, nos. 4–5 (September 2011): 534–47.

Y Combinator. "Mark Zuckerberg at Startup School 2013." Paper 160. *Zuckerberg Transcripts*, October 25, 2013. http://dc.uwm.edu/zuckerberg_files_transcripts/160.

Zimmer, Michael. "Facebook's Zuckerberg: 'Having Two Identities for Yourself Is an Example of a Lack of Integrity.'" Michael Zimmer. May 14, 2010. https://www.michaelzimmer.org/2010/05/14/facebooks-zuckerberg-having-two-identities-for-yourself-is-an-example-of-a-lack-of-integrity/.

6

PROCESSING IS NOT JUDGMENT

On a dark night in March 2018, forty-nine-year-old Elaine Herzberg was pushing her bike across a boulevard in Tempe, Arizona, when she was struck and killed by a self-driving Uber car. Just seconds before the fatal crash, video shows a human driver looking down as the fully autonomous Volvo XC-90 SUV was cruising at 43 miles per hour. Sensors in the car had spotted Herzberg six seconds before hitting her, but the system's algorithms decided to engage the brakes just 1.3 seconds before hitting her. By design, the system's emergency braking functions are disabled when Uber vehicles are under computer control, leaving potentially dangerous last-second maneuvers to the discretion of human drivers. Also by design, the system does not alert the driver. In this case, the driver took control less than a second before hitting Herzberg, and engaged the brakes only after impact (Associated Press 2018).

Uber is only one among many companies racing to enter the market for autonomous vehicle systems. Most of these are automotive giants like Toyota, BMW, Nissan, GM, and Volvo. But other tech companies like Google, Apple, Microsoft, Cisco, and even Amazon are also developing autonomous systems or system components. Several years before the Uber accident, critics speculated about the life-or-death predicaments soon to be faced not only by pedestrians but by car owners:

> Your car is speeding along a bridge at fifty miles per hour when an errant school bus carrying forty innocent children crosses its path. Should your car swerve, possibly risking the life of its owner (you) in order to save the children, or keep going, putting all forty kids at risk? If the decision must be made in milliseconds, the computer will have to make the call.
>
> (Marcus 2012)

Such are the moral burdens with which programmers of autonomous systems are tasked. This is a modern version of the classic "trolley problem" first outlined by Philippa Foot (1967) and elaborated by others. But the rapid development of automated vehicles adds urgency and complexity to such problems. Under product liability law, for example, drivers could sue manufacturers for negligence if these scenarios are not anticipated and addressed algorithmically (Bonnefon et al. 2015, p. 2). The stakes are even higher in the case of autonomous military robots, drones, and other automated weapons under development at the U.S. Department of Defense. Given the potential for "unintended engagements," Pentagon policy dictates that such systems incorporate "appropriate levels of human judgment" (Department of Defense 2012, p. 2). One wonders, though, that if a split-second intervention is unlikely to stop a car on a dark boulevard in Tempe, Arizona, how likely is it to stop an attack on the battlefield? (see Marcus 2012).

Whether for traffic flows or military engagements, engineers tout increased accuracy and efficiency as a benefit when "neutral" code displaces the irrational emotions and sluggishness that compromise flesh-and-blood decision-making (Vaidhyanathan 2011, p. 62). This perspective frames moral choices as a matter of simple rule-following or calculation. But since Aristotle, philosophers of virtue ethics have argued against simplistic formulas, insisting instead on "good judgment in specific situations" (Weston 2001, p. 99). Even when making informed decisions, it is nearly impossible to predict every long-term consequence of new technologies. If the most important consequences of combustion-engine automobile production were unforeseen (e.g., the emergence of suburbs), those of self-driving cars will be exponentially more complex (Goldhill 2018).

And despite the fact that safety protocols include an element of human judgment, it matters how, and by whom, "appropriate" levels of human intervention are determined. Every technological object "embodies decisions to develop one kind of knowledge and not some others, to use certain resources and not others" (Christians 1989, p. 125). In other words, human operators stand ready to intervene in systems that are already value-laden. In this sense, processing is a type of judgment but not the type required for effective self-governance.

The Perils of Pre-judgment

In the early 1960s, Martin Luther King Jr. outlined a prescient distinction between *pre-judgment* and *post-judgment*: "The tough-minded person," he argued, "always examines the facts before he reaches conclusions; in short, he post-judges. The tender-minded person reaches a conclusion before he has examined the first fact; in short, he prejudges and is prejudiced" ([1963] 1986, p. 493). Like the tender-minded person, computer processing encodes decisions that have been made beforehand, outside the context of real-time situations, even supposing that engineers genuinely embrace the responsibility of careful forethought. Algorithmic processing is a form of prejudgment or prejudice. Human operators may monitor and intervene, but the values embedded in the systems are foregone conclusions. To the extent that we acquiesce to the pre-judgments of such systems, assuming their beneficence and trusting their judgment, we become tender-minded in the manner that King described. As we will see in this chapter, the consequences of such tender-mindedness are directly related to the racial injustice that King so passionately fought against during his lifetime.

In this chapter, we do not argue against any and all instances of algorithmic decision-making. Algorithmic processing is here to stay and can be developed and managed ethically, provided that pre-programmed judgments are reached through a transparent process that reflects the interests of all relevant stakeholders. Since most stakeholders are excluded from initial decision-making processes, judgment of a sort is present but not what we would call meaningful judgment (Morozov 2013, p. 179). As status-quo values solidify in the form of proprietary and opaque algorithms, an intellectual ethic of tender-mindedness prevails. Critical reflection, which is the lifeblood of democratic culture, is diluted and diminished. The potential benefits of processing systems accrue disproportionately to those who own them. The trolley is programmed, wittingly or unwittingly, to protect and empower the trolley-maker. If we do not shine a light on this process, the rest of us will surely be taken for a ride, and a bumpy one. In some cases, as Elaine Herzberg discovered, the ride turns deadly.

The Catechism: Processing Is Judgment

The catechism supports the belief that algorithmic processing of data is more efficient and simply better than human judgment when it comes to making decisions about news to consume, legal decisions about crimes committed, and personal decisions about whom to date, to name but a few. Users too often acquiesce to this gatekeeping power on the assumption that software programs are morally neutral and data sets comprised objective facts. Rather than amplify pre-existing racial prejudice and gender stereotypes in unanticipated and disturbing ways, we assume quite the opposite, namely, that algorithms tamp down or can potentially eliminate such injustices. We assume algorithms are an inherently benevolent, a kind of all-knowing and guiding hand designed to keep our highs and lows in check. If we are suspicious at all, we eventually dismiss our concerns once we realize we will probably never see (or be able to recognize if we did see) an actual algorithm anyway. Algorithms become the secret recipes in the most abundantly available and affordable food. Rather than go hungry for social interaction and online information, we shrug our shoulders and swallow the sweet with the sour.

But our personal and social well-being is indeed at stake, and we risk ill health by assuming too much. To continue the food analogy, "Raw data is both an oxymoron and a bad idea; to the contrary, data should be cooked with care" (Bowker 2005, pp. 183–4). Or as one critic suggests, "every algorithm has values baked into it" (Keen 2011). But who are the cooks in the kitchen? Data are not simply found or discovered. They have to be created, generated, or "imagined" before they can have meaning (Gitelman and Jackson 2013, p. 3). We must therefore ask, Where did this particular set of data come from? Who imagined it? What does all this data mean? Who has access to it? How is it deployed, and to what ends? (Boyd and Crawford 2012, p. 664).

The Dogma of Data Fundamentalism

The problem with how engineers and users alike think about data and algorithmic processing is that such questions as those above are often considered irrelevant. Too often we proceed with the assumption that data are transparent and information is self-evident. If we assume that data are "the fundamental stuff of truth itself," its accumulation becomes more than merely helpful; it becomes a moral imperative. In turn, "our zeal for more and more data can become a faith in their neutrality and autonomy, their objectivity" (Gitelman and Jackson 2013, p. 3). Taken together, these assumptions are referred to as "Big Data fundamentalism," that is, "the idea [that] with larger data sets, we get closer to objective truth" (Hardy 2013).

To challenge Big Data dogma and to suggest that data or coding can be biased can elicit dismissiveness and even contempt. In a conversation with writer Ta-Nehisi Coates, U.S. Congresswoman Alexandria Ocasio-Cortez argued that software platforms have "racial inequities that get translated" because their algorithms "are still made by human beings. ... If you don't fix the bias, then you're automating the bias" (Molloy 2019). *Daily Wire* columnist Ryan Saavedra promptly dismissed the Congresswoman's comments by claiming that since algorithms are "driven by math," they could not be biased (Molloy 2019). But experts quickly offered support for Ocasio-Cortez's argument. Safiya Umoja Noble, author of *Algorithms of Oppression*, suggested that Saavedra's misunderstanding is based on pervasive cultural assumptions about the moral neutrality of math and computer science. Technologies are not "value-free," she explained, adding that "my own research reveals the ways that racism and sexism are reinforced in digital technologies" (Molloy 2019). Racial and gender discrimination is a well-documented problem in artificial intelligence (AI) research (McDonough 2019).

The political contentiousness surrounding this issue underscores a key point: data and algorithmic processing are not neutral but are sites of cultural struggle. There is general agreement that bias is possible and indeed already present, but there is disagreement about its primary victims. A few months earlier Saavedra himself had warned of potential anti-conservative political bias in Facebook's News Feed algorithms and called for "oversight of FB's algorithms, operations, & news distribution" (Molloy 2019).

The silver lining is that there is clear potential for bipartisan agreement on the need to understand and address the issue. In late 2017, lawmakers began to move in that direction with the Fundamentally Understanding the Usability and Realistic Evolution of Artificial Intelligence Act, or the FUTURE of AI Act, a bill that drew support from both Democrats and Republicans in the U.S. House and Senate. While embracing the potential of AI for economic growth, this legislation clearly identifies, and aims to protect, the individual rights of users (Breland 2017).

Reflecting on this bill co-sponsor Pete Olson, a Republican Congressman from Texas, remarked that "the Congressional dialogue has only just begun, and we have much more to accomplish to embrace the future and potential of AI" (Cullen 2018). Meanwhile, as debates unfold on Capitol Hill, evidence indicates support among both Republican and Democratic voters for legislation to delay or restrict potentially discriminatory technologies like facial recognition software (Lannan 2019).

Given the complexity of these debates, our working definition of Big Data must include both technical and philosophical dimensions. To be sure, Big Data is a technological endeavor, with the maximization of processing power as an overarching goal. It is also a scholarly and scientific endeavor, insofar as such data-processing power is leveraged to identify and understand patterns in our economic and social environment. But importantly, it is a cultural endeavor because it is inseparable from our often-unstated beliefs about what knowledge and information are, and how they contribute to wisdom. When we talk about Big Data, then, we are always already talking about a broader cultural "mythology" of data, namely, "the widespread belief that large data sets offer a higher form of intelligence and knowledge that can generate insights that were previously impossible, with the aura of truth, objectivity, and accuracy" (Boyd and Crawford 2012, p. 663). Recalling our historical discussion in Chapter 2, recent enthusiasm for Big Data carries the legacy of the computational imperative, which asks us to define ourselves through the lens of digital technology. When we acquiesce to this imperative, we render cultural struggles invisible and sideline non-computational approaches to our own thinking.

A growing number of voices insist on our collective resistance to this dogma of data fundamentalism. "Do numbers speak for themselves?" they ask, answering clearly, "We believe the answer is 'no'" (Boyd and Crawford 2012, p. 666). Ironically, blind faith in numbers tosses aside the objectivity that "raw" data allegedly provide. "Computationality" is a kind of "onto-theology" (Berry 2011, p. 12)—a reference to transcendental proofs of God based not on experience but on conceptual inference. We are asked to believe that data, when processed effectively, will provide insight into the very nature of being, if not God *per se*. This over-emphasis on data reinforces the type of "faith" embraced throughout Silicon Valley, which tends to flourish "when you can pretend that computers do everything and people do nothing" (Lanier 2011, p. 16). This faith relinquishes cultural and technological power to the gatekeepers whose expertise consists of one set of methods to the exclusion of many others.

The Legal Injustices of Algorithms

The common saying, "justice is blind" means that legal codes are interpreted and applied by people with the capacity to exercise prudent judgment in preserving the integrity of the law while treating individual defendants fairly. Importantly, it does not mean that laws are executed without attention to the context and consequence of their application. As described in the examples that follow, the assumption that data and algorithms are morally neutral often leads juries and judges to ignore their own prejudice or the systemic injustice of the culture in which we live. As the U.S. Supreme Court Chief Justice John Roberts noted in the spring of 2017, the day is already here when algorithms and artificial intelligence play a key role in the judicial process, "and it's putting a significant strain on how the judiciary goes about doing things" (Liptak 2017).

Consider the following contrasting cases. The first case, which we call the bicycle case, involves Brisha Borden and Sade Jones, who were arrested for stealing a six-year-old's bicycle, estimated to be worth about $80. Borden had committed misdemeanors as a juvenile, while Jones had never been arrested. The second case, which we call the Home Depot case, involves Vernon Prater, who had been arrested a year prior for shoplifting tools from Home Depot. The value of the shoplifted tools in the Home Depot case roughly equaled that of the bicycle case.

And yet, when computer programs assessed each of these defendants for their potential risk of re-offence, the algorithms gave Prater a low risk score of 3, Jones a medium score, and Borden a high-risk score of 8 out of 10. Though the judge in the bicycle case said he often releases first-time and low-level offenders without bond, he decided to raise each of these women's bonds from the recommended $0 to $1,000. The main difference between the two cases is that Borden and Jones (bicycle case) are African American while Prater (Home Depot case) is white (Angwin et al. 2016).

In their investigative report on "machine bias" in the criminal justice system, the non-profit newsroom ProPublica determined that in this case, "the computer algorithm got it exactly backward" (Angwin et al. 2016). Two years after their arrests, neither Borden nor Jones (bicycle case) had been charged with any new crimes. At the time of their report, however, Prater (Home Depot case) was serving an eight-year prison term for "breaking into a warehouse and stealing thousands of dollars' worth of electronics." The judge in the bicycle case claimed to have no memory of the case and declined to say whether the computerized risk scores influenced his bond decision. Struggling to find work during her probation, Jones told ProPublica, "I went to McDonald's and a dollar store, and they all said no because of my background" (Angwin et al. 2016).

These types of risk scores are used in courtrooms all across the United States. In the case of ProPublica's report, the calculations that comprise such scores are proprietary and unavailable for analysis. The for-profit company who developed the scoring software, Northpointe, disputed ProPublica's report but did not make their underlying algorithms available. A defendant's attorneys, not to mention the judge in their case, see only the results of risk calculations and not the calculations themselves. Northpointe's developers, Tim Brennan and Dave Wells, had only intended for the scores to be used to determine whether, and what kind, of services a defendant might need, for example, drug treatment or mental health counseling. Nevertheless, many judges use the scores to make sentencing decisions, and when they do so, the algorithms often recommend harsher penalties for black defendants (Angwin et al. 2016).

As judges began to use the COMPAS software system for sentencing decisions, attorneys took aim at this apparent abuse of due process. In arguments that reached the State Supreme Court of Wisconsin all the way to the U.S. Supreme Court, attorneys for one man argued on behalf of strict rules that would limit use of programs like COMPAS, the system sold by Northpointe. They argued that, given the proprietary status of the algorithms, such systems lack transparency and therefore should be used only in decisions about treatment and probation eligibility. Under no circumstance, they argued, should judges base the length of a defendant's sentence solely or even primarily on computerized risk scores. The Wisconsin court argued that such systems do not violate due process rights "if used properly," and the U.S. Supreme Court declined to hear the defendant's appeal (Wisconsin v. Loomis 2016, p. 5).

As if to underscore the ambiguity involved in the word "properly," Florida Judge John Hurley, who is the same judge who had raised the recommended sentence for defendants in the bicycle case, later issued a statement stressing the importance of human judgment. While Hurley found computerized risk scores helpful to him as a new judge, "now that he has experience he prefers to rely on his own judgment," according to the report from ProPublica (Angwin et al. 2016). To borrow Martin Luther King Jr.'s words introduced at the beginning of this chapter, the judge was no longer "tender-minded."

Readers who have little contact with the criminal justice system, or who do not belong to a racial minority group, should not assume immunity from these types of problems. Broadly speaking, algorithms are often used to identify our networks and predict our behavior based on those networks. Many large organizations use AI systems to make important decisions that impact whether we are considered and hired for a job position. These systems have proven to be unreliable as well and often discriminate on the basis of gender. In the United States, it is still legal for employers to make hiring decisions on the basis of personal networks. This process can easily lead to discrimination when employers use Facebook or the popular job-networking site LinkedIn to decide if a job candidate will be a "good fit" for their company (Boyd et al. 2014, pp. 54–55).

Increasingly, applicant tracking and screening software is used in place of time-intensive work by flesh-and-blood application reviewers. As reported originally by Reuters, when Amazon implemented an AI system in 2014 to assist in its head-hunting endeavors, it quickly became clear that its algorithms discriminated against women. By 2015, Amazon realized its system was favoring male candidates and down-grading women's applications. The engineers had apparently fed the system applications from past successful applicants and, as one observer noted, "because of the tech world's well-known gender imbalance, those past hopefuls tended to be men" (Weissman 2018). The AI system learned, in other words, that it should favor men.

It decided, for example, that skills in programming and coding were not as impor-tant as candidates' use of masculine terms like "executed" and "captured." Here again, male readers should not rest assured that they will not face such discrimination. As Reuters reported, "Gender bias was not the only issue. Problems with the data that underpinned the models' judgments meant that unqualified candidates were often recommended for all manner of jobs" (Dastin 2018). Faced with the sheer complex-ity of addressing these systemic problems, Amazon gave up on the project in 2017.

Personalized Data and Data-fied Persons

The most insidious forms of algorithmic bias arise from hugely popular platforms like Google, Facebook, Instagram, and Twitter that appear to cater to our personal interests and values. But as these platforms personalize content, an algorithmically friendly version of ourselves often comes back to haunt us in ways we may not directly perceive or understand. This algorithmic haunting is what makes our digital lives so frequently "creepy." When our social values and our technical capabilities are misaligned, when the values of engineers are far afield from those of the general public, we experience a deep unease whose source we cannot always pinpoint (Tene and Polonetsky 2013, p. 2). As one tech insider explains, "Creepiness is when information systems undermine individual human agency. It happens when you feel violated because the flow of information disregards your reasonable attempts to control your own information life" (Lanier 2013, pp. 305–6). We usually only see the end result of having been pigeonholed into certain identity categories. We typically cannot connect the dots directly to anything specific we have said or done. We feel creepiness in retrospect, knowing now that our experience all along has been premised on questionable motives and behavior of which we were unaware.

The identities that arise out of data aggregation and algorithmic processing, which come back to haunt us in this way, are called "passive online identities" (Balick 2014, p. 111). They are identities that others construct for us, categories into which platforms and third-party companies place us without our knowledge or understanding. These identities are used to make judgments about us, but the decision-making process is not transparent to us. The paradoxical result is that while control over our online profiles may increase, our ability to control others' perceptions of us is "far less under our control—than ever before" (Palfrey and Gasser 2008, p. 34).

Socio-economically marginalized groups are more vulnerable to passive online identities. Users often serve as unwitting guinea pigs for banks, insurance companies, and other commercial organizations who wish to identify patterns of potential profit or risk among users of Facebook, Instagram, and any number of other popular social media platforms. When we use such sites, we are literally being scored in ways similar to how defendants in the criminal justice system are scored for their relative level of risk. We are sorted into silos or categories constructed by insurance companies and banks whose exploitation of user data often amounts to economic coercion. Welfare recipients, for example, may be targeted with predatory financial instruments and economic surveillance programs, while religious or racial minorities may be subject to law enforcement profiling. Facebook even patented a technology allowing lenders to review credit ratings for users' authorized connections (i.e., "friends") and reject loan applications if the average credit rating is below a minimum score. Critics have decried this program as discriminatory because it makes vulnerable users "more prone to using alternative predatory systems such as payday loans" (Zombeck 2015; Sullivan 2015). If risk scores in law enforcement cases are often wrong, how accurate could such scores be when banks or insurance companies base them on the behavior of our "friends"?

Notwithstanding Twitter's superiority in tracking breaking news, better filtering algorithms cannot address the shifting market dynamics that make substantive investigative reports less likely to appear online in the first place. Sources that still hold fast to basic principles of editorial discretion and public service scramble for lost revenue as advertisers bypass them in favor of direct deals with social media platforms or third-party ad-placement services. This situation places downward pressure on the quality of content, as exemplified by the proliferation of "content farms" and sites such as Gawker, which base production decisions on real-time search trends and traffic patterns (McChesney 2013, p. 185).

Faced with overwhelming amounts of content, as well as difficult-to-navigate privacy and personalization settings, users bear an unwieldy burden in fostering an ethos of meaningful judgment in the digital rainforest. Serving up content that is interesting and useful often devolves into pandering to users' worst fears and prejudices. This problem came to a head in the aftermath of the 2016 U.S. presidential election, when Facebook was forced to admit that its News Feed was filled with Russian propaganda aimed at influencing the outcome of the election. As described in detail in Siva Vaidhyanathan's book *Anti-Social Media: How Facebook Disconnects Us and Undermines Democracy* (2018) and in the two-part investigative *Frontline* documentary, *The Facebook Dilemma* (2018), the problem was not that a foreign government had stolen user data but that it had used the platform in the exact manner for which it had been built: to target specific niche audiences with carefully crafted messages. Before Donald Trump began using it to engage his critics, the term "fake news" referred to misleading or false content disguised as trustworthy reporting. With the help of News Feed algorithms, Facebook users had unwittingly descended into a rabbit hole of tribalism, partisanship, and self-delusion, what we might call the "personalization of truth" (Healey 2013, p. 182).

Here again, the presumption of objectivity and neutrality in code undermines meaningful judgment by relieving tech companies from responsibility. Facebook's primary defensive response to the Russian exploitation of its platform has been to deny that it is a media company in the first place. In doing so, it follows Google, Uber, and other tech companies in claiming that it is simply a neutral technology platform. Its users, in this argument, are responsible for whether the platform is used for good or evil. This is another variation on the refrain that commercial media simply "give the people what they want"—a self-serving myth debunked years ago (McChesney 2004, pp. 198–205).

Perhaps the most important judgment we exercise is whether to sign up for an online service in the first place. Even that judgment is tightly controlled, since digital media companies often have near-monopoly status and users have little choice for alternatives. The choice we face is often to get the service on the company's terms or to get no such service at all. This is partly why users throw up their hands or shrug their shoulders each time Facebook reveals yet another data breach. Where else are people going to go if they want to use a social media platform?

Alternatives like Diaspora exist, but hardly anyone uses them. This is a typical example of what scholars call network effects. Once you click "agree" to a user-end agreement you likely did not read (and which is typically written not for the sake of clarity but for the sake of protecting the service from lawsuits), you then enter an architecture in which your judgment is confined to a range of preferences and choices that are relevant to the business model driving the platform.

For example, Mark Zuckerberg and Sheryl Sandburg of Facebook like to speak about privacy in terms of the "control" that users have. However, they are referring mainly to controls that determine what friends see online, not whether data are consolidated across Facebook's apps, and not whether third parties can leverage sets of aggregated data to influence users. Social media companies stress social privacy but downplay informational privacy. Users exercise judgment with regard to whether and with whom they share personal information. But Facebook is notorious for leaving users out of controversial business decisions like the ill-fated Beacon program, which revealed users' online purchases to their friends without their consent (Zuckerberg 2007). The idea of personalization, then, is problematic even when users do exhibit some level of judgment. The contours and confines of users' decisions rest within what scholars call choice architecture, a pre-defined set of choices designed to nudge users toward certain behaviors.

Thanks to the work of investigative reporters, it is clear that companies cannot bootstrap their way out of these issues by piecing together a ragtag team of employees to serve as content moderators. After the white-nationalist rallies in Charlottesville, Virginia, in 2017, Reddit CEO Steve Huffman vowed to address the problem of how his platform is implicated in speech "glorifying violence" (Brancaccio et al. 2018). To his credit, he acknowledged that AI algorithms were not equipped to properly identify and address hate speech. AI could serve some role in the process, Huffman said, "but a motto we've always had at Reddit is 'let humans do the hard part'" (Brancaccio et al. 2018). "We have a whole team dedicated" to harassment, incitement of violence, and bullying. But he also noted that he is "actually a huge proponent of how do we share that burden with our community? Because the only thing that scales with users, is users" (Brancaccio et al. 2018).

No matter how well-intentioned such efforts may be, two things have become clear especially in the aftermath of Facebook's role in the spread of Russian propaganda during the 2016 presidential election. First, while users are indeed responsible for their behavior online, they cannot be responsible for cleaning up messes that emerge as a predictable result of the platform's design. Sharing responsibility is one thing; shifting blame to avoid accountability is quite another.

Second, content moderation by teams of employees is often best described as a thumb in the dike. The above-mentioned investigations by *The Verge* (Newton 2019) and *Frontline* (Bourg et al. 2019) suggest that Facebook's moderators, in particular, are unqualified, inexperienced, and prone to stress and anxiety. Prudent judgment cannot be an afterthought. It must be integrated into the very design, development, deployment, use, and regulation of a platform. Otherwise the production of "personalized data" will hinge on the data-fication not only of users but employees. We "personalize" our experience of a platform, to be sure. But the platform also asks us, nudges us, to become a certain kind of person, too, and usually one that enjoys being entertained and is in a good, consumer-friendly buying mood.

Algorithmic Coercion

Platforms like Facebook that offer "personalized" content are ripe for exploitation by ill-intentioned third parties. They only defer or cater to the judgment of users in limited ways. Too often, they pander to users' anxieties, fears, anger, prurience, and tribalism. But what about services like Uber, Lyft, Airbnb, or Tinder? These too are designed for our personal use. We might assume these familiar platforms amplify our own judgment. If we are a looking for work, they give us the option to use our vehicle to earn extra cash on our own time. If we need a ride, they show us what options are available, and we choose among them. If an app demonstrates bias of some sort, it must be the fault of the users, and not the software engineers.

Once again, we tend to assume that platforms like Uber, Lyft, Airbnb, and Tinder, to name several, are simply "giving the people what they want," as the saying goes. Is that right? Yes and no. Even in cases where user judgment and choice are allowed into a process, such judgment is allowed only within boundaries that keep algorithms and their engineers in the "driver's seat," to use an apt metaphor. Ultimately, these platforms provide examples of how *not* to involve user judgment, that is, after the fact. User judgment is not always ignored or abandoned. But platforms see great benefit in nudging, corralling, commodifying, and exploiting (a/k/a, "coercing") user judgment in ways that are ethically suspect. A report by *The New York Times* showed that many features within the apps are designed to emulate addictive video games like Tetris by leveraging well-researched psychological dynamics. Though there is plenty of historical precedent where companies use such techniques to nudge consumers, their use in nudging employees is likely to become the future norm (Scheiber 2017).

Ride-sharing services like Uber and Lyft leverage the power of algorithms to nudge drivers to work more often, or in certain places, or for longer periods at a time. Drawing directly from behavioral science research, these companies developed gamification methods that coerce drivers to internalize the company's values. Engineers at Lyft devised one algorithmic experiment that showed some drivers how much money they could gain by moving to Fridays instead of Tuesdays, while showing others how much they were losing by sticking to Tuesday schedules. The experiment showed that the latter approach worked better in terms of motivating drivers to change their work-schedule preferences consistent with similar research in behavioral economics (Scheiber 2017).

Other Uber app features encouraged drivers on a daily basis by questioning their judgment about when to quit for the day. The app would calculate a seemingly arbitrary dollar amount the driver had almost, but not yet, reached, and then ask the driver if they really wanted to quite before achieving that goal. Uber thus conducts real-time experiments. In addition, it uses its treasure-trove of user/driver data to conduct other offline experiments and studies to determine details about driver behavior, which it then leverages in revising its app design (Scheiber 2017).

Both Uber and Lyft have a feature called forward dispatch, which identifies and assigns a new ride for a driver before their current ride is complete. Again, company executives say this feature is meant to respond to drivers' complaints about idle time, but some critics suggest that its primary benefit to the platform is that "it overrides self-control" (Scheiber 2017). This disconnect, between a feature's stated function and its surreptitious function, creates what we might call a façade of judgment. The rhetoric from engineers and executives frames such behavioral strategies not as manipulation but as deference to drivers' preferences. For example, Uber wanted drivers to reach a 25-ride threshold (at which point they earn a signing bonus), so it implemented a gamification feature in its app to encourage drivers as they moved closer to that goal. One Uber spokesman framed coercive psychological techniques as an effort to "make the early experience as good as possible" because "we want people to decide for themselves if driving is right for them" (Scheiber 2017).

Consider the problems related so-called "sharing economy" services like Airbnb. Research and news reporting demonstrates that if unregulated by the companies or by law, then the algorithms driving such platforms will cater to and amplify pre-existing racial preferences, or prejudices, of users. Plaintiffs in at least two different lawsuits against Airbnb claim that hosts regularly deny requests on the basis of prospective renters' race. Until a policy change, the platform had required renters to upload a photograph and to use their real name. Hosts had been allowed to use both to make their decisions. One African-American plaintiff claimed that after being denied a rental through his authentic profile, he was able to secure the same rental by using a fake profile with a white man's photo (King 2016). A formal study by Harvard Business School confirmed these allegations, reporting that African-American names were 16 percent less likely to be accepted as renters (Edelman et al. 2016). This problem may reflect the racial imbalance among hosts. The same study found that 63 percent of hosts were white, and only 8 percent were black. No one is arguing that Airbnb discriminated directly against African-American renters by coding racial prejudice into its algorithms. Nevertheless, Airbnb may be legally at fault for indirectly enabling discrimination on the part of its hosts. As one report submits, Airbnb's original hosting policies "unwittingly enabled people to act on their biases" (Guynn 2017; Stevens 2018).

Airbnb and other such companies leverage the assumption of technology's neutrality to deny and avoid responsibility when such issues arise. As *The New York Times* reporter Claire Cain Miller put it, Airbnb demonstrates certain "core business principles that have become a religion in Silicon Valley": that companies are morally neutral; that everything can be automated through algorithms; and that therefore humans should be employed sparingly in favor of more technology. Airbnb's terms of service position the company as a neutral "middleman" between users (hosts and renters) (Miller 2014). While the U.S. law does protect tech companies from liability with regard to online speech, such protections do not extend to transgressions in the real world. Yet companies and users fail to make, or willfully blur, this important distinction. When real-world instances of racial discrimination, vandalism, or even violence reach a crisis point (i.e., the problem can no longer be ignored), companies often fall back on the assumption that technical solutions—especially algorithms— can protect the company from liability. For example, in response to complaints of vandalism by hosts, Brian Chesky, Airbnb's co-founder and chief executive, argued that in addition to teams of human monitors, the company had employed "algorithms that identify suspicious behavior" (Miller 2014).

Catering to Prejudice

Let us turn to an example of user-oriented platforms where algorithmic processing is clearly intrinsic to the service: the case of online dating. Here the problems are more ethically complex, yet similar problems of discrimination are evident. Unlike car-sharing or apartment-sharing services, it is more socially acceptable for dating platforms to cater to the preferences of users. Specialized sites have been available from the earliest days of online dating. Since 1996 Jewish singles have used JMatch, and more recently websites like MazalTov provide services for Jewish singles with special needs. Similarly, specialized sites are available for Christians and a host of other special-interest groups: people over fifty, farmers, marijuana smokers, people who like snakes, people who like spicy food, and more.

But even if we set aside these specialized sites, inclusive dating platforms like Tinder, OkCupid, and Grindr can amplify racial and ethnic prejudice. Like Airbnb, most dating websites are not intentionally programmed to match same-race couples (Notopoulos 2016). Even if sites are coded to ignore the race of users when making match suggestions, the platforms may amplify prejudice by allowing users to explicitly state racial preferences in their profiles. Many users have announced explicitly they will not date a black or Asian person. Additionally (and in contrast to how rental hosts deny services to minorities), some dating-service users actually seek out racial minorities on the basis of fetishized stereotypes. One African-American woman describes being propositioned by a white man who wanted "a taste of jungle fever" (Petter 2018). Researchers have confirmed that such anecdotal reports reflect a broad pattern. For instance, black users are ten times more likely to send a message to white users than whites are to message blacks (Lefkowitz 2018).

As with Airbnb, the point here is that online dating services are not neutral with regard to users' judgment. Those who harbor some measure of prejudice have largely found ample room to indulge it online, even in ostensibly neutral or inclusive platforms. Platforms can enable discrimination insofar as they allow prejudice to masquerade as a "preference." In such cases, algorithms serve to amplify prejudice, not accidentally but through a combination of intentional design and plausible deniability. But, like Airbnb, dating websites have a responsibility to understand and manage the impact of platform architectures on user behavior. Users are responsible as well, of course, but platforms cannot simply blame users and proclaim their own innocence in the face of evidence of persistent discrimination. For this reason, some critics have argued that dating sites are obligated to encourage a general ethos of inclusiveness pro-actively, if not interracial communication *per se* (Hutson et al. 2018).

Like car and apartment-rental apps, dating websites include the judgment of human users as an integral part of their service and in this sense are quite different from third-party services that screen job applicants or assess the risk of legal defendants. Nevertheless, the inclusion of user judgment does not protect platforms from the pitfalls of algorithmic discrimination. As we argued at the beginning of this chapter, it matters not just that judgment is involved, but when and how we introduce human judgment into a complex process. It matters in part because both engineers and (perhaps more importantly) users assume that processing and judgment are at least interchangeable, if not equivalent. Knowing little or nothing about the algorithms on which they rely, users nevertheless place enormous trust in algorithms to match them with potential romantic partners, no less than to find relevant web content. Much of the impact of algorithmic processing depends on the presence of this trust, and the extent to which it is either justified or misplaced.

The problem of blind trust in algorithmic processing extends beyond the specter of user manipulation by software engineers. If users of dating platforms can be influenced by misleading results of algorithmic processing, so too can scientists. This problem has led to what one statistician calls a "crisis in science" (Ghosh 2019). Machine-learning software, which is specifically designed to identify patterns in large sets of data, often produces results with little or no relation to the real world. This is why many studies based on machine-learning cannot be reproduced, that is, performed again with the same results. The problem here, writes one reporter, is that "experiments are not designed well enough to ensure that the scientists don't fool themselves and see what they want to see in the results" (Ghosh 2019). The primary question for us to consider, then, is "can we really trust those findings?" (Ghosh 2019).

Challenging the Catechism: Processing Is Not Judgment

Recall the argument articulated by Martin Luther King Jr. earlier in this chapter. To lead ethical lives, to create an ethical society, requires tough-mindedness. That means being able, individually and collectively, to exercise prudent judgment in context. When we make judgments out of context, beforehand or without relevant knowledge, we may unwittingly allow injustice to continue. This is not an argument against rules or laws by itself. It is merely a recognition of their limitations as forms of pre-judgment. As in the case of jury trials, it is certainly important to know the law as it exists and as it has been applied in the past. But it would be folly, and manifestly unjust, to turn over a legal system wholesale to automated bots that execute rules blindly and uncaringly. This is why juries, judges, and attorneys are an integral part of the process: ideally, they function to integrate existing rules with reasoned argument and prudent, contextual judgment.

The problems we have identified in the previous several sections arise not from the mere existence of algorithms or data-processing systems. Our goal here is not to argue against them or to eliminate algorithms or their role in our daily lives. As in previous chapters, the problems we face arise largely because we wittingly or unwittingly misunderstand what algorithmic processing can and cannot do, and indeed what it should and should not be trusted to do. These misunderstandings feed into imprudent design, improper use, and lack of appropriate regulation. To borrow King's terms, when it comes to development of algorithmic systems, an ethos of tender-mindedness, or soft-mindedness, too often prevails.

The question then is how we can demand and exercise proper judgment as users, developers, and policy makers. How do we disrupt the tendency toward blind faith?

What practices help us develop tough-mindedness? What practices help us avoid unwittingly creating, or the creeping haunting by, passive identities? As in the past, we will leave broad-stroke policy solutions for Chapter 9. In the concluding section of this chapter, we will look first at practices whose goal is to put the user in the position of reflecting upon his or her own data and to process it by exercising his or her own judgment.

Poetic Processing

Most of our students grew up amid a flurry of algorithmic nudging, where commercial platforms leverage data-processing power to corral and coerce human judgment. We wanted to create a simple exercise to address the question, "What does it feel like to take the wheel, to process data, and exercise judgment with regard to it, on my own terms?" To this end, we created two exercises that put users back in the driver's seat with regard to their own "data." We put "data" in quotes here because the exercises involve working with content we do not usually think of as data, including analog content like hand-written letters and postcards.

To release us from the rut of habitual content consumption, we built these exercises on a unique method of analysis called poetic transcription. In arts-based research, poetic transcription is a way of discovering hidden patterns of meaning within a collection of documents. It is often paired with traditional qualitative content analysis but goes beyond it by engaging the aesthetic and emotional sensibilities of both the researcher and their target audience. The main goal is not simply corralling and reporting information but interpreting and communicating meaning.

It is a good idea to have students read about, and see examples of, poetic transcription before conducting these exercises. This way, students understand the broader purpose and benefit of arts-based work. As one expert in this field, Patricia Leavy (2015), helpfully explains, "Poetry can interrupt traditional ways of knowing and help us see differently and thus may be particularly appealing to those conducting identity research or seeking to express alternative or non-dominant viewpoints" (p. 299). The expression of non-dominant viewpoints, especially those that challenge the catechism of Silicon Valley, has been a central goal of this book.

In the first exercise, students create their own online data (in this case, their blog posts on a dedicated course website) based on assigned readings. We explored several variations of this exercise using different types of readings, including published interviews with Silicon Valley executives as well as chapters from scholarly books. In our courses, which focus specifically on media, the readings usually relate directly to ethical issues in digital culture; faculty in other disciplines may just as easily adapt this exercise with different materials. After completing the assigned readings, each student writes a reflective essay summarizing and commenting on the central ideas. So far, this is a typical read-and-reflect exercise.

Here is where the poetic transcription begins. To underscore the purpose of the exercise, which again is to put users in the driver's seat in processing data, we like to call this part of the activity "poetic processing." In pairs of two each student reads, and prints out in hard-copy form, their partner's blog entry, thus moving the "data" from digital into analog form. Now (having seen and discussed examples previously), each student is asked to create a poetic transcription of their partner's post. As poets, students position themselves as analysts and interpreters of their classmates' online "data" (the written blog posts). They perform the process of poetic transcription either in-class or more often outside of class and return prepared to share their poems. Ideally, students read aloud the poems they have transcribed from their partner's blog post.

It is important to discuss, as a class, the experience of being both a poet who interprets and communicates meaning about their partner's data, and a writer who hears or reads a transcribed version of their blog piece. Discussion usually reveals that students better understand and appreciate the meaning of the original assigned reading. Moreover, the aesthetic dimension of the exercise puts students into a much more meaningful dialogue not only with the original text but with each other as learners and as writers. The transcribed poem becomes more than a response or critique; it becomes a gift given from one student to another. One benefit of doing this partner exercise first is that students can communicate directly, in person, about their experience of being a poet as well as about the subject of another person's poem. Especially insightful is the experience of reading, or hearing read aloud, a poem that someone else has created from one's own published content.

FIGURE 6.1   A student's blog post, printed and marked to "discover" a hidden poem.

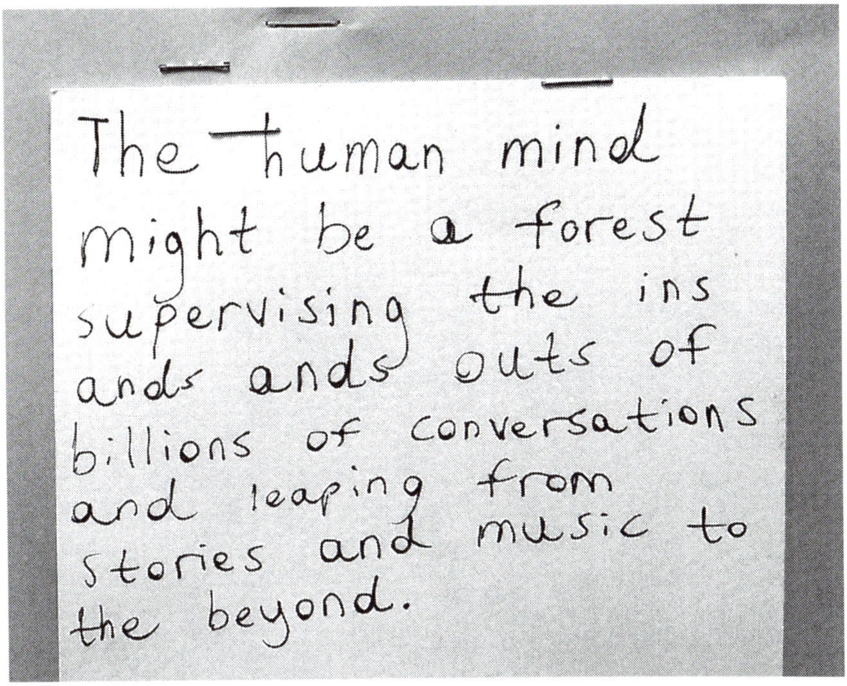

The human mind
might be a forest
supervising the ins
ands ands outs of
billions of conversations
and leaping from
stories and music to
the beyond.

FIGURE 6.2 A student's final poem, transcribed from the printed blog post.

The second exercise builds on this face-to-face experience but now expands the focus of poetic inquiry to include well-known tech leaders and their public critics. Instead of using peers' blog entries, in this exercise students transcribe, or poetically process, the words of people like Mark Zuckerberg and public intellectuals who have criticized them. For example, in a seminar on digital history we asked students to read and perform poetic transcriptions of two texts: one was Zuckerberg's (2019) widely read Facebook post celebrating the fifteenth anniversary of the website; the other was an essay by media and technology scholar Siva Vaidhyanathan (2019) which directly criticizes Zuckerberg's statement. Some students felt a negative response to engaging so closely with a text authored by someone like Zuckerberg whom most did not like personally. Perhaps because of their need to push through such a visceral response, students reported that they both (1) empathized and understood Zuckerberg's position better and (2) better understood why they disliked it so intensely and so were able to articulate their critique more effectively.

Both of these exercises ask students to engage with online content in ways that platform engineers did not intend. Students engage their own content, and that of others, in ways that subvert the process of data mining and the creation of passive online identities. The objective, to restate, is to help students position themselves as analysts who process online content in a way that is meaningful to them, effectively taking back the power to create, interpret, and communicate meaning, even as popular platforms compete to position themselves as the gatekeepers of judgment and meaning.

It is worth noting that in both exercises, the activity of poetic processing generates surprising and unforeseen insights. It does so because it subverts the notion of authorship. With regard to their transcribed poems, we ask students, Who wrote this poem? Was it your partner who wrote the blog? Was it Mark Zuckerberg? Or was it you, the poet who found new meaning in the data? Poetic transcription works well as a contemplative exercise because in the best-case scenario both the poet, and the subject of the poem, realize that authorship is a process that exceeds their individual sense of self. Something larger is at work, which opens up a space for empathy and for transformation.

In contrast to the personalization of data, which we have argued is concurrent with the data-fication of persons, these types of practices represent a transformative *humanization* of data.

In the commercial personalization of data, the whole is often less than the sum of its parts. As noted earlier in this chapter, algorithmic processing tends to "chop up a network of individuals so finely that you end up with a mush" (Lanier 2011, p. 17). By contrast, these practices create a sense of shared authorship in which the whole is more than the sum of its parts. The poem is something we both wrote, and yet it is more than either of us could have done individually. Through engaging in these types of practices we begin to understand, often quite viscerally, that "the network by itself is meaningless. Only the people were ever meaningful" (Lanier 2011, p. 17). In Chapter 9, we will discuss how to translate these micro-level insights into broad-stroke policy initiatives.

Conclusion

In a flurry of Silicon Valley self-justification , the National Transportation Safety Board (NTSB) reported that Elaine Herzberg had tested positive for marijuana and methamphetamine, was wearing dark clothing, and had no side-reflectors on her bicycle. Apparently, NTSB would have us believe that if Herzberg had not tested positive, or had been wearing light clothing, and her bicycle had had side reflectors, then the accident might have been avoided. Before the month's end following the accident, Uber halted its self-driving car-testing program and conducted an audit of its safety policies before resuming testing in December of that year (Associated Press 2018).

Without question, "every algorithm has values baked into it" (Keen 2011). The construction of Google's algorithms, for instance, involves numerous decisions about what users want and how to provide it most efficiently: there are many cooks in Google's kitchen. Google's own goals of increased revenues and market expansion also impact these decisions. As media scholars have long known, companies like Google do not simply respond to what users want; they also shape users' perceptions of their own needs and wants. This complex give-and-take makes media companies politically, economically, and culturally powerful. Google's "process of collecting, ranking, linking, and displaying knowledge determines what we consider to be good, true, valuable, and relevant"; "The stakes," as one critic observes, "could not be higher" (Vaidhyanathan 2011, p. 7). Elaine Herzberg would agree.

Simply put, "Data require our participation. Data need us" (Gitelman and Jackson 2013, p. 6). To say that an algorithm is biased is not to suggest that a computer program harbors feelings of animosity toward minorities. Nor does it necessarily suggest that software engineers harbor such feelings and deliberately code them into their programs, although that is certainly possible. More often, algorithms reflect or amplify pre-existing prejudice in the contexts where they are developed and deployed. Oversights on the part of well-meaning but naïve and relatively privileged programmers exacerbate this problem.

Years ago, the streaming music service Spotify ran an advertisement claiming that its personalization algorithm was so uncannily intelligent that listening to a stream of music was like hearing "you" in musical form. But the algorithms we use are using us as much as we are using them to collect data, to gather attention, and to sell these things to advertisers. On one earnings call, Facebook CEO Mark Zuckerberg explained that "our goal here is to make ads as interesting and useful as your friends' content" (Facebook 2014). Similarly, since introducing search personalization in 2009 Google shifted its specialization from "delivering information to satiate curiosity" toward doing so "to facilitate consumption" (Vaidhyanathan 2011, p. 201).

Searching for information has given way to browsing for products. The consumerist element in personalization is significant because, beyond simply responding to users' demands, companies actively shape users' perceptions of their own needs and wants. In the final analysis, commercial interests impinge on the dynamics of identity formation in ways that are difficult to discern. When we use the word "personalize," therefore, the action goes both ways. It is a two-way street of identity formation. And, as in any two-way street, the potential for deadly collision exists, no matter how much algorithms might suggest otherwise.

References

Angwin, Julia, Jeff Larson, Surya Mattu, and Lauren Kirchner. "Machine Bias: There's Software Used across the Country to Predict Future Criminals. And It's Biased against Blacks." ProPublica. May 23, 2016. https://www.propublica.org/article/machine-bias-risk-assessments-in-criminal-sentencing.

Associated Press. "Uber's Self-Driving SUV Saw the Pedestrian in Fatal Accident But Didn't Brake, Officials Say." CNBC. May 24, 2018. https://www.cnbc.com/2018/05/24/ubers-self-driving-suv-saw-the-pedestrian-in-fatal-accident-but-didnt-brake-officials-say.html.

Balick, Aaron. *The Psychodynamics of Social Networking*. London: Karnac Books, 2014.

Berry, Wendell. *What Are People For?* New York: North Point Press, 1990.

Bonnefon, Jean-François, Azim Shariff, and Iyad Rahwan. "Autonomous Vehicles Need Experimental Ethics: Are We Ready for Utilitarian Cars?" ArXiv.org. October 13, 2015. http://arxiv.org/pdf/1510.03346v1.pdf.

Bourg, Anya, and James Jacoby [producers]. *The Facebook Dilemma*. Boston: WGBH Educational Foundation, 2018.

Bowker, Geoffrey C. *Memory Practices in the Sciences*. Cambridge, MA: MIT Press, 2005.

Boyd, Danah, and Kate Crawford. "Critical Questions for Big Data." *Information, Communication & Society* 15, no. 5 (May 10, 2012): 662–79.

Boyd, Danah, Karen Levy, and Alice Marwick. "The Networked Nature of Algorithmic Discrimination." In *Data and Discrimination*, 53–57. New York: Open Technology Institute, 2014.

Brancaccio, David, Ali Oshinskie, and Danielle Chiriguayo. "The CEO of Reddit: 'We Are Not the Thought Police … But We Do Care about How You Behave.'" Marketplace. July 2, 2018. https://www.marketplace.org/2018/07/02/business/ceo-reddit-we-are-not-thought-police-we-don-t-want-control-what-you-believe-we.

Breland, Ali. "Lawmakers Introduce Bipartisan AI Legislation." *The Hill*, December 12, 2017. https://thehill.com/policy/technology/364482-lawmakers-introduce-bipartisan-ai-legislation.

Christians, Clifford G. "A Theory of Normative Technology." In *Technological Transformation: Contextual and Conceptual Implications*, edited by Edmund F. Byrne and Joseph C. Pitt, 123–39. Boston: Kluwer Academic Publishers, 1989.

Cullen, Cate. "Olson Thanks Delaney for His Leadership." Congressional Artificial Intelligence Caucus. December 13, 2018. https://artificialintelligencecaucus-olson.house.gov/media-center/press-releases/olson-thanks-delaney-for-his-leadership.

Dastin, Jeffrey. "Amazon Scraps Secret AI Recruiting Tool That Showed Bias against Women." *Reuters*, October 9, 2018. https://www.reuters.com/article/us-amazon-com-jobs-automation-insight/amazon-scraps-secret-ai-recruiting-tool-that-showed-bias-against-women-idUSKCN1MK08G.

Department of Defense. "Autonomy in Weapon Systems." Directive No. 3000.09. 2012. http://www.dtic.mil/whs/directives/corres/pdf/300009p.pdf.

Edelman, Benjamin G., Michael Luca, and Daniel Svirsky. "Racial Discrimination in the Sharing Economy: Evidence from a Field Experiment." Harvard Business School. January 25, 2016. https://hbswk.hbs.edu/item/racial-discrimination-in-the-sharing-economy-evidence-from-a-field-experiment.

Facebook. "Facebook Q2 2014 Earnings Call." *Zuckerberg Transcripts*. Paper 152. 2014. http://dc.uwm.edu/zuckerberg_files_transcripts/152.

Foot, Philippa. "The Problem of Abortion and the Doctrine of the Double Effect." *Oxford Review* 5 (1967): 5–15.

Ghosh, Pallab. "AAAS: Machine Learning 'Causing Science Crisis.'" BBC News. February 16, 2019. https://www.bbc.com/news/science-environment-47267081.

Gitelman, Lisa, and Virginia Jackson. "Introduction." In *"Raw Data" Is an Oxymoron*, edited by Lisa Gitelman, 1–14. Cambridge, MA: MIT Press, 2013.

Goldhill, Olivia. "Philosophers Are Building Ethical Algorithms to Help Control Self-Driving Cars." Quartz. February 11, 2018. https://qz.com/1204395/self-driving-cars-trolley-problem-philosophers-are-building-ethical-algorithms-to-solve-the-problem/.

Guynn, Jessica. "NAACP Is Trying to Help Airbnb Be Less White." *USA Today*, July 26, 2017. https://www.usatoday.com/story/tech/2017/07/26/naacp-trying-help-airbnb-less-white/513024001/.

Hardy, Quentin. "Why Big Data Is Not Truth." *New York Times*, June 1, 2013. http://bits.blogs.nytimes.com/2013/06/01/why-big-data-is-not-truth/.

Healey, Kevin. "You Are Not a Gadget: Prophetic Critique in the Age of Google." In *Prophetic Critique and Popular Media: Theoretical Foundations and Practical Applications*, edited by Robert H. Woods Jr. and Kevin Healey, 171–91. New York: Peter Lang, 2013.

Hutson, Jevan, Jessie G. Taft, Solon Barocas, and Karen Levy. "Debiasing Desire: Addressing Bias & Discrimination on Intimate Platforms." *Proceedings of the ACM on Human-Computer Interaction* 2, CSCW, Article 73 (November 2018), 18 pages. https://doi.org/10.1145/3274342.

Keen, Andrew. "Yes, Google Is a Monopolist (and Why We Should Worry)." Tech Crunch [Video Interview]. March 22, 2011. http://techcrunch.com/2011/03/22/keen-on-yes-google-is-a-monopolist-tctv/.

King, Hope. "Airbnb Sued for Discrimination." CNN. May 18, 2016. https://money.cnn.com/2016/05/18/technology/airbnb-lawsuit-discrimination/index.html.

King, Martin Luther, Jr. "The Strength to Love." In *A Testament of Hope: The Essential Writings of Martin Luther King, Jr.*, edited by James M. Washington, 491–517. 1963. Reprint ed., San Francisco: Harper & Row, 1986.

Lanier, Jaron. *You Are Not a Gadget: A Manifesto*. New York: Vintage Books, 2011.

———. *Who Owns the Future?* New York: Simon & Schuster, 2013.

Lannan, Katie. "Poll: Voters Want Checks on Face Recognition Technology." WGBH News [Boston]. June 18, 2019. https://www.wgbh.org/news/local-news/2019/06/18/poll-voters-want-checks-on-face-recognition-technology.

Leavy, Patricia. *Method Meets Art: Arts-Based Research Practice*. New York: The Guilford Press, 2015.

Lefkowitz, Melanie. "Redesign Dating Apps to Lessen Racial Bias, Study Recommends." *Cornell Chronicle*, September 27, 2018. http://news.cornell.edu/stories/2018/09/redesign-dating-apps-lessen-racial-bias-study-recommends.

Liptak, Adam. "Sent to Prison by a Software Program's Secret Algorithms." *New York Times*, May 1, 2017. https://www.nytimes.com/2017/05/01/us/politics/sent-to-prison-by-a-software-programs-secret-algorithms.html.

Marcus, Gary. "Moral Machines." *New Yorker*, November 27, 2012. http://www.newyorker.com/online/blogs/newsdesk/2012/11/google-driverless-car-morality.html.

McChesney, Robert W. *The Problem of the Media: U.S. Communication Politics in the Twenty-First Century*. New York: Monthly Review Press, 2004.

———. *Digital Disconnect: How Capitalism Is Turning the Internet Against Democracy*. New York: New Press, 2013.

McDonough, Annie. "MIT Study Backs AOC on Algorithm Bias." City & State New York. January 28, 2019. https://www.cityandstateny.com/articles/policy/technology/mit-study-backs-alexandria-ocasio-cortez-algorithm-bias.html.

Miller, Claire Cain. "When Uber and Airbnb Meet the Real World." *New York Times*, October 17, 2014. https://www.nytimes.com/2014/10/19/upshot/when-uber-lyft-and-airbnb-meet-the-real-world.html.

Molloy, Parker. "What *the Daily Wire* Gets Wrong (and Alexandria Ocasio-Cortez Gets Right) about Algorithms and Racism." MediaMatters. January 24, 2019. https://www.mediamatters.org/blog/2019/01/24/what-daily-wire-gets-wrong-and-alexandria-ocasio-cortez-gets-right-about-algorithms-and-racism/222629.

Morozov, Evgeny. *To Save Everything, Click Here: The Folly of Technological Solutionism*. New York: Public Affairs, 2013.

Newton, Casey. "Bodies in Seats." The Verge. June 19, 2019. https://www.theverge.com/2019/6/19/18681845/facebook-moderator-interviews-video-trauma-ptsd-cognizant-tampa.

Notopoulos, Katie. "The Dating App That Knows You Secretly Aren't into Guys from Other Races." BuzzFeedNews. January 14, 2016. https://www.buzzfeednews.com/article/katienotopoulos/coffee-meets-bagel-racial-preferences.

Palfrey, John, and Urs Gasser. *Born Digital: Understanding the First Generation of Digital Natives.* New York: Basic Books, 2008.

Petter, Olivia. "Racism Is Rife on Dating Apps—Where Does It Come From and How Can It Be Fixed?" *Independent.* August 24, 2018. https://www.independent.co.uk/life-style/love-sex/dating-apps-racism-tinder-bumble-grindr-online-dating-a8504996.html.

Scheiber, Noam. "How Uber Uses Psychological Tricks to Push Its Drivers' Buttons." *New York Times*, April 2, 2017. https://www.nytimes.com/interactive/2017/04/02/technology/uber-drivers-psychological-tricks.html.

Stevens, Suzanne. "Oregon Judge Denies Airbnb Motion to Dismiss Lawsuit Alleging 'Intentional Discrimination.'" *San Francisco Business Times*, November 1, 2018. https://www.bizjournals.com/sanfrancisco/news/2018/11/01/oregon-judge-denies-airbnb-motion-discrimination.html.

Sullivan, Mark. "Facebook Patents Technology to Help Lenders Discriminate against Borrowers Based on Social Connections." Venture Beat. August 4, 2015. https://venturebeat.com/2015/08/04/facebook-patents-technology-to-help-lenders-discriminate-against-borrowers-based-on-social-connections/.

Tene, Omer, and Jules Polonetsky. "A Theory of Creepy: Technology, Privacy and Shifting Social Norms." *Yale Journal of Law and Technology* 16 (September 16, 2013): 59–134.

Vaidhyanathan, Siva. *The Googlization of Everything (And Why We Should Worry).* Berkeley, CA: University of California Press, 2011.

———. *Anti-Social Media: How Facebook Disconnects Us and Undermines Democracy.* New York: Oxford University Press, 2018.

———. "Dear Mr. Zuckerberg: The Problem Isn't the Internet, It's Facebook." *The Guardian*, February 4, 2019. www.theguardian.com/technology/2019/feb/04/facebook-15-anniversary-mark-zuckerberg.

Weissman, Cale Guthrie. "Anonymous Is Supporting a New Privacy-Focused Social Network That Takes Aim at Facebook's Shady Practices." *Business Insider*, June 15, 2015. http://www.businessinsider.com/facebook-competitor-mindscom-launches-with-help-from-anonymous-2015-6.

Weston, Anthony. *A 21st Century Ethical Toolbox.* New York: Oxford University Press, 2001.

Wisconsin v. Loomis. "State of Wisconsin, Plaintiff-Respondent, v. Eric L. Loomis, Defendant-Appellant." Case No. 2015AP157-CR. Opinion filed: July 13, 2016. https://www.documentcloud.org/documents/2993525-Wisconsin-v-Loomis-Opinion.html.

Zombeck, Richard. "Facebook Patents Technology That Could Allow Banks and Businesses to Discriminate Based on Social Connections." *Huffington Post*, August 7, 2015. http://www.huffingtonpost.com/richard-zombeck/facebooks-patenttechnolo_b_7956820.htm.

Zuckerberg, Mark. "Thoughts on Beacon." *Zuckerberg Transcripts.* Paper 14. December 5, 2007. http://dc.uwm.edu/zuckerberg_files_transcripts/14.

———. Untitled Facebook Post. February 4, 2019. https://www.facebook.com/zuck/posts/10106411140260321.

7

STORAGE IS NOT MEMORY

In Samuel Beckett's one-act play "Krapp's Last Tape," a ragged old man named Krapp rummages obsessively through reels of recorded tapes from years past. On the tapes, his voice relates broken stories of romantic encounters and addiction to bananas, alcohol, sex, and the very process of recording and listening to oneself. In one passage, the voice from the tape paints a grim picture of lonely isolation: "Past midnight. Never knew such silence. The earth might be uninhabited." As the tapes roll, he sits "staring vacuously before him" before breaking out a virgin reel on which he records his newfound hatred for "that stupid bastard I took myself for thirty years ago" (Beckett 1976, p. 495).

The scene reveals Beckett's long preoccupation with what he called "that double-headed monster of damnation and salvation—Time—and its necessary corollary, Memory." He regarded the latter with some suspicion, describing it as "a clinical laboratory stocked with poison and remedy, stimulant and sedative" (p. 477). Penned in 1959, shortly after the arrival of the tape recorder, "Krapp's Last Tape" highlights Beckett's particular concern for the impact of electronic media on individual and cultural processes of memory.

Today, data processing and storage combine to produce tragic scenes not unlike Beckett's. When Facebook's 2014 Year in Review presented blogger Eric Meyer with images of his deceased six-year-old daughter, his complaints of "algorithmic cruelty" went viral (Meyer 2014). Other users related similar experiences. Researchers have begun to ask whether the vast storage capacity of networked technologies threaten to send us unsuspectingly into a tailspin of regret similar to that suffered by old man Krapp. Life-logging devices like Autographer, Memoto, and SixthSense aim to capture every waking moment. Google's Eric Schmidt touts an intelligent future in which cloud systems will provide us with "infinite memory" (*The Colbert Report* 2013).

One wonders whether the proliferation of unsorted images on our smartphones and in proprietary clouds might undermine our ability to let go of the past and construct more meaningful long-term memories (Parker-Pope 2010). More than a mere problem of accuracy in storage and retrieval, memory requires the skillful exercise of selective judgment. It requires meaningful participation in decisions about what and how to remember, as well as what and how to forget.

This is the skill that Krapp sorely lacks. As the old man's late-night reminiscence suggests, one's ability to return to accurate and abundant images at a later date does not necessarily aid the process of one's personal narrative. In the networked era, Krapp's box of reels becomes a bottomless fount wherein he encounters others' images of him as well as his own, with commercial entities, known and unknown, having access to the same. Schmidt's optimism notwithstanding, we might do well to recall a prophetic admonition from German-American Christian existentialist Paul Tillich. In an essay aptly titled "Frontiers," the noted theologian warned that "in many Christian lands a superstition has developed inside and outside the churches which misinterprets eternal life as endless duration, and does not perceive that an infinity of the finite could be a symbol for hell" (Tillich [1966] 1999, p. 248).

Krapp's Last Tweet?

Beckett's concern about electronic media's impact on memory is still relevant. Of course, if recalling everything is dangerous, so too would be an inability to remember anything at all. With total erasure or amnesia on one hand, and total recall on the other, how do we forge a meaningful middle ground?

In each previous chapter, we stressed that technology is not morally neutral. As Krapp came to see, the choice to store everything is not a neutral choice. It changes one's present and one's future with cascading effects. As researchers and scholars are just beginning to understand, memory is not a mental function separate from judgment; rather, it presupposes and depends upon judgment. Nor is memory separate from our understanding of wisdom. In fact, contrary to the catechism of Silicon Valley, wisdom emerges over time through the judicious exercise of both remembering and forgetting.

Also as in previous chapters, our approach here is to insist on a correct understanding of both memory and data storage: what they are, and perhaps more importantly what they are not. As we will argue, your brain does not store memories like a computer stores data. By the same token, we cannot replicate or otherwise outsource memory to clouds of data because storage is not the same as memory. As with other aspects of the catechism, the assumption that storage and memory are coequal, or interchangeable, is not only faulty, but it is also ethically and politically fraught.

While new technologies of memory clearly impact individual processes of remembering, their collective impact is of equal importance and includes, among other things, the historical development of commercial and administrative systems and the extension of corporate and state power (Olick 2007, pp. 27–28).

The outsourcing of individual and institutional memory to commercial data storage platforms is therefore a political, and not merely technological, development. As this happens, users cede active judgment about the relative importance of specific events to the software applications and proprietary clouds that are supposedly designed to help them "remember" but whose contents are subsequently mined, aggregated, and commodified by commercial enterprises and law enforcement agencies with memory projects of their own.

One critic summarizes the problem directly, noting that "storage of information without selection is not memory—at least not as we use the term when we speak of the human condition" (Morozov 2013, p. 278). The mere fact of better, faster, and deeper storage is not in itself reason for celebration. The question of who has assumed the power of selection in the expanding trove of stored data, and for what purpose, is the key to understanding the shifting politics of cultural memory in the digital era.

The Catechism: Storage Is Memory

Nuance of the sort described above is lacking in the pronouncements of tech leaders, who tend to focus primarily on the benefits of new technologies for individual consumers. On a raft trip through the Grand Canyon with Luc Vincent, manager of Google's Street View imagery and mapping applications, reporter Adam Fisher recalls the "trippy moment" when he realized that "I was going to be able to look back at my own outsourced memory one day" (Fisher 2013).

Having noted the beauty of the surroundings, Fisher told Vincent, "I'm trying to burn these images into my retinas, so I never forget this place" (Fisher 2013). In reply, Vincent reassured the reporter, "you never will, because Street View is there to help you to remember" (Fisher 2013). If psychologists are correct, however, Fisher was straining not simply to capture the raw data of the senses for later access but to integrate, in that moment, the most important aspects of his sensory, aesthetic, and emotional experience. Stored imagery can surely help one to remember, but it is the narrative and emotional dimensions that will ensure that Fisher never forgets the experience, not the data itself.

While reminding us that computers cannot literally remember anything, critics argue that such metaphors have come to assume a literal meaning in part because such assertions serve the professional interests of technology celebrants (Searle 2008, p. 71). The self-interested equation of storage and memory is a common theme in Google's projects. Describing the transition from traditional print to digital news, Larry Page touted the benefits of personalization via mobile devices, arguing, "it will remember what you know" and "will suggest things that you might want to know" (Pariser 2011, pp. 61–62). Google chief executive officer Eric Schmidt muddied the water further, arguing that in the future "computers are going to do what they do well, which is, they have infinite memory—they remember everything—and people are going to do very well what we're good at, which is judgment" (*The Colbert Report* 2013).

While we might applaud Schmidt for acknowledging the limitations of digital technologies and underscoring the role of human judgment, his reassurances are disingenuous. First, he fails to acknowledge what we established in Chapter 6 of this book, namely, that algorithmic processing is itself a form of pre-judgment with political implications. Second, like Vincent, he moves beyond mere metaphor to a literal assertion that storage equals memory, a rhetorical sleight of hand that obscures the cultural politics of memory. To be more precise, Schmidt creates a false distinction between memory and judgment. As we will make clear in the discussions below of life-logging devices and digital cameras, whether in relation to individuals or entire nations, memory without judgment is meaningless. Memory itself is a process of judgment. In addition, advances in neuroscience undermine the catechism's insistence that forgetting is somehow a technical glitch or gross inefficiency that must be overcome. While researchers recognize the importance of remembering to remember, they have also come to recognize that remembering to forget may actually be the beginning of wisdom and human flourishing and not their end.

Logging Your Life

The merging of storage and memory is arguably most pronounced in the marketing of life-logging devices such as Autographer, Memoto, and SixthSense. Some devices, such as Autographer, are autonomous photo-capturing devices that operate without the conscious involvement of the user by snapping images at predetermined intervals. Others allow users to operate the device in a hands-free manner using intuitive gestural interfaces. By allowing users to behave in a more natural manner, these devices ostensibly avoid the pitfalls of distraction that accompany conventional cameras and thereby allow users to remain in the moment (Northcote et al. 2014). Pranav Mistry, who frames his SixthSense technologies as a means of bridging the "digital divide" between the physical space and cyberspace, argues that such devices may "help us, in some way, to stay human, to be more connected to our physical world" (Mistry 2009).

Psychologists, though, caution that we have yet to generate definitive research about a range of related issues, including the effects of exposure to "hybrid" information during daily activity, the best design practices for reducing users' "cognitive load," and the impacts of these technologies on social interaction (Gaggioli 2012, p. 444). Marketers urge us to jump into life-logging on the pretext that memory is a mere storage function of the brain, readily outsourced to commercial devices.

More broadly, the rhetoric surrounding ostensibly "natural" interfaces hides their political-economic dimensions. Embodying the lofty goal of perfect memory, wearable technologies entrench the computational metaphor by offering the possibility of augmenting the mind, where the mind itself is understood as a computer (Northcote et al. 2014; see our discussion in Chapter 2). Implicit in these kinds of assumptions is the corollary notion that forgetting is a disability.

Consider the implications of this notion in the case of the Autographer. The device was initially sold without Internet connectivity (all data were stored on the device), creating a misleading sense of user privacy. As commercial industries move toward networked cloud storage, it is likely that user data on the Autographer and similar devices will be available for use by third parties for data mining and marketing opportunities. Since user data are the lifeblood of the digital economy, commercial life-logging devices provide the means for extended data extraction, aggregation, and commodification. Consequently, the "natural" design of autonomous and gestural interfaces is not only, or even primarily, a benefit to users. The unbounded storage of data in perpetuity generates unprecedented opportunities for integrating individuals more seamlessly into regimes of consumer and political surveillance. While data mining for national security is typically understood as an effort to find the proverbial needle in a haystack, the possibility arises that political elites may exploit troves of data on an as-needed basis to impugn activists and dissidents through selective exposure of apparently damning behavior or associations. Surveillance in the era of Big Data is a matter of finding "haystacks about needles" (Meyrowitz 2014). If storage without selection is not memory, the power of selection is key to the cultural politics of remembering.

Attempts to ease such concerns often lead to contradictory statements from corporate executives. After reassuring users that Google is legally required to "forget" their data, Schmidt suggested that the essential nature of computer systems is to "remember forever" (*The Colbert Report* 2010). He sees this characteristic as a net positive, however, suggesting that perpetual data storage is tantamount to immortality. By equating storage with memory and positing the development of perfect memory as a techno-historical inevitability, Schmidt thus admits that while Google maneuvers around legal frameworks for public relations purposes, its long-term goal is to render such constraints technically and ideologically obsolete.

The goal of rendering regulations obsolete brings special urgency to the technical and legal battles that characterize the politics of memory in the digital age. Applications such as SnapChat have attempted to incorporate user-driven preferences for forgetting into interface designs, but security experts note that such applications often fail to delete data completely or remain vulnerable to hackers (Guynn 2013). While such technical proposals may be helpful, they represent yet another instance of the technological "solutionism" that characterizes Silicon Valley culture (Morozov 2013, pp. 279–80). By focusing on technical solutions to these issues, commercial firms sidestep the political and legal aspects of development.

Digital Cameras: Distracting or Not Distracting Enough?

In recent years, digital camera technology has veered in two opposite, but perhaps equally problematic, directions. The first direction is toward constant and distracting image-taking. Smartphones with easy access to image-taking, filtering, and sharing apps invite users to document quite literally anything and everything by hand. This direction echoes the era of film photography, when Kodak had marketed itself as "the platform for nostalgia" and urged users to seek out and capture "Kodak moments" in their personal lives (Sturken 2015, p. 100). But the obvious limitations of analog film (the limited number of images one can take, the inability to see a captured image immediately) acted as a kind of speed bump, forcing users to be selective rather than indiscriminate. By contrast, digital devices, with their unlimited storage capacity and instantaneous image production, promise to make every moment a Kodak moment. This promise may turn out to be a curse: if every moment is equally laden with meaning, then perhaps there are no Kodak moments. Put another way: if everything is important, nothing is important, because nothing stands out as different or unique.

The shift to Facebook and Google as platforms for photographing and curating images of one's personal history is considered "the death of the analog photographic-film industry" (Sturken 2015, p. 103). As one insider explains, "the concept of the Kodak moment is increasingly obsolete" since social media encourages self-documentation with constant updates rather than "the unique photo moment" (Sturken 2015, p. 104). Unlike analog photography, which is often understood in terms of the loss of a moment as it slips into the past, in digital platforms "the *update* is its primary mode" (Sturken 2015, p. 106, emphasis original).

Research shows that there are clear downsides to such persistent image-taking when it becomes a compulsive habit. Laboratory experiments reveal what psychologists call a "photo-taking impairment effect," in which people remember fewer—and fewer details about—objects they photograph ("Overexposed?" 2014). Over-reliance on hand-held devices leads to a lack of mindful attention that undermines the meaningful formation of memory. Users are left with many images on file but rarely attempt to sort, order, or discard them. This problem is compounded as the ubiquity of recording devices, which makes all manner of joyful and embarrassing events fodder for public scrutiny in perpetuity (Tsesis 2014). Researchers suggest the proliferation of unsorted images on our smartphones and Flickr accounts undermine our ability to let go of the past and construct more meaningful long-term memories (Parker-Pope 2010). In essence, always-available hand-held cameras and sharing apps can impede judicious attention to our environment, thereby undermining memory skills.

The second and more recent direction of digital image technology is toward devices that are less intrusive, if not completely outside of one's immediate attention. GoPro comes to mind as a popular gadget in this vein, although it is not intended for constant, daily use. Constant use that is seamless with our daily activities is the point of the life-logging SixthSense device. Mistry's device frames the device as a way of being more in touch with the physical world. Since users will not have to attend constantly to their device either cognitively or physically, the device will reinforce their memory of meaningful moments without distracting from them. At least, that is the rationale.

Interestingly, the idea that new technology can allow us to remain in the moment, and avoid distraction, predates digital computers. In contrast to Kodak, the Polaroid Corporation was always less about nostalgia and the family and more about hipness, spontaneity, and art (Sturken 2015, p. 100). In its early marketing materials, Polaroid aimed to "change the person who takes pictures from a harried off-stage observer into someone who was a natural part of the event" (Sturken 2015, pp. 101–2).

It is possible that devices like SixthSense take this logic to such an extreme that it backfires. Ironically, Mistry's gadget might not enhance but undermine memory because, by design, it suggests to users that they do not need to engage in mindful moments of judgment to create lasting memories.

Is there a potential middle ground between a hands-off device that captures everything (where our exercise of judgment and mindful attention begins to atrophy) and a hand-held device that ends up distracting us (what Polaroid described, above, as "the harried off-stage observer")?

Celebrations of the death of analog photography may have been premature. It is true that both Kodak and Polaroid declared bankruptcy just as Facebook was in its ascendance. Facebook's Timeline feature was in a sense the final nail in the coffin, at least in terms of the prior regimes of commercial amateur photography (Sturken 2015, pp. 95–96). But this is only part of the story. It is clear that the consumer market harbors demands that harken back to the analog era, even as consumers embrace the digital.

Consider how platforms like Instagram (owned by Facebook) and Hipstamatic cater to users' nostalgia for analog-era photography. Both offer multiple filters that echo the days of Polaroid snapshots. Hipstamatic sells itself on the slogan "digital photography never looked so analog" (Sturken 2015, p. 105). Analog cameras apps like Huji, Calla, and Feelm are designed to simulate the low, variable image quality of old-style film cameras including random light leaks and date stamps. Especially popular among these apps is Gudak Cam, which recreates not only the image quality of film but also the uncertainty and delay that comes with analog cameras. The app simulates the limitations of a 24-image roll of analog film by forcing users to wait three days for their images to "develop" before they can view them and begin using another "roll." Here again, the app is merely simulating analog cameras. Other apps, like the now-defunct White Album, literally made users wait for their digitally captured images to be developed on actual film, which would be delivered to a user's home in a box. The price tag of $20 per "roll" of 24 photos may have been what sealed the White Album's fate.

These tools respond to users' desire to relate to the present moment more meaningfully. But they can only provide so much by simulating the material, hands-on quality of the analog. These shortcomings may explain renewed interest in instant photography devices. At the time of this book's publication, the local Rite Aid, CVS, and Walgreens each carry several different brands of instant photo-devices including Fujifilm and, yes, Polaroid. Interest in such devices is not so much about instantaneity as materiality (Draper 2019). It is similar to why people have revived interest in type-writers and vinyl records. The speed is human-speed and the capacity for attention is human-capacity.

The Cultural Politics of Memory

While the above-mentioned examples in the previous two sections focus chiefly on individual users' privacy, other questions arise with regard to how digital platforms impact the collective memory of entire nations and cultures. A case in point is the effort within the United States to revise history curricula in public schools, much of which tends to marginalize ethnic, racial, and religious minorities. As evidenced by debates over ethnic studies programs in Arizona and California public schools, such struggles are political hotbeds (Caesar 2014). Such efforts are prime examples of the cultural politics of memory. Given the nation's shifting demographics, which portend a more diverse population in the coming decades, educational curricula are a significant site of struggle in the process of cultural memory formation. According to some critics, such debates are driven in part by a growing sense of despair among some white Americans (Ehrenreich 2015). In the United States, it is as if non-Hispanic whites have begun to feel the same brooding, spiteful resignation epitomized by old man Krapp, when he opines with despair, "Perhaps my best years are gone." In other words, the politics of memory is sometimes driven by xenophobic resentment. From this perspective, efforts to undermine or end ethnic studies programs may constitute what one observer describes as a form of forgetting called "repressive erasure" (Connerton 2008), that is, an effort to impose one's privileged view of identity on cultural constructions of memory.

Digital media platforms can exacerbate such reactionary or repressive tendencies. When protests in Ferguson, Missouri, erupted after the shooting of Michael Brown in August 2014, Twitter feeds lit up, but Facebook's News Feed reportedly failed to prioritize coverage (Tufekci 2014). That discrepancy is perhaps unsurprising, given Mark Zuckerberg's infamous offhand quip that "a squirrel dying in front of your house may be more relevant to your interests right now than people dying in Africa" (Kirkpatrick 2010, p. 181). Moreover, despite Facebook's arguments to the contrary, the company's own research suggests that its News Feed tends to increase political polarization modestly (Sandvig 2015). And while Twitter may serve more effectively in broadcasting breaking news, it also tends toward polarization when it comes to politically charged issues (Barberá et al. 2015). In other words, at the very moment when digital capitalism is exacerbating class inequality, social media is catalyzing attitudes of racism, sexism, and nativism among those who fear losing the socioeconomic privilege they once enjoyed.

The Science of Memory

Scientific understanding of memory is arguably still in its infancy. Yet we know enough to say that the simple equation of memory and storage is incorrect. One neuroscientist explains it this way:

> When you dig into molecules, and the states of ion channels, enzymes, transcription programs, cells, synapses, and whole networks of neurons, you come to realize that there is no one place in the brain where memories are stored.
>
> (Stockton 2017)

In a very real sense, as one *Wired* reporter explains, "The memory is the system itself" (Stockton 2017). Our brains are not static, mechanical formations—a bolt here, a screw there, holding together until the rust prevails and the system decays. Instead, our brains are constantly changing. This is called the principle of neuroplasticity. And memory is part of the holistic, system-wide process. Even neuroscientists are quick to express considerable humility in the breadth and depth of their understanding of this complex process, which begs the question: if we do not yet understand what memory is, or how it works, how can we claim that computers are better at it? More importantly, what do we stand to lose when we acquiesce to such premature claims? Another way of putting it is, who stands to gain? When companies impose their own metaphors, for instance, a timeline, or a stream, and ask us to think of our own memories through that lens, we begin to think and remember in ways that serve a platform's ends rather than our own (Sturken 2015, p. 106).

Current neuroscience research offers a helpful corrective to the false distinction between memory and judgment noted earlier. Neuroscientists argue that we should not think of memory "simply as a means for high-fidelity transmission of information through time" (Siegfried 2019). Instead, they say, "the goal of memory is to guide intelligent decision making" (Siegfried 2019). The implication here is that simplification, or the ability to reduce memories to their most important characteristics, is essential for memory to work for us rather than against us as it did for Beckett's old man Krapp. Another neuroscientist argues as much:

> An overly precise memory is maybe not really what we want in the long term, because it prevents us from using our memories to generalize them to new situations. ... If our memories are too precise and over-fitted, then we can't actually use them to ... make predictions about future situations.
>
> (Siegfried 2019)

Memory is effective when we engage in the moment to grasp the gist of an experience. This way, we can generalize the insights of experience for future events that are similar but not exactly the same, which is a chief component of what we understand as wisdom.

Our very use of the word "memory" to describe mere information storage is "baffling" at times since computers "lack a basic feature of memory, the ability to select" (Todorov 1996, p. 8).

Memory requires the skillful exercise of "narrative imagination" through selective judgment and meaningful participation in decisions about what and how to remember, as well as what and how to forget (Morozov 2013, p. 277). One's ability to return to accurate and abundant images at a later date does not necessarily aid the narrative process. Human memory is far more dynamic than mere photographs. A photograph is not a memory, because remembering requires that we actively integrate past and present, not passively retrieve and display static sets of data. The integrity of personal identity is achieved through an ongoing process of storytelling wherein the details, plot, and normative content change as the author's experience and worldview develops through subsequent experience (Olick 2007).

This way of viewing memory upends the catechism, which sees forgetting as a case of mechanical or system failure, malfunction, or decay. On the contrary,

"Forgetting is good and an adaptive thing" (Siegfried 2019). "It's been shown over and over in computational models and also in animal work that an intelligent memory system needs forgetting," neuroscientists explain (Siegfried 2019). There is a certain irony here, considering our earlier exploration of life-logging devices, namely, if we build machines so they do not (or cannot) forget, perhaps we are not building machines that we can properly call "intelligent." Forgetting serves an important purpose by expunging old or outdated information that "would hamper sound judgment" (Siegfried 2019). Memory serves an adaptive function provided that we remember actively and judiciously. Researchers argue that our brain's default mode is to let go of, or jettison, memories unless we actively intervene in the process. In the words of one expert, "We might have a slow chronic forgetting signal in our brains that basically says, let's erase everything, unless a judge … comes to intervene and says, 'This memory is worth saving'" (Siegfried 2019).

The fact that forgetting may be a helpful, adaptive function does not necessarily mean that the technical capacity for infinite data storage is lacking any possible benefit. But these neuroscientific insights do suggest that such technical capacities should be developed and used judiciously and not as a go-to consumer service or product. Furthermore, it all suggests that memory is a learned skill requiring the ongoing exercise of attention and judgment. As such, it cannot be wholly outsourced to mere storage devices. The ubiquity and ease-of-use of hand-held devices tempts us to do so, however, with effects that are not always obvious.

Challenging the Catechism: Storage Is Not Memory

In my writing, I remember so I can then forget. Of course, I do not mean that I erase my memory like a computer hard drive.

(Leggo 2015, p. 158)

The poet Carl Leggo explains that remembering and forgetting are not really opposites but more like two sides of the same coin: one does not exist without the other. One depends on the other. When we write, he explains, we actively remember not to ensure that we never forget but to shave off those parts of our experience that we no longer need, leaving the essence of what provides a meaningful life for us. But forgetting does not mean denying or ignoring. "My ways of forgetting," he explains, "involve acknowledging the hole [in your heart], not seeking to fill it in or patch it up." When writing serves effectively as a practice of both remembering and judiciously forgetting, "the hole remains like a wound that helps spell all that is not the hole. My writing is forgetting, *for getting* on with the journey" (Leggo 2015, p. 158; emphasis original).

When we juxtapose the proverb "storage is not memory" with the corollary "remember the virtue of forgetting" (which we elaborate on in Chapter 8), we intend to capture the nuanced dialectic Leggo describes above. The injunction to "remember" is active and engaged, not passive. The proverb and its corollary remind us to keep in mind actively what really matters, to make sound judgments about what memories we do and do not keep as we build our relationships.

In the spirit of Leggo's practice of writing "for getting on," we have developed classroom exercises that build upon the method of poetic transcription described in Chapter 6. As you may recall, poetic transcription is an arts-based research (ABR) method wherein researchers translate or transcribe an existing data set (usually content like interview transcripts, written essays, and the like) into a poem or series of poems. In the exercises described in Chapter 6, students use poetic transcription to exercise greater control in how they read and find meaning within online content, including their own blog posts as well as published interviews with tech executives. In the exercise described here, using this same arts-based method, students focus instead on offline content, namely, hand-written letters, and leverage poetry as a method of finding and integrating meaning into memory. If the poetic processing illustrated in Chapter 6 is one step removed from algorithmic gatekeeping (printing and transcribing online content), then the current exercise is further removed from those algorithms (transcribing off-line communication with social media "friends").

The premise of the exercise described here echoes the argument of the neuro-scientists cited above, who argue that the purpose of memory is not total recall but the ability to generalize insights from prior experiences to future ones. As a research method, poetic transcription is similarly aimed at grasping the gist of a broad swath of written material or other content in a way that is aesthetically and emotionally evocative so that deeper meanings become apparent. The purpose of ABR is "to make conscious and to give clarity, form, and meaning to the human phenomena under investigation" (Gerber and Myers-Coffmann 2018, p. 596). Poetic transcription acknowledges emotional and sensory-based ways of knowing. "It's from these ways of knowing," explains one leading proponent, "that our values and memories come, and those in turn inform how we live in the world" (Gerber and Myers-Coffmann 2018, p. 592).

In our classroom exercises, we have students identify people with whom they communicate primarily, if not exclusively, through social media platforms like Facebook or Instagram. They reach out to one or two of these people, whether family or friends, and make an agreement to shift their communication offline to entirely hand-written forms for a few weeks. We ask them to document the process by taking digital photographs of their hand-written letters, their envelopes and stamps, the letters they receive in return, and even (in one of our seminars) the campus mailbox where we all put our first set of letters to be mailed. Even before poetic transcription takes place, students find the process of letter-writing meaningful, even "magical," as one wrote. One student noted that she "was careful with what words I used and how I phrased my sentences," adding, "I never do that when I text." Students respond with surprise and delight when they move to an analog medium that is disconnected, and which therefore cannot be processed, mined, or otherwise commodified through some form of digital surveillance and processing. Communication that would have been saved and stored for processing, only to resurface later (e.g., as a Facebook "memory"), is now content over which the letter-writer takes greater control and ownership.

At the end of two or three weeks, when students have material to work with from both letter-writers, we engage in a process of poetic transcription. This process puts the student, or "poet," in a position that is a human analog to the algorithmic scripts that process our online "memories." The goal here is to make the process of memory-formation explicit and meaningful, without outsourcing it to platforms or apps.

To create a model of poetic transcription for his class, one of your authors (Kevin) chose to work with letters he had accumulated over the years from his late grandmother Rose Notari, who died in 1999. He first printed several hard copies of her letters. Sitting down with a highlighter and pen, he read through the letters and circled or highlighted phrases, words, or themes that were most evocative, such as the pain of arthritis and the sadness of a rainy day spent alone. Then he assembled the best, or most meaningful, of these into a Word document. He performed minor edits to correct spelling or to make phrases grammatically consistent. After composing the transcribed poem, he created a set of collage images in Photoshop, superimposing the poem over photographs of his grandmother's handwriting. The final piece, which he titled "Scranton Is Getting Bad," appears in the online poetry journal *Typishly* (Healey 2018; see Figure 7.1). We encourage students to create something similar

FIGURE 7.1   The opening verse from Kevin's poem "Scranton is Getting Bad," transcribed of hand-written letters he received from his late grandmother.

and either share it on social media (thus returning from analog to digital) and/or send it back to their letter-writing partner via snail mail.

For Kevin, the process of transcribing dozens of letters from his grandma Rose was indeed one of remembering in order to forget, for "getting on," to borrow Leggo's phrase. Kevin relates being able to let go of the many details in the letters, because although he had kept them for years he had only given them their due attention in this exercise. He was able to "distill the 'gist' of Rose." Our students offer similar reports as they take part in their own version of this exercise. Poet letter-writers will likely preserve the materials as keepsakes but feel less of a need to re-read them. In sharing these transcribed poems (especially with photo-collage pieces) online through social media, we manage to integrate analog and digital in more meaningful ways—not either/or, but rather both/and. The exercise is thus an example of data storage *in service of* memory, in keeping with our description of the proverbs in this book's Introduction, where we note that memory formation requires judgment, wisdom, and even courage. These are virtues that human users must bring to the platforms they use; the platforms cannot provide them, but they can provide an avenue to share the meaningful work users have created through their own sweat and tears.

The letter-writing practice we describe here helps restore an important sense of control and ownership among social media users. Too often, platforms like Facebook do not show us things we do not want to see, even if our awareness of them might make us better citizens. This is where our dual roles of citizens and consumers come into conflict, and commercial platforms nudge us to embrace the latter at the expense of the former. In avoiding issues or events that might make us uncomfortable (racism, economic injustice, opposing but legitimate political points of view), personalization algorithms acquiesce to our own sense of humiliation when confronting a cultural and social taboos. In this way, the personalization of news and personal content distorts both individual and cultural memory, resulting in what one onlooker describes as "humiliated silence," which is a form of forgetting (Connerton 2008, pp. 67–69). In other words, insofar as commercial algorithms cater or pander to our unease and unwillingness to confront difficult emotions, or hold difficult conversations, they may enable a deafening silence about social injustice. As one practitioner of this form of forgetting explains, "few things are more eloquent than a massive silence" (Connerton 2008, p. 68). A collective silence about those who are vulnerable, or victims of violence, is all the more regrettable when propelled by profit-driven algorithms that have so much power to direct public attention.

From a more theological standpoint, we might say that consumer culture is organized against history. It nudges us toward the loss of identity through the abandonment of community traditions that value human relationships over market values. In this context, there is a depreciation of memory and a ridicule of hope. Everything must be held in the now, either an urgent now (e.g., constant news feeds, updates to our Instagram selfies) or an eternal now (e.g., the "mindless mindfulness" or spiritual bypassing of Wisdom 2.0 discussed in Chapter 3). Rather than energizing memories, we are bombarded by algorithmically selected memories that calm and soothe us into complacency.

For Old Testament theologian and author Walter Brueggemann, our contemporary dominant consciousness can be described as the "ethos of consumerism" (2001, p. 1). It parallels the Solomonic royal consciousness and even exceeds its commitment to "achievable satiation" and a "subjective consciousness concerned only with self-satisfaction" (Brueggemann 2001, p. 42). This dominant consciousness denies us the "legitimacy" of any tradition, religious or otherwise, that calls us to reflect on the past and actively cultivate an adaptive memory that enables human flourishing (Brueggemann 2001, p. 43). Such memories, after all, have the potential to dilute one's devotion to the idol of the consumer dollar or to the belief that progress and innovation are always the best ways to solve our greatest problems. "One thing we learn from religious traditions," explains media scholar Quentin J. Schultze, "is the importance of habits of remembering" (Schultze 2002, p. 81) as a source of wisdom to aid our present crises and future movements. And even though our remembrances at times and in unfortunate ways can be "corrupted by nostalgic yearnings, by intentional alternations of history, and simply by faulty memories," they nonetheless provide a proven way of "recalling the virtuous deeds of past generations and thereby being inspired by them again and again" (Schultze 2002, p. 81).

Rabbi Gavriel Goldfeder's discussion of Sabbath in relation to digital media is quite appropriate here:

> The Sabbath spoken about in Jewish tradition is not, simply, a day to step away from the desk. It is a day of resonance with something much bigger than ourselves. It is a day that is not only concerned with my rest, but with the rest of those around me. In the Torah, the Sabbath includes memory. The memory in Deuteronomy demands that I remember slavery—let my brief respite from email and office have more of an effect on me than the simple realization that "the more time I spend away from my work, the better that work will be, most often." Let it remind me of slavery and its evils, and let my rest on that day serve as a portal for inspiration to end slavery not just for myself but for all.
>
> (Goldfeder 2019)

A community rooted in energizing memories and summoned by radical hopes is a curiosity and a threat to commercial culture (Brueggemann 2001, p. 11). The exercises outlined above represent a step toward a renewed sense of agency as digital citizens. They help to recognize the hole in our heart, to remember what matters and to get on with the project of wisdom and flourishing for all.

Conclusion

Beckett's portrayal of the despairing Krapp is a caveat to all those living in a media- and technology-saturated era. We do not want to become like old man Krapp, spiteful and unpleasant as we remember our lives. Yet even now, decades after Beckett's prescient and determined play, we see symptoms of a creeping despair. Like the revived interest in vinyl records and typewriters we discussed in Chapter 5, the up-tick in sales for instant film cameras is symptomatic of the catechism's failure. On some level we intuitively know, individually and collectively, that storage and memory are related but not equivalent. Consumer markets have begun to respond to a latent desire for attention and judgment in the process of memory formation. This is because, as the many examples in this chapter demonstrate, data storage actually works against the grain of adaptive memory since the latter generally wants to forget unless there is good reason to remember.

Theoretically we can "recall" everything with the touch of a button, but that is precisely why we cannot afford to outsource the process of memory formation. We need to be more, not less, involved in the formation of memory, understood properly as a process of contextual judgment. By relying on Google Street View or SixthSense, we are not really outsourcing memory. Instead, we are postponing and outsourcing judgment, for instance, to Facebook's memory algorithms. As one columnist writes:

> In its early days, media pundits hailed Facebook as the social application of the future, and yet what it really does is change our relationship to the past. Facebook makes contact so casual that it allows people to leapfrog back instantly to a former you, one you thought you had left behind—maybe one you had worked hard to put firmly in the past.
>
> (Dominus 2014)

Relentless increases in storage capacity and the ready availability of stored data has become a "burden imposed on memory" and "a problem for society in general" (Connerton 2008, pp. 65–66). Consequently, "genuine skill in conducting one's life may come to reside less and less in knowing how to gather information and more and more in knowing how to discard information" (Connerton 2008, pp. 65–66). Understood as "simplification" or "getting the gist" of something, memory requires the careful execution of judgment and ultimately serves as the foundation of wisdom. "Forgetting" can sometimes be an accident, but often it is an ethical choice. It can make us more human in relation to one another. It helps our stories jive insofar as it helps us tell our story in a way that is dignifying to all of us. Forgetting, as much as remembering, can be a success, an achievement, a virtue. It takes wisdom and judgment to know the difference—two virtues that Krapp could never muster.

References

Barberá, Pablo, John T. Jost, Jonathan Nagler, Joshua A. Tucker, and Richard Bonneau. "Tweeting from Left to Right: Is Online Political Communication More Than an Echo Chamber?" *Psychological Science* 26, no. 10 (October 2015): 1531–42. doi:10.1177/0956797615594620.

Beckett, Samuel. "Krapp's Last Tape." In *I Can't Go On, I'll Go On: A Samuel Beckett Reader*, edited by Richard W. Seaver, 479–99. New York: Grove Press, 1976.

Brueggemann, Walter. *The Prophetic Imagination*. 2nd ed. Minneapolis, MN: Fortress Press, 2001.

Caesar, Stephen. "El Rancho Schools Don't Wait on State, Adopt Ethnic-Studies Curriculum." *The Los Angeles Times*, July 7, 2014. http://www.latimes.com/local/education/la-me-ethnic-studies-20140708-story.html.

The Colbert Report. Episode 771. Directed by Jim Hoskinson. Written by Stephen Colbert. *Comedy Central*, September 21, 2010. http://thecolbertreport.cc.com/videos/tnb3an/eric-schmidt.

———. Episode 1182. Directed by Jim Hoskinson. Written by Stephen Colbert. *Comedy Central*, April 23, 2013. http://thecolbertreport.cc.com/guests/eric-schmidt-2/54pqtc/eric-schmidt.

Connerton, Paul. "Seven Types of Forgetting." *Memory Studies* 1, no. 1 (January 2008): 59–71.

Dominus, Susan. "Can Facebook Be Your Friend?" Real Simple. August 17, 2014. https://www.realsimple.com/work-life/technology/communication-etiquette/facebook-friend.

Draper, Nora A. Personal conversation with Kevin Healey. University of New Hampshire. Durham, NH, May 7, 2019.

Ehrenreich, Barbara. "America to Working Class Whites: Drop Dead!" TomDispatch.com. December 1, 2015. http://www.tomdispatch.com/blog/176075/.

Fisher, Adam. "Google's Road Map to Global Domination." *New York Times*, December 11, 2013. http://www.nytimes.com/2013/12/15/magazine/googles-plan-for-global-domination-dont-ask-why-ask-where.html.

Gaggioli, Andrea. "Cybersightings." *Cyberpsychology, Behavior, and Social Networking* 15, no. 8 (August 2012): 444–45.

Gerber, Nancy, and Katherine Myers-Coffman. "Translation in Arts-Based Research." In *Handbook of Arts-Based Research*, edited by Patricia Leavy, 587–607. New York: Guilford Press, 2018.

Goldfeder, Gavriel. "Shabbat Mindfulness." Unpublished manuscript. 2019. Cited with permission of the author.

Guynn, Jessica. "Privacy Watchdog EPIC Files Complaint against Snapchat with FTC." *The Los Angeles Times*, May 17, 2013. https://www.latimes.com/business/la-xpm-2013-may-17-la-fi-tn-privacy-watchdog-epic-files-complaint-against-snapchat-with-ftc-20130517-story.html.

Healey, Kevin. "Scranton Is Getting Bad." Typishly. April 26, 2018. https://typishly.com/2018/04/26/scranton-is-getting-bad/.

Kirkpatrick, David. *The Facebook Effect: The Inside Story of the Company That Is Connecting the World*. New York: Simon & Schuster, 2010.

Leggo, Carl. "Loving Language: A Poet's Vocation and Vision." In *Arts-based and Contemplative Practices in Research and Teaching*, edited by Susan Walsh, Barbara Bickel, and Carl Leggo, 143–68. New York: Routledge, 2015.

Meyer, Eric. "Inadvertent Algorithmic Cruelty." meyerweb.com. December 24, 2014. http://meyerweb.com/eric/thoughts/2014/12/24/inadvertent-algorithmic-cruelty/.

Meyrowitz, Joshua. "Snowed-in by Surveillance: Technopoly and the Social Reconstruction of Reality." Plenary address at the Fifteenth Annual Convention of Media Ecology Association. Toronto, Ontario, 2014, June 19, 2014.

Mistry, Pranav. "The Thrilling Potential of SixthSense Technology." TEDIndia. November 2009. http://www.ted.com/talks/pranav_mistry_the_thrilling_potential_of_sixthsense_technology/transcript.

Morozov, Evgeny. *To Save Everything, Click Here: The Folly of Technological Solutionism*. New York: Public Affairs, 2013.

Northcote, Graeme, Lauren Rabindranath, and Stephen Trothen. "The Anti-Life Logger: Remapping Memory, Re-membering Meaning." Panel presentation at the Fifteenth Annual Convention of Media Ecology Association. Toronto, Ontario, June 19, 2014.

Olick, Jeffrey K. *The Politics of Regret: On Collective Memory and Historical Responsibility*. New York: Routledge, 2007.

"Overexposed? Camera Phones Could Be Washing Out Our Memories." NPR. May 22, 2014. http://www.npr.org/2014/05/22/314592247/overexposed-camera-phones-could-be-washing-out-our-memories.

Pariser, Eli. *The Filter Bubble: What the Internet Is Hiding from You*. New York: Penguin Press, 2011.

Parker-Pope, Tara. "An Ugly Toll of Technology: Impatience and Forgetfulness." *New York Times*, June 6, 2010. http://www.nytimes.com/2010/06/07/technology/07brainside. Html.

Sandvig, Christian. "What Facebook's 'It's not Our Fault' Study Really Means." *Wired*, May 8, 2015. https://www.wired.com/2015/05/facebook-not-fault-study/.

Schultze, Quentin J. *Habits of the High-Tech Heart: Living Virtuously in the Information Age*. Grand Rapids, MI: Baker Academic, 2002.

Searle, John R. *Philosophy in a New Century: Selected Essays*. New York: Cambridge University Press, 2008.

Siegfried, Tom. "Why Forgetting May Make Your Mind More Efficient." *Knowable Magazine*, January 14, 2019. https://www.knowablemagazine.org/article/mind/2019/why-we-forget.

Stockton, Nick. "Your Brain Doesn't Contain Memories. It Is Memories." *Wired*, July 19, 2017. https://www.wired.com/story/your-brain-is-memories/.

Sturken, Maria. "Facebook Photography and the Demise of Kodak and Polaroid." In *Images, Ethics, Technology*, edited by Sharrona Pearl, 94–110. New York: Routledge, 2015.

Tillich, Paul. "Frontiers." In *The Essential Tillich: An Anthology of the Writings of Paul Tillich*, edited by F. Forrester Church, 239–49. 1966. Reprint ed., Chicago: University of Chicago Press, 1999.

Todorov, Tzvetan. "The Abuses of Memory." *Common Knowledge* 5 (Spring 1996): 6–26.

Tsesis, Alexander. "The Right to Erasure: Privacy, Data Brokers, and the Indefinite Retention of Data. *Wake Forest Law Review* 49 (2014): 443–84.

Tufekci, Zeynep. "What Happens to #Ferguson Affects Ferguson: Net Neutrality, Algorithmic Filtering and Ferguson." The Message. August 14, 2014. https://medium.com/message/ferguson-is-also-a-net-neutrality-issue-6d2f3db51eb0.

PART III

8

HOW TO THINK DIFFERENTLY ABOUT TECH

Corollaries to the Proverbs

In Chapter 1, we argued that the current crisis of digital media is multi-dimensional: it is ideological, psychological, moral, and spiritual. It is *ideological* because it posits as obvious truth some very misleading and misguided notions about technology and tech's relationship to human happiness. It is *psychological* because the devices and platforms we use are, on one hand, powerful extensions of our intellectual capabilities; on the other hand, they are powerful forces that also shape how we think and communicate, and they do so in ways that benefit some people over others. The crisis is *moral* because these ideological and psychological dimensions collude to mask and displace moral responsibility for the problems we face. Finally, it is *spiritual* because the Silicon Valley catechism asks us to treat something (our technology) as sacred and infinite when it is merely finite and of limited value.

Insofar as tech leaders are guilty of idolatry and hubris, we all lose track of our priorities. Ironically, constant connectivity keeps us, as users, disconnected from ourselves. Connectivity will undermine our own agency if it consists primarily in handing over to coders and engineers the keys to judgment and wisdom. The worship of tech undermines the quest for human flourishing, for authentic living, for a life of integrity. All the while, tech elites may seem to get the better end of this deal, living lives of relative economic privilege at the expense of others. To update a quote by Fannie Lou Hamer (1971), who famously argued that "nobody's free until everybody's free," we might say that no one truly flourishes in the digital age until everyone does.

That brings us to the current chapter, in which we begin to connect the dots between the proverbs and their corollaries. If the proverbs say "no" to the catechism (e.g., Information Is Not Wisdom), the corollaries seek a path to which we can say "yes" (e.g., So Inform Wisely). A key theme throughout this book has been the importance of distinguishing private or commercial gain from the public good, or the welfare of all. This distinction is not either/or, but both/and: we embrace both commercial markets and the public good. The former is a powerful tool that can serve the latter. The problem is that, as it stands, our priorities are out of whack.

For the remainder of the book, as we move from saying no to saying yes, we will argue that the path forward is complex and nuanced but achievable nevertheless. It is complex because, as we begin to show in this chapter, the virtues we have discussed in previous chapters overlap considerably. Wisdom requires judgment, for instance, judgment about information, including what information should remain private. Judgment, in turn, requires memory, because remembering means connecting back to values we have claimed to hold dearly. To remember is to connect back to stories we began to tell in the past and that we need to continue telling. Often this means finding gems of insight hidden in the rubble of history's past sins, as Martin Luther King Jr. often did in his speeches and essays (Simpson 2002, p. 127). These are stories about who we truly are individually and collectively—in other words, about our being authentic.

Some philosophers argue that integrity is the highest virtue, and there is much to be gained by seeing it this way. When we remember our deepest commitments, acting judiciously and wisely in relation to them, things begin to fit together not just in our own lives but also across cultures and nations and in harmony with the earth's complex ecological systems. We are only deceiving ourselves when we rewrite history in a way that renders invisible those human beings who suffered to get us to this point, telling misleading stories about things, machines, and bots rather than flesh-and-blood people. Such stories are disingenuous because those who tell them, and ask us to believe them, are ultimately angling to establish their own power even as they keep them hidden behind curtains, like Wizards from a digital Oz.

While fleshing out the corollary to each proverb, this chapter seeks to remember the nearly forgotten role of institutions that have, at least in theory, always aimed to serve the public good: journalism, education, and politics. Such institutions can, if stewarded faithfully, cultivate virtues like wisdom, authenticity, integrity, judgment, and memory.

Information Is Not Wisdom, So Inform Wisely

The grand mission of Google, namely "to organize the world's information and make it universally accessible and useful," is certainly compelling (http://www.google.com/about/company/). The problem is that tech companies tend to imagine the consequences of their work from a naïve and privileged position. In Chapter 3, we defined informationism as "faith in the collection and dissemination of information as a route to social progress and personal happiness" (Schultze 2002, p. 21). The problem with informationism is that it places too much blind trust in technology. It tends toward technological solutionism. It ignores other important human factors, and in doing so it exacerbates pre-existing social problems. This is why critics express such concern when companies like Google assume that good coding is the same as good morals.

If our goal is to create a world where computers flourish in their pursuit of happiness, perhaps we would be on track with informationism. As long as humans are still part of the picture, however, things are much more complicated. It is not enough simply to collect data and make it accessible in some theoretical sense. Not all data are the same. A collection of true statements is data; a collection of false statements is also data. Even if both sets of statements are publicly available, that does not mean everyone has the time or capacities of judgment to compare the two and make a reasonable decision about what to believe. Theoretically, this aspect of the problem is covered by the "universally accessible" part of Google's mission statement. But that mission is a fantasy, at least in the hands of a single, commercial organization. How could one company possibly ensure universal access to information, never mind the capacity for proper judgment about that information? And why would it be appropriate for one company to fulfill that mission?

While Facebook's platform has been a financial success by some measures, it has been a socio-political disaster because it fails to put information into meaningful context that attends to the truth of claims and the sincerity of claim-makers. From a business standpoint, this is not a bug but a feature, because it caters to users' individual preferences. By positioning itself as merely a tech company, and quite specifically not as a media company, Facebook cedes ground to other third-party players who have the capacity to create meaningful but not necessarily truthful contexts. By design, tech companies put the burden of judgment on users, thus avoiding responsibility for the consequences of their success until those consequences pile up, of course, and there is a kind of "Facebook Chernobyl" where the systemic issues can no longer be ignored.

We are beginning to reach such a moment as it becomes clear that the mission of these companies requires the active participation of stakeholders whose values and interests are directly at odds with their business models. Do we want humanity to realize Google's mission collectively? Or Facebook's mission? After all, how could we reject calls for things like connectedness, openness, or accessibility? Explicitly or implicitly, these companies' mission statements claim to espouse the universal virtues we have been exploring throughout this book—that is, wisdom, authenticity, integrity, memory, and judgment. The dirty secret we have aimed to reveal is that realizing such virtues may require a political-economic context in which companies like Google and Facebook no longer exist—at least not in their current form. And there is another dirty secret here: tech leaders know this and are scrambling to respond. The situation has become increasingly clear through the hard work of technology journalists, who have exposed the inner-workings (and inner turmoil) of Silicon Valley elites in the wake of data breaches and electioneering scandals (Solon and Farivar 2019; Bourg and Jacoby 2018).

As a public good, journalism is a potential counter-force to the information ideology of Silicon Valley. Journalists attend to a key question we are raising here: How do we harness the power of information in service of wisdom knowing that wisdom requires not just information, but also judgment, courage, humility, tenacity, persistence, and grit? As we argued in Chapter 6, ethics is more than a simple explication of rules or codes. Rules are good, but they are not good enough. What we need are principles and virtues. While rules are externally imposed, principles and virtues are internally generated (Elliott and Spence 2017, p. 186).

To the extent that journalists aspire to embody such virtues, they serve as "wise watchdogs," holding those in power accountable (Elliott and Spence 2017, p. 187). As "informational agents," journalists commit themselves to the ethical values of truth, accuracy, truthfulness, honesty, reliability, and trustworthiness (Elliott and Spence 2017, p. 184). As a profession, the institution of journalism understands that information seeking must be anchored to a concern for well-being. Information should support the pursuit of happiness (p. 185).

Attending to that overarching goal, journalists have a responsibility to evaluate "the impact of information, including digital information, on the well-being and happiness of citizens" (p. 185), precisely what tech companies have thus far refused to do, or have failed to do well. When it works well, professional journalism serves to enable wisdom. Journalists are charged with the normative values associated with information as information (accuracy, truth) and with information as action (do no harm), and with the responsibility of discerning how to use and disseminate information on behalf of the public good. Commercial markets provide little support for broad-based coordination, and in fact tend to incentivize the privatization of user data within the bounds of "walled gardens" (McChesney 2013, p. 135). Therefore, non-market measures are necessary to support reporting and analysis as public goods and connectivity as a right rather than a privilege (Andrews 2011, p. 67).

Like journalism, education is a public good that, at its best, leverages information and knowledge in service of wisdom. Children who grow up with digital tools are arguably more sophisticated than their elders in terms of visual-spatial intelligence, which digital media are good at cultivating. But that type of intelligence is meaningless without the type of "deep processing" required for "mindful knowledge acquisition, inductive analysis, critical thinking, imagination, and reflection" (Greenfield 2009, pp. 69–71). As we noted in Chapter 3, there is reason to believe that as we spend more time online, we lose our capacity for deep reflection, imagination, and original thought. This is a concern among neuroscientists who study the cognitive impact of multitasking (Tapscott 2009, pp. 108–9). But it is also a concern among business leaders and researchers who study entrepreneurship and innovation (Tse and Esposito 2014). Perhaps this is also why, as we discussed in Chapter 5, many tech leaders prefer to send their children to private schools where access to technology is restricted or forbidden (Weller 2018).

Even as Silicon Valley elites send their kids to tech-free schools, public schools acquiesce to pressures and incentives from tech companies and tech-friendly state legislatures, adopting devices and platforms designed by, or in connection with, companies like Facebook, Google, and Apple. Students at one Brooklyn public school complained bitterly that they were spending far too much time staring at screens after their school adopted the Facebook-designed Summit Learning platform. In November 2018, nearly 100 students walked out of the Secondary School for Journalism in Park Slope to raise awareness about the issue (Edelman 2018).

And so, there is a sense even among students that as the amount of information explodes, we have yet to understand how to inform wisely.

To inform wisely, we need not just knowledge but judgment, courage, and grit. The most effective journalists, teachers, and parents do not just accumulate information and knowledge. They understand what it means in the broader context of our lives. They communicate that meaning in a way that allows others to develop the same capacity—even when the implications are far-reaching and disruptive. To inform wisely is a service, a gift, through which we begin to live well and flourish together.

Transparency Is Not Authenticity, So Strive for Authentic Transparency

"How could anyone be against transparency?" Its benefits "seem so crushingly obvious." So begins Lawrence Lessig's (2009) widely cited essay "Against Transparency," which he penned over ten years ago for *The New Republic*. But transparency, Lessig argues, had become something more than a mere operating principle or ethical guidepost for business and tech development. Instead it had become a movement unto itself, a movement of "naked transparency" by which titillating phrase he meant to suggest immodesty and imprudence. Whether the proliferation of information leads to more efficient markets, more accountable governments, or more honest citizens depends on much that this techno-centric movement failed to consider.

It is all well and good to issue targeted mandates for the release of information, enabling public scrutiny about the ebbs and flows of money between government and industry. But it remains a question whether the depth and quality of scrutiny, and the intentions driving it, can "reveal something real" (Lessig 2009). It is just as likely that public debates would devolve into comparisons of data that are at best not meaningful and at worst downright disingenuous. Picking up this thread nearly ten years later, one critic argues that the proliferation of data and speech will more often than not "become instruments in the production of the very inequalities (economic, political, educational) that the gospel of openness promises to remove" (Fish 2018).

One of our goals in Chapter 4 was to point out the hypocrisy of tech companies that urge users to share more, even as they hide proprietary code and business machinations from public scrutiny. In this context, the catechism's claim that an authentic life depends on full personal transparency rings hollow. In fact, sociologists argue that an individual's control over the relative openness of one's personal boundaries is central to the achievement of autonomy and authenticity (Trepte and Reinecke 2011, p. 62). A similar argument holds in the business realm, in the sense that innovation may require a certain degree of secrecy during early phases of technical development and after an algorithm is deployed. Nevertheless, policy makers "should ensure elemental transparency in such technologies and their general effects on information in ways that do not disclose the proprietary information itself, such as through labelling requirements and media literacy education" (Picard and Pickard 2017, p. 30).

In other words, authenticity actually requires some measure of privacy or hiddenness, whether we are talking about our personal lives, business innovation, or politics. The question here is one of balance: how do we cultivate real intimacy in our personal lives? Genuine competition in the marketplace? True democratic freedom? Put simply, to live authentically requires that we exercise meaningful agency in determining who sees what and when—and by "meaningful," we mean something more than misleading claims about how Facebook, for example, has rolled out more "controls" for users.

By arguing on behalf of "authentic transparency," we are not taking an extreme approach of full informational awareness of all data, by all people, at all times. That radical view is the catechism in a nutshell, at least when its proponents are not being hypocritical. What we mean by authentic transparency is fairness and justice in both personal and collective decision-making about data and information.

There are two main ways that such fairness is undermined under the guise of accountability in commercial digital culture. First, rather than transforming the status quo, companies have capitalized on the public's legitimate concerns about privacy. What we see too often is yet another commercial product or service, packaged and sold to us as a solution, which is actually another way of profiting from customers' personal data. Instead of offering genuine solutions, companies see users' concerns as another market niche to be tapped, turning anxiety into a commodity to be packaged and sold back to them without fundamentally altering the systems that gave rise to those worries in the first place. Nora A. Draper (2019) discusses this issue at length in *The Identity Trade*.

Second, companies like Acxiom, Facebook, and Google have developed tools that ostensibly aim to amplify users' ability to understand and manage their data, but they are designed as much to obfuscate and conceal as to reveal. In their analysis, Draper and Joseph Turow (2019) put the word "transparency" in scare quotes when referring to such tools, underscoring that such initiatives are often disingenuous (pp. 8–9). Companies position these tools as tools of empowerment for users, but they generally "give little insight into the firm's actual practices" and therefore fail to represent "actual transparency" (p. 9). Buttressed by branding campaigns and slick promotional language, these tools are ultimately a kind of architectural or procedural rhetoric designed to cultivate an ethos of "digital resignation" (Draper and Turow 2019, pp. 9–10). Companies benefit when users decide that fighting for a balance of power in the digital economy is not worth the time or effort.

What does is look like, then, to argue for transparency not as an end in itself, but in service of authenticity, if authenticity means more than full exposure? Here the phrase "in service of" intentionally suggests limits and parameters for how, when, why, and to whom to release information. One supporter puts this dilemma in terms of the virtue of honesty, which she believes is "powerfully challenged by the techno-social developments of the last century." Honesty, she argues, "is about the *appropriate and morally expert* communication of information" (Vallor 2016, p. 21, emphasis added). Information and communication technologies have radically altered the landscape in which we decide what is appropriate, and who qualifies as morally expert in such communication. We have yet to create a system of legal regulations, design strategies, business ethics, and social norms where our communication serves the commitments we claim to hold dear: genuine democracy, personal sincerity, and real competition in commercial markets. In part this is because these goals are always in tension with each other. But that does not mean we must toss one or more aside.

As we discussed in Chapter 4, connection and understanding is a key component of authentic relationships. One measure of how well we are leveraging transparency in service of authenticity is whether we can truly say that we are cultivating compassion and empathy by exploring and moving through our deeply held values, biases, and preferences. Being authentic means more than revealing our gut reactions. It takes courage and vulnerability, a willingness to stand in a space of uncertainty about our views. That is unpleasant, which is why social media companies prefer to frame authenticity in more simplistic, self-serving terms like personalization and sharing. It is also why most companies' and governments' policies regarding organizational "transparency" deserve scare quotes: they simply do not reflect a genuine effort to face the kind of sustained scrutiny that might demand substantive change.

On a broader scale, authentic transparency requires a more nuanced understanding of "objectivity" with regard to the truth and the facts of any particular matter. Too often, the norm of objectivity is used as a bludgeon by those in power to maintain the status quo, while silencing voices who wish to tell a different story. This happens when reporters defer to official sources in business or politics, allowing those stakeholders to set the agenda. It happens as well when news reports default to a simplistic he-said, she-said model when covering a contentious issue. This can create a false equivalency between arguments driven merely by self-interest and short-term gain and arguments supported by evidence and long-term planning.

As we discuss the important role of journalists and news reporters here in Chapter 8 and further in Chapter 9, we are indebted to scholars who articulate a more nuanced view of objectivity. Sandra Borden's (2010) application of virtue ethics to journalistic practice, especially her discussion of authenticity, integrity, and epistemic responsibility, is helpful, as is Stephen J. A. Ward's (2005) notion of pragmatic objectivity (pp. 259–316). Similarly, Clifford G. Christians warns that rather than reducing social problems to "financial and administrative problems defined by politicians," we must understand "truth in journalism as authentic disclosure" (Christians 2003, p. 300; 2004, p. 46). As Geert Lovink and Patrice Riemens (2013) argue, journalism involves not simply the collection of facts but their systematic verification and contextualization into "an understandable discourse" (p. 248).

Similar to the quest to inform wisely, in the search for authentic transparency we cannot underestimate the importance of interpretation, meaning, and context. The facts do not always speak for themselves, in part because someone must always decide which facts are important in the first place. Someone is always writing a story. If living authentically means holding the pen while writing the story of your life, then in the digital age authentic transparency is a matter of justice and equity in the telling of our stories as communities and nations as one species among many on this planet. Transparency is authentic when it is more than a one-way street, allowing the powerful to peer into the lives of the less powerful. We might think of authentic transparency as an information-based version of market-based concepts like fair trade or equal exchange: these are ethical frameworks for avoiding exploitation and enabling justice for all stakeholders.

Convergence Is Not Integrity, So Integrate Divergent Elements

In Chapter 5, we talked about how artists strive to maintain their integrity in the face of adversity and even existential threats. They cannot do so alone, however. Scholars, industry leaders, and legislators must be willing to intervene on behalf of policies and institutional reforms that yield greater integrity for systems of creative production. System integrity in this sense consists of coherence between the diverse goal-strivings of artists, industry professionals, and other cultural stakeholders (Emmons 1999, p. 113). Artistic integrity is something we can all aspire too, even if we are not chart-topping artists or musicians. All human beings desire, and are capable of, something akin to artistic expression and creativity. This is a primary point of Ellen Langer's (2005) book *On Becoming an Artist*, which suggests that the point of artistic creation is the process itself, not the outcome. Not whether we sell a gold record, or have a piece of art hung in a gallery, but whether we feel that we have envisioned a life for ourselves and for our fellow human beings; that we are "walking the walk" and "talking the talk" in realizing that vision; that the pieces of our lives fit together; and that we are working toward a world in which different communities of people, of nations, fit together as well.

Recall our discussion of type-writing as a counter-practice in Chapter 5. The reason typewriters have enjoyed a renaissance of sorts is because they are designed to accomplish one task. Initially this form of dedicated practice was simply a measure of technical limitations. Even if a convergence machine could be imagined, inventors had few resources to build one.

Multitasking is an affordance of convergent, digital technologies. But not all affordances are desirable features. Just because you can multi-task does not mean you should, at least not always. When the songwriter John Mayer writes lyrics, he uses a typewriter not because it is faster or more efficient, not because it has more storage capacity, not because it can cross-reference words or ideas, but precisely because it lacks all of those qualities. Paradoxically, the freedom to create, in fact, to realize and embody one's artistic integrity, depends on a willingness and an ability to work within certain limitations insofar as they distill a practice into its essence— into what really matters in the moment of creation. Convergence may be useful in some contexts, but blurring or erasing boundaries between tasks, between social roles, between organizational functions merely for the sake of doing so, or because we have the technical capacity to do so, makes little sense as a general rule. Through simple practices like using a typewriter, we are protecting the integrity of the creative process, and by doing that we cultivate and protect the integrity of the artist.

So how do we translate typewriting as a personal practice into a humane philosophy that can at least supplement, if not replace, Silicon Valley's techno-utopian ideology? What is the sound of a thousand typewriters? Like John Mayer, we do not want the whole web converging on our thoughts. We want space to think. We want time to be a parent, time to be an employee, time for ourselves. From a broader perspective, typewriting is not just a strategy for avoiding distraction. It is a political practice in the sense that it asserts the power of the individual over and against the gatekeeping power of coders, platform developers, and advertisers. As in our discussion of transparency, what is at issue here is a matter of balance of power and of responsibility.

The personal concerns driven by convergence (e.g., the problem of how to integrate our personal and professional lives) are echoed a thousand times over on the collective scale of today's digital economy. If technical convergence merely catalyzes government and corporate surveillance, and thereby increases inequality and social divisions, it cannot be said to enhance the integrity of a democracy. Healthy self-development involves not total transparency (as Mark Zuckerberg would have us believe) but defensive maneuvers of concealment that protect us against impingement from outside threats, virtual or otherwise (Balick 2014, p. 114). The ability of users to assert control over their own data, their own thoughts, their own ideas and conversations is fundamental to our personal integrity, and indeed to the integrity of digitally mediated democracies. As one observer argues, "liberty and prosperity in any state depend on the existence of a wise balance between groups and classes in society, as well as on a wise architecture of power that includes balance/separation of powers" (Craiutu 2017). What we seek is not the elimination of difference, but the celebration of it through integration into a more complex whole.

This is what we mean by coupling the proverb, "convergence is not integrity" with its corollary "integrate diverse elements." Let each thing have its own purpose, let each be what it is, and see how they fit together. Do not just blend everything together. Fit together different things. Complexity is key. Integrity is complex. There are many moving parts. Your body has integrity because its different systems fit together coherently. And within that complex system of systems, each organ does its own thing. Each has its own integrity.

As a framework for applying these ideas on a collective or institutional scale, we point to what Helen Nissenbaum, a professor of information science at Cornell Tech, calls "contextual integrity." As she explains:

> The practice of harvesting information from social networking sites by third-party aggregators as well as by social networking site operators, job recruiters, and employers is morally troubling because it threatens to disrupt the delicate web of relationships that constitute the context of social life, injecting into workplace and business contexts information of the wrong type, under inappropriate transmission principles.

> (Nissenbaum 2010, p. 228)

The principle of contextual integrity underscores a key argument from Chapter 5: our personal and social lives are complex. They cannot, and should not, be reduced or flattened into a particular kind of coherence that primarily serves the interests of business. The principle of contextual integrity is precisely what Zuckerberg profoundly gets wrong when he claims that "having more than one profile for yourself is an example of a lack of integrity" (Kirkpatrick 2010, p. 199). On the contrary: when a company like Facebook insists on collapsing the boundaries that users seek to maintain in their personal and professional lives, Facebook's assertion of its financial interests ultimately violates the integrity both of its users and of the broader economy in which they live and work. Its business model is, in other words, unsustainable in the long run.

In his map of the human life cycle, the psychologist Erik Erikson outlines a final stage usually experienced when individuals have reached their senior years: a stage in which, looking back upon their lives, they experience a sense of integrity, on the one hand, or, on the other hand, a feeling of disgust and despair. In his own words, Erikson defines integrity as "a sense of comradeship with men and women of distant times and of different pursuits, who have created orders and objects and sayings conveying human dignity and love" (1968, p. 139). This vision is a far cry from the machinations of Facebook executives and researchers, who imagine themselves as somehow qualified to perform psychoanalysis "outside the clinic" (Healey and Potter 2018). Arguably, integrity is the highest virtue, that is, a state of being wherein one's personality, one's life narrative, succeeds in "holding in synthesis the virtues of the eight [developmental] stages, hope, will, purpose, competence, fidelity, love, care and wisdom" (Hampden-Turner 1981, p. 135). Integrity is a thoroughly social virtue as well, since it depends "not so much on understanding who one is and what one believes and is committed to, but rather understanding what one's society is and imagining what it could be" (Babbitt 1997, p. 118).

We therefore see the rising ethos of "digital resignation" as symptomatic of a political economy that is lacking in integrity (Draper and Turow 2019). The risk in this scenario is that quite contrary to the catechism, users of digital media will chose to engage in more performative forms of online expression; that is, personal branding of a stereotypical, socially scripted nature (Nissenbaum 2010, p. 230). Put another way, we will become less, not more, authentic.

The problem Big Tech's convergence not merely of gadgets and data but of economic and social power is that it espouses a kind of cultish fanaticism with regard to its techno-centric worldview. But as philosophers of ethics note, "fanatics lack one very important quality" that is "centrally important to integrity: they lack proper respect for the deliberations of others" (Cox et al. 2017). Voluntary initiatives and self-regulation on the part of businesses will not be sufficient to address the crises we face, because companies have little incentive to weigh the public's long-term interests against their own financial ones. We will return to this issue in Chapter 9 when we address structural solutions.

In the digital era, the mere fact of technical convergence, no matter its speed or power, cannot by itself guarantee equity among different groups of stakeholders in the digital economy. Integrity in the digital era requires us to keep some things smaller and slower, and to keep some things separate and distinct even as we piece them together into a bigger picture. To integrate divergent elements means that we understand and respect the dignity of each component within a complex whole.

Processing Is Not Judgment, So Process Judiciously

Let us pick up the idea about self-driving cars that we discussed at some length in Chapter 6. These are products of interest to general consumers as well as to companies like Uber. In Chapter 6, we discussed some ongoing research into the ethics of self-driving cars. For example, the University of Washington's Ryan Calo studies how ride-sharing apps use data collection and algorithmic processing to "channel the behavior of the driver in the direction they want it to go" (Scheiber 2017). Research like Calo's aims to help the public make informed decisions about policy. Such critical investigations are especially important given the difficulty of predicting long-term consequences of new technologies. Research data in experimental ethics certainly contribute significantly to emerging legal frameworks for algorithmically driven software (Bonnefon et al. 2015, p. 8).

Such research also shows that companies intend to do more than simply nudge or coerce the behavior or individual users (whether drivers or riders). Perhaps more importantly, they intend to influence how people think about the implications of their products. They do this in two ways. First, they frame the long-term consequences of their products as easily predictable, universally beneficial, and virtually inevitable. Second, to the extent that others' interests are different from their own, they aim to deprive users and other stakeholders of any meaningful role in predicting and shaping their products' actual consequences. The two strategies go hand-in-hand, and together represent a powerful marketing and branding strategy if not a sustainable long-term strategy for developing tech in the public interest.

The presence of three human capabilities determines the outcome of new technological developments: intention, discernment, and self-control (Toyama 2015, p. 165). Those concepts deserve a longer explication than what we can provide here (see Toyama's book for a full discussion). Suffice it to say that these three elements resonate with the virtue concepts we have outlined in this book, especially wisdom and judgment. Kentaro Toyama's point is that these human capabilities, or virtues, must be in place if new technical developments are to bring about consequences that can meaningfully be called "good." As one tech reporter suggests, when companies design apps to "gamify" drivers' choices, the apps' choice architecture "overrides self-control" (Scheiber 2017). Companies leverage code as a form of procedural rhetoric (a kind of coercive argument embedded in software) in a way that benefits the company while undermining one of the key elements of user or human-centered technical development in the public interest. As ride-sharing companies move toward self-driving vehicles, this problem will take a slightly different form, creating a "moral crumple zone" (Elish 2019). Automobiles have long been designed to include a physical "crumple zone" that protects the driver and passengers in the event of a collision. In the era of automated systems, commercial developers have come up with rhetorical and legal strategies for protecting themselves against liability. "While the crumple zone in a car is meant to protect the human driver," explains one critic, "the moral crumple zone protects the integrity of the technological system, at the expense of the nearest human operator" (p. 41).

Research in other areas of technical development supports the existence and pervasiveness of this problem. Hany Farid, professor of computer science and digital forensics at Dartmouth College, developed software to filter out child pornography despite claims from tech companies that it could not be done. His research shows that when commercial values drive tech development, organizations are often disincentivized from producing technologies that serve the public good. These types of public-good benefits may be neglected or sidelined to the extent that the public acquiesces to the moral catechism of Silicon Valley (Farid 2011).

One reason why users feel cynical, resigned, and even disoriented is that the programing code that underlies our favorite platforms is both persuasive and mysterious. Code compels and coerces behavior but does so in ways that (by design) are unknown to us and unknowable (or at least hidden) by the legal standards of copyright and intellectual property. The ubiquity of code, and its ever-present malleability, creates spaces that are as unstable as the shifting staircases that Harry Potter encounters at Hogwarts. As companies conduct real-time research and modify their algorithms for greater efficiency in an ongoing way, software code is like sand shifting under our virtual feet. When Facebook decided to publicize users' retail purchases, and later re-structured its default privacy settings to nudge users toward more public sharing, users understandably revolted. A class action suit shut down the former program. Disruptions in the built structures of our lives cause a dreaded sense of return to primordial chaos (Eliade [1957] 1987, p. 48).

By coupling the proverb, "processing is not judgment" with the corollary "process judiciously," we mean to highlight the importance of fairness and equity in collective decision-making about the development and deployment of systems driven by algorithmic processing, including emergent forms of artificial intelligence (AI). An important element of media policy in the digital era involves "providing information to ensure that consumers understand algorithms and other automated technological influences on content choice" (Picard and Pickard 2017, p. 10).

We also mean to underscore the risk of technological solutionism mentioned earlier in this chapter. It is tempting to try to solve the problem of algorithmically propagated hate speech and misinformation by implementing a more sophisticated algorithm, a kind of watchdog algorithm to monitor the other algorithms. The potential here to spiral into absurdity is apparent to some executives and engineers. In a discussion about combatting hate speech and propaganda online, Reddit CEO Steve Huffman notes:

A motto we've always had at Reddit is "let humans do the hard part." And so when we're talking about things like classification and setting standards for discourse and policy enforcement, I'm actually a huge proponent of [asking] how do we share that burden with our community? Because the only thing that scales with users is users. And I think we've got a long way to go. When my spellcheck, when autocorrect gets a little better on my phone, then we can start talking about, you know, AI is the solution to all of our problems.

(Brancaccio et al. 2018)

Here again a caveat is in order. As we noted in Chapter 6, sharing responsibility is good but not if it means shifting the blame to avoid accountability. Content moderation (i.e., prudent judgment) by teams of humans (i.e., employees or an assemblage of employees and user-volunteers) is good in principle but not if it is an afterthought intended to plug the hole in a leaking dike. Judgment must be integrated into the very design, development, deployment, use, and regulation of a platform.

Similar problems arise even in areas ostensibly shielded from the pressures of the commercial market where, following Toyama's model, the intention to serve the public interest appears well-established among stakeholders. Consider the case of automated grading of standardized tests in public schools. Utah and Ohio have already implemented automatic grading of standardized tests. Initially, the schools followed Huffman's model of letting humans do the "hard part" by coupling automation with human scorers. But eventually the schools moved to a model of letting computers grade tests and letting the computers decide whether and when to outsource judgment to a human (Smith 2018). Institutional and financial pressures favor automation, and here administrators concluded that the computer systems could be trusted to perform well on the task at hand.

The naiveté of such trust has become apparent as students and critics have tested the limits of such systems. Les Perelman, a research affiliate and former Dean at MIT, is a noted critic of automated grading systems. Perelman developed the satirically named Babel (Basic Automated Essay Language) as a means of demonstrating the absurdity of outsourcing the scoring of written essays to automated systems. His tests show that computer-generated essays that are specifically designed to be meaningless have nevertheless received perfect scores from automated grading systems like e-Rater (used by the Educational Testing Service) (Smith 2018). From a different angle, Orion Taraban, executive director of Stellar GRE (a tutoring company in San Francisco), says when students devote energy to crafting meaningful and aesthetically resonant essays they are essentially casting "pearls before swine" because machines cannot understand or appreciate meaning (Smith 2018). One problem here is that teachers may shift how and what they teach, losing the very essence of the educational process; another is that students may simply learn to write in ways that please or trick the system. For such reasons, groups like the National Council of Teachers of English and Professionals Against Machine Scoring of Student Essays have organized against the use of machine scoring in high-stakes student tests, citing research that shows such methods are a poor substitute for human judgment.

What does is look like to develop practices, policies, or initiatives that prioritize the use of algorithmic processing in service *of* human judgment? One component of a holistic strategy is to update outdated legal and social models that fail to account for network dynamics. One observer points out that "our social and legal models focus on the individual" even though "networks are at the base of data analytics" (Boyd et al. 2014, p. 56). Legal models tend to focus on preventing individual harm, protecting individual rights, and asserting individual control over data. More than this, we need an ethical and legal framework that attends to how data analytics can discriminate based on an individual's position within a network. Social biases are "baked into algorithmic decision-making," in essence. Therefore, "not only must such practices be made legible, but we must also develop legal, social, and ethical models that intentionally account for networks, not just groups and individuals" (Boyd et al. 2014, p. 56).

Notwithstanding Huffman's quip about letting humans "do the hard part," processing judiciously means more than hiring a team of underpaid, inexperienced employees to monitor the social fallout from social media algorithms. To process judiciously requires a certain kind of "tough-mindedness," to recall Martin Luther King Jr.'s (1986, p. 493) discussion of judgment and prejudice from Chapter 6, a willingness to include the concerns of all relevant stakeholders. As we will discuss in Chapter 9, that may mean outsourcing judgment of proprietary algorithms to third-party auditors and policy makers.

Storage Is Not Memory, So Remember the Virtue of Forgetting

In Chapter 7, we began our discussion of memory with Samuel Beckett's one-act play "Krapp's Last Tape," in which we witness an old man suffering through his final days in a state of complete despair and disgust. It is the portrait of an individual who has failed to achieve that final developmental stage of integrity as described by psychologist Erik Erikson. And it is a portrait in which technologies of memory feature prominently. In Chapter 7, we suggested that Krapp's suffering epitomizes theologian Paul Tillich's argument that "an infinity of the finite could be a symbol for hell" ([1966] 1999, p. 248).

The personal hell suffered by Beckett's old man Krapp symbolizes a collective hell that activists and lawmakers rightly seek to avoid as the politics of memory unfolds in the digital era. Issues of personal memory construction are all the more complicated at the level of communities and nations. Cultural memory certainly involves different media forms and images, but it is ultimately a social and institutional process, not merely a technological one. Memory is a defining element of group identity, and as such it is entrusted to specialized professionals like teachers, journalists, and religious leaders who, presumably, are equipped with the requisite tools of discernment and judgment. Like individual memory, though, cultural memory shifts over time, rightfully so, and not without struggle.

Social media platforms have labored to position themselves as powerful gatekeepers of both personal and cultural memory. Facebook's memory architecture (e.g., the inclusion of "Your Memories on Facebook" in News Feed) is problematic insofar as it imposes constructed notions of relevance with little transparency. As one critic notes, "companies like Facebook organize many people's digital memories for the benefit of remote clients who want to manipulate what's put in front of those people" (Lanier 2013, p. 313). The digitization of memory is not a morally neutral process (Healey and Woods 2017). This is not to say that we should reject tech-enabled narrative constructions of identity. But such platforms need to be more flexible and open, since individuals' life stories are social processes that change over time. Digital platforms should reflect a nuanced understanding of memory rather than constructed notions that reflect the interests of commercial gatekeepers.

Two complimentary markets have emerged in recent years, one of which thrives on collecting user data while the other grows by assuaging users' anxiety about data privacy. Platforms like Facebook and Google, along with products like Autographer, Memoto, and SixthSense, aim to collect and store data for users. As the problems related to such data storage have become evident (e.g., employers who scour applicants' social media profiles in search of unsavory behavior), a corresponding industry has developed to leverage users' concerns about privacy and reputation. Reputation management has for years been a burgeoning (if narrow and commercially friendly) sector of the digital memory economy. It is simply easier and cheaper to save data by default rather than develop tools to manage it judiciously (or enable users to do so) (Draper 2019, p. 156). Instead of curating as we go along, we store everything and then manage which aspects of our data are most publicly visible and accessible. A company like Reputation.com, for example, does not just protect and repair identity; it promotes identity in the sense of encouraging users to position their online profiles as brands (Draper 2019, p. 147).

The synergy between social media and reputation management is clear: their business models feed off of, and indeed depend upon, each other. Within this context, online visibility is encouraged, but of a kind that is much easier to navigate for users who fall within the bounds of privilege. Cultural norms tend to flow from, and reinforce, dominant racial and gender identities, so people who belong to a cultural minority are more likely to be seen as transgressing those norms. It is hard to be both authentic and culturally appropriate (key characteristics of a good brand) if, for example, you are an African American (Draper 2019, pp. 147–48). This is why then-candidate Barack Obama was perceived as being "too black" by some white voters in the 2008 U.S. Presidential election (see Zacharias and Arthurs 2008, p. 425). Industrial models of reputation management do not recognize these fine distinctions, and therefore tend to amplify a particular privileged range of identities.

A holistic approach to digital memory rests on a "three-legged stool" where regulation, technology, and cultural norms each serve as a solid support (Draper 2019, p. 218). To some extent, our focus on counter-practices at the end of each of our proverb chapters (Chapters 3–7) addresses the cultural dimension. Practices like poetic transcription and letter-writing serve to aid the personal process of remembering and forgetting, where each means something more than the mere storage and deletion of data. Such practices allow us to practice memory in new ways, fulfilling the call to develop "notions of forgiveness despite the impossibility of forgetting" in the digital era (Wagman 2016, pp. 120–21).

Legislation that compels companies to delete data, or remove it from search results, will likely be imperfect (e.g., the so-called "right to be forgotten" regulations we discuss in Chapter 9). We therefore need robust cultural norms to compliment whatever regulatory measures we put into place. To extend our proverb, if storage is not memory, deleting is not forgetting. Paradoxically, forgetting is often a compassionate form of remembering. It is a kind of forgiveness. As the poet Carl Leggo

(2015) suggests in a clever turn-of-phrase, "my writing is forgetting, *for getting* on with the journey" (p. 158, italics original).

Rabbi Gavriel Goldfeder, a colleague whom we cite in Chapter 7, reminds us that within the Judaic tradition, the Genesis memory includes an awareness of one's social obligations and connectedness to others. "The memory in Deuteronomy demands that I remember slavery," Gavriel notes. In the context of digital media, what this means for Rabbi Goldfeder (2019) is that when we engage in simple, restorative counter-practices, we should do more than let ourselves relax:

> Let my brief respite from email and the office have more of an effect on me than the simple realization that "the more time I spend away from my work, the better that work will be." Let it remind me of slavery and its evils, and let my rest on that day serve as a portal for inspiration to end slavery not just for myself but for all.
>
> (Goldfeder 2019)

To recall our opening statements in this chapter, judgment and wisdom require memory in so far as remembering means connecting back to values we, or our ancestors, have claimed to hold dearly. From the Latin root *memorari*, meaning "be mindful of," to remember means to bring to mind once again that which truly matters, because that is what carries us forward together. The corollary injunction to "remember the virtue of forgetting" is intentionally twofold. First, it is: knowing when and what to remember, and second, when and what to forget, which is a key measure of wisdom and prudent judgment.

Conclusion

The corollaries are a strategy for restoring a balance that has been lost or distorted as digital technologies have disrupted traditional patterns of social and moral gate-keeping. They point to public-good institutions like government by consent, news reporting in the public interest, and education for all. The catechism is ultimately a rhetorical strategy for consolidating public trust in the new digital gatekeepers and undermining trust in public-good institutions.

The integrity of democracy itself is at stake. As we demonstrated in Chapter 5, technical convergence is a way of consolidating corporate and economic power. The logic of the market is toward economic consolidation, which means oligopoly if not monopoly. But monopoly control is not the same as integrity. It is quite the opposite. As we noted in the Chapter 2, Adam Smith knew this very well when, in the revolutionary year of 1776, he penned *The Wealth of Nations*, the foundational text of modern capitalist economics. Chapter 9 will outline some specific strategies for keeping the power of today's digital gatekeepers in check and for revitalizing these public-interest institutions.

We live in an era where moral risk-taking is a necessity. Being courageous means becoming vulnerable. Disruption without risk and vulnerability is just hubris and recklessness. On the path to integrity, the tiny moral bubbles of Silicon Valley must burst. To the extent that our strategies embrace a holistic commitment to both personal and civic mindfulness, the emerging digital economy may yet fulfill what one scholar describes as the primary goal of every economic system, namely "to promote widespread and sustainable human flourishing" (Loy 2013, p. 420).

References

Andrews, Lori. *I Know Who You Are and I Saw What You Did: Social Networks and the Death of Privacy*. New York: Free Press, 2011.

Babbitt, Susan E. "Personal Integrity, Politics, and Moral Imagination." In *A Question of Values: New Canadian Perspectives on Ethics and Political Philosophy*, edited by Samantha Brennan, Tracy Isaacs, and Michael Milde, 107–31. Atlanta, GA: Rodopi, 1997.

Balick, Aaron. *The Psychodynamics of Social Networking*. London: Karnac Books, 2014.

Bonnefon, Jean-François, Azim Shariff, and Iyad Rahwan. "Autonomous Vehicles Need Experimental Ethics: Are We Ready for Utilitarian Cars?" ArXiv.org. October 13, 2015. http://arxiv.org/pdf/1510.03346v1.pdf.

Borden, Sandra. *Journalism as Practice: MacIntyre, Virtue Ethics and the Press*. New York: Routledge, 2010.

Bourg, Anya, and James Jacoby [producers]. *The Facebook Dilemma*. Boston, MA: WGBH Educational Foundation, 2018.

Boyd, Danah, Karen Levy, and Alice Marwick. "The Networked Nature of Algorithmic Discrimination." Open Technology Institute, Washington, DC. October 2014, 53–57.

Brancaccio, David, Ali Oshinskie, and Danielle Chiriguayo. "The CEO of Reddit: 'We Are Not the Thought Police . . . But We Do Care about How You Behave.'" Marketplace. July 2, 2018. https://www.marketplace.org/2018/07/02/business/ceo-reddit-we-are-not-thought-police-we-don-t-want-control-what-you-believe-we.

Christians, Clifford G. "Cross-Cultural Ethics and Truth." In *Mediating Media: Studies in Media, Religion and Culture*, edited by Jolyon P. Mitchell and Sophia Marriage, 293–303. Edinburgh: T. & T. Clark, 2003.

———. "The Changing News Paradigm: From Objectivity to Interpretive Sufficiency." In *Qualitative Research in Journalism: Taking It to the Streets*, edited by Sharon Hartin Iorio, 41–56. Mahwah, NJ: Lawrence Erlbaum, 2004.

Cox, Damian, Marguerite La Caze, and Michael Levine. "Integrity." *The Stanford Encyclopedia of Philosophy*, Spring 2017 edition, edited by Edward N. Zalta. https://plato.stanford.edu/archives/spr2017/entries/integrity/.

Craiutu, Aurelian. "Moderation May Be the Most Challenging and Rewarding Virtue." Aeon. July 17, 2017. https://aeon.co/ideas/moderation-may-be-the-most-challenging-and-rewarding-virtue.

Draper, Nora A. *The Identity Trade: Selling Privacy and Reputation Online*. New York: New York University Press, 2019.

Draper, Nora A., and Joseph Turow. "The Corporate Cultivation of Digital Resignation." *New Media & Society* 21 (2019): 1824–39.

Edelman, Susan. "Brooklyn Students Hold Walkout in Protest of Facebook-Designed Online Program." *New York Post*, November 10, 2018. https://nypost.com/2018/11/10/brooklyn-students-hold-walkout-in-protest-of-facebook-designed-online-program/.

Eliade, Mircea. *The Sacred and the Profane: The Nature of Religion*. 1957. Reprint ed., New York: Harcourt, 1987.

Elish, Madeleine Clare. "Moral Crumple Zones: Cautionary Tales in Human-Robot Interaction." *Engaging Science, Technology, and Society* 5 (2019): 40–60.

Elliott, Deni, and Edward H. Spence. *Ethics for a Digital Era*. Hoboken, NJ: John Wiley & Sons, 2017.

Emmons, Robert A. *The Psychology of Ultimate Concerns: Motivation and Spirituality in Personality*. New York: The Guilford Press, 1999.

Erikson, Erik. *Identity: Youth and Crisis*. New York: W.W. Norton, 1968.

Farid, Hany. "Automating the Hunt for Child Pornographers." *New Scientist*, April 6, 2011. https://www.newscientist.com/article/mg21028075-000-automating-the-hunt-for-child-pornographers/.

Fish, Stanley. "'Transparency' Is the Mother of Fake News." *New York Times*, May 7, 2018. https://www.nytimes.com/2018/05/07/opinion/transparency-fake-news.html.

Goldfeder, Gavriel. "Shabbat Mindfulness." 2019. Unpublished manuscript. Cited with permission of the author.

Greenfield, Patricia. "Technology and Informal Education: What Is Taught, What Is Learned." *Science* 323 (January 2, 2009): 69–71. DOI: 10.1126/science.1167190.

Hamer, Fannie Lou. "Nobody's Free Until Everybody's Free." In *The Speeches of Fannie Lou Hamer: To Tell It Like It Is*, edited by Maegan Parker Brooks and Davis W. Houck, 134–39. Jackson, MI: University Press of Mississippi, 2010.

Hampden-Turner, Charles. "Generativity and the Life-Cycle: Erik Erikson's Concept of Identity." In *Maps of the Mind: Charts and Concepts of the Mind and Its Labyrinths*, edited by Charles Hampden-Turner, 132–35. New York: Collier Books, 1981.

Healey, Kevin, and Robert H. Woods Jr. "Processing Is Not Judgment, Storage Is Not Memory: A Critique of Silicon Valley's Moral Catechism." *Journal of Media Ethics* 32, no. 1 (2017): 2–15.

Healey, Kevin, and Richard Potter. "Coding the Privileged Self: Facebook and the Ethics of Psychoanalysis 'Outside the Clinic.'" *Journal of Television and New Media* 19, no. 7 (2018): 660–76. https://doi.org/10.1177/1527476417745152.

King, Martin Luther, Jr. "Love, Law, and Civil Disobedience." In *A Testament of Hope: The Essential Writings of Martin Luther King, Jr.*, edited by James M. Washington, 43–53. San Francisco: Harper & Row, 1986.

Kirkpatrick, David. *The Facebook Effect: The Inside Story of the Company That Is Connecting the World*. New York: Simon & Schuster, 2010.

Langer, Ellen. *On Becoming an Artist: Reinventing Yourself through Mindful Creativity*. New York: Ballantine Books, 2005.

Lanier, Jaron. *Who Owns the Future?* New York: Simon and Schuster, 2013.

Leggo, Carl. "Loving Language: A Poet's Vocation and Vision." In *Arts-based and Contemplative Practices in Research and Teaching*, edited by Susan Walsh, Barbara Bickel, and Carl Leggo, 143–68. New York: Routledge, 2015.

Lessig, Lawrence. "Against Transparency." *The New Republic*, October 9, 2009. https://newrepublic.com/article/70097/against-transparency.

Lovink, Geert, and Patrice Riemens. "Twelve Theses on WikiLeaks." In *Beyond WikiLeaks: Implications for the Future of Communications, Journalism and Society*, edited by Benedetta Brevini, Aren Hintz, and Patrick McCurdy, 245–53. New York: Palgrave Macmillan, 2013.

Loy, David R. "Why Buddhism and the West Need Each Other: On the Interdependence of Personal and Social Transformation." *Journal of Buddhist Ethics* 20 (2013): 401–21.

McChesney, Robert. *Digital Disconnect: How Capitalism Is Turning the Internet against Democracy*. New York: The New Press, 2013.

Nissenbaum, Helen. *Privacy in Context: Technology, Policy, and the Integrity of Social Life*. Stanford, CA: Stanford University Press, 2010.

Picard, Robert G., and Victor Pickard. "Essential Principles for Contemporary Media and Communications Policy," 1–48. Oxford: Reuters Institute for the Study of Journalism, 2017.

Scheiber, Noam. "How Uber Uses Psychological Tricks to Push Its Drivers' Buttons." *New York Times*, April 2, 2017. https://www.nytimes.com/interactive/2017/04/02/technology/uber-drivers-psychological-tricks.html.

Schultze, Quentin J. *Habits of the High-Tech Heart: Living Virtuously in the Information Age*. Grand Rapids, MI: Baker Academic, 2004.

Simpson, Gary. *Critical Social Theory: Prophetic Reason, Civil Society, and Christian Imagination*. Minneapolis, MN: Fortress Press, 2002.

Smith, Tovia. "More States Opting to 'Robo-Grade' Student Essays by Computer." NPR, Weekend Edition Saturday. June 30, 2018. https://www.npr.org/2018/06/30/624373367/more-states-opting-to-robo-grade-student-essays-by-computer.

Solon, Olivia, and Cyrus Farivar. "Mark Zuckerberg Leveraged Facebook User Data to Fight Rivals and Help Friends, Leaked Documents Show." NBC News. April 16, 2019. https://www.nbcnews.com/tech/social-media/mark-zuckerberg-leveraged-facebook-user-data-fight-rivals-help-friends-n994706.

Tapscott, Don. *Grown Up Digital: How the Net Generation Is Changing Your World*. New York: McGraw Hill, 2009.

Tillich, Paul. "Frontiers." In *The Essential Tillich*, edited by F. Forrester Church, 239–49. 1966. Reprint ed., Chicago: University of Chicago Press, 1999.

Toyama, Kentaro. *Geek Heresy: Rescuing Social Change from the Cult of Technology*. New York: PublicAffairs, 2015.

Trepte, Sabine, and Leonard Reinecke. "The Social Web as a Shelter for Privacy and Authentic Living." In *Privacy Online: Perspectives on Privacy and Self-Disclosure in the Social Web*, edited by Sabine Trepte and Leonard Reinecke, 61–73. New York: Springer, 2011.

Tse, Terence, and Mark Esposito. "Want More Innovation Driven Entrepreneurship? Go Low-Tech. *European Business Review*, January 20, 2014, 45–47.

Vallor, Shannon. *Technology and the Virtues: A Philosophical Guide to a Future Worth Wanting*. New York: Oxford University Press, 2016.

Wagman, Ira. "Forgiving without Forgetting: Contending with Digital Memory." In *Image, Ethics, Technology*, edited by Sharrona Pearl, 111–25. New York: Routledge, 2016.

Ward, Stephen J. A. *The Invention of Journalism Ethics: The Path to Objectivity and Beyond*. Montreal: McGill-Queen's University Press, 2005.

Weller, Chris. "Silicon Valley Parents Are Raising Their Kids Tech-free—and It Should Be a Red Flag." *Business Insider*, February 18, 2018. https://www.businessinsider.com/silicon-valley-parents-raising-their-kids-tech-free-red-flag-2018-2.

Zacharias, Usha, and Jane Arthurs. "Introduction: Race versus Gender? The Framing of the Barack Obama–Hillary Clinton Battle." *Journal of Feminist Media Studies* 8, no. 4 (2008): 425–33.

9

PROPHETIC IMAGINATION AND INSTITUTIONAL CHANGE

On an infrequent visit to the nearby shopping mall, we came across a backlit billboard featuring a public service ad from the Ad Council's *Discover the Forest* campaign. The ad depicts two images: one of a young boy sitting cross-legged while staring at a hand-held screen and the other of the same boy sitting in a forest, intently studying a fern that he holds in his hands. The caption reads simply, "Unplug."

Not surprisingly, this seemingly rare message imploring children to step away from networked screens and into the natural environment was funded not by Silicon Valley but by a non-profit public interest organization. As we have shown throughout this book, big tech marketing and other commercial content touts the benign, if not salvific, powers of connectivity. In natural settings like a forest, then, solitude becomes paradoxical as one becomes comfortable enough in one's aloneness to realize the commanding presence of life—even something as small as a fern—that surrounds us. We believe we are alone amid the trees until we realize the imposing presence of the trees themselves. As Jewish theologian Martin Buber (1958) describes, in such moments the "it" becomes a "Thou": "It can, however, also come about, if I have both will and grace, that in considering the tree I become bound up in relation to it. The tree is now no longer *it*. I have been seized by the power of exclusiveness" (p. 7).

To be seized in this, this way requires that we extricate ourselves, at least for a time, from the pressing demands of networked devices. This explains some recent, eloquent calls for a return to the institution of the Sabbath, that is, the intentional respite from both commerce and state power. On the Sabbath, "the practical benefits of technology are laid aside, and one tries to stand in the cycle of natural time, without manipulation or interference" (Fishbane 2008, p. xi). It is the kind of practice that may serve not merely as a stress reliever but also as a form of political and social resistance (Brueggemann 2014; Levy 2006).

As tech leaders exhibit pride and reckless hubris, users increasingly feel "digital resignation" (Draper and Turow 2019, pp. 9–10). It is this kind of disposition, this cynical malaise, that so often keeps users from recognizing the fern among the forest, as the case may be, or resisting the catechism. Companies actively cultivate this disposition. By placating users' concerns, diverting their attention, using confusing or reassuring jargon, or deliberately misnaming technical features, companies engage in an effective strategy that "prevents individual frustration from being transformed into collective anger that might encourage institutional change" (Draper and Turow 2019, p. 11). The average user becomes comfortably numb to the possibility of real structural change that might affect him or her on a daily basis. Consumer-oriented measures like increasing users' awareness of data privacy issues, or providing new "tools" or "controls," tend to deepen attitudes of resignation or numbness (p. 11). By shifting responsibility and placing the burden on individual users when it comes to changing the status quo, such "solutions" actually become part of the problem.

As Old Testament theologian and author Walter Brueggemann explains, "The task of prophetic imagination is to cut through the numbness, to penetrate the self-deception" (2001, p. 45). One who speaks in the prophetic mode does not take for granted an already-scripted vision (read: the catechism) and ask how to implement it. If a new vision is to emerge, imagination must come first. Silicon Valley's "royal consciousness" prioritizes implementation including a set of changes to one's privacy settings, or a new set of plug-ins or tools that one can download and install because in a culture of royal consciousness "imagination is a danger." This, Brueggemann says, "is why every totalitarian regime is frightened of the artist." Prophetic imagination is also "poetic imagination." He continues: "It is the vocation of the prophet to keep alive the ministry of imagination, to keep on conjuring and proposing alternative futures to the single one the king wants to urge as the only thinkable one" (Brueggemann 2001, p. 40).

As noted in this book's Introduction, we can find parallels to this Judeo-Christian framework in a Buddhist context. In his discussion of Thich Nhat Hanh, for example, Strain (2014) emphasizes the importance of practice. Buddhist ethics are not about following rules or moral algorithms to make incremental, stepwise progress toward a goal. The process and the practice of virtue is, in itself, the point. Nhat Hanh calls this "being peace" (2005, pp. 13–18). Along the same lines Arthur Zajonc (2010), Director of the Center for Contemplative Mind in Society, argues that the goal of mindfulness meditation is to create an orientation to the world "that is not imprisoned or distorted by mental habits or emotional desires. When free of these, we are opened to a richer exploration to reality that presents to us new insights into self and world" (p. 153). The upshot here is that contemplative practices, though anchored in the individual, have social and political implications. Mindfulness practices can help individual citizens understand their long-term self-interest so as to avoid the mistaken assumptions that led to the recent economic collapse (Bush 2011, p. 195).

Moving from Personal Frustration to Civic Mindfulness

The types of counter-practices we have described create an opening to imagine new ways of engaging with digital media that engineers had not intended. Moving forward, this productive interaction between individual practice and collective action is essential. We are arguing for a dual approach that includes both personal counter-practices as well as collective action through policy initiatives and structural reform. The first without the second can devolve into "spiritual bypassing" of the kind we describe in Chapter 3. On the other hand, the second without the first tends to produce pseudo-solutions that leave the status quo unchallenged. Practices, even counter-practices of the type we are recommending, are not enough on their own. But collective action, especially as typically conceived (i.e., institutional reform, policy measures, etc.) needs to be informed by practice. Practice puts us on top of the world, where we become humble in ways that Red Bull and stuntman Felix Baumgartener are not (see Chapter 1). And yet, we must take action. We must leap. Just like Felix.

In this current chapter, we argue that individual and collective solutions can, and must, go hand in hand. Throughout this book, we have outlined specific counter-practices for each tenet of Silicon Valley's moral catechism: from contemplative reading exercises to type-writing and poetic transcription. What makes these practices different is that they are not merely designed to placate or deflect users' feelings of concern and cynicism. They do not simply prescribe a recipe (i.e., an algorithm) for a changing one's privacy settings. They are designed instead to cultivate prophetic imagination.

In the sections that follow, we will flesh out the remaining aspects of a tri-part strategy for holistic reform involving technological, regulatory, and cultural dimensions. We will think about these dimensions in terms of initiatives emerging in industry, in politics, and in civic organizations. These dimensions overlap, of course, and we will highlight some of their connections. What we have seen throughout this book is that virtues (wisdom, authenticity, integrity, judgment, and memory) overlap. They are not mutually exclusive and cannot be defined separately. They hold together as a web of values. It is no longer possible to make a clear distinction between the tech industry and journalism. We are aware of this situation, and in fact the problems arising from this blurring of boundaries is one of the issues we address. By discussing industry and journalism separately, we do not mean to ignore or neglect this development. Our argument is that we must regain some distinction between the two in order to preserve the integrity of each.

Suffice it to say that, if our prior chapters concluded with personal, contemplative counter-practices, here we argue that the application of such micro-level principles (attention, compassion, discernment) on an institutional level is necessary if we wish to move toward what we have called *civic mindfulness*, defined as the presence of institutional and cultural systems that cultivate and sustain collective attention toward, and responsiveness to, the structural sources of suffering in the body politic. Civic mindfulness describes a set of "principles and practices aimed at addressing stress in the body politic, including abuses of power and breaches of the public trust" (Healey 2013). Such systems, aimed at facilitating the recognition of digital capitalism's shadow-side, would provide robust affordances for quality investigative journalism, corporate and political whistleblowing, and grassroots activism.

Business and Commerce

For years the tech companies like Google have been "searching for integrity" with regard to their social and political responsibilities (Healey 2013). In this section, we wish to move beyond the narrow focus of media ethics research, which tends to focus on the behavior of individuals while neglecting questions of collective responsibility. Specifically, we wish to avoid a kind of Trojan horse argument of the type articulated by Google's Chade-Meng Tan. With regard to corporate mindfulness programs like Google's Search Inside Yourself, proponents like Tan often claim that therapeutic mindfulness programs can generate transformative change within dysfunctional systems (see Ng 2016, pp. 10–11). On the contrary, because of their individualist focus such programs strip contemplative practices of the ethical components that might otherwise address the systemic causes of human suffering (Forbes 2019, pp. 58–60). Along these lines, we have argued that tech executives who espouse the benefits of such corporate mindfulness programs should aim to develop platforms, devices, and services that enhance mindfulness among users as well, while catalyzing an ethos of civic mindfulness in the body politic as a whole (Healey 2015, p. 963).

To some extent, technology executives have begun to demonstrate concern for the integrity of their organizations by attending to the cognitive and socioeconomic impact of their products, and not merely to their financial bottom line. This is evident in the industry's move away from corporate social responsibility (CSR) campaigns that often enhance brand image while neglecting the root causes of social problems in favor of so-called "social innovation" campaigns. Scholars rightly critique the former, arguing that CSR programs like Bono's Red campaign often enhance brand image while neglecting the root causes of social problems. The latter, by contrast, seeks to ensure that an organization's business practices enhance the well-being of local communities as well as the sustainability of the broader global economy (Einstein 2012). These are steps in the right direction.

The pursuit of a more sustainable digital economy has become a central concern for many former Silicon Valley entrepreneurs. Jaron Lanier, a tech pioneer whom we have cited throughout this book, issued a call for such humane design roughly eight years ago. In his quirky yet deeply insightful book *You Are Not a Gadget* (2011), Lanier argued that as we face the rising tide of digital data, we humans should insist on remaining human. This means protecting ourselves against the pressure to think the way social media platforms want us to think. In the face of smart machines and artificial intelligence, we should struggle to remain authentically human, or analogue beings in a digital world. An early pioneer of virtual reality (VR) and still an active computer scientist (working most recently for Microsoft Research), Lanier is no enemy of tech. But his book was a prophetic plea for balance in an imbalanced digital economy.

It is heartening that former code engineers and corporate executives have begun to heed Lanier's prophetic call. Some of the original, pioneering employees from companies like Facebook, Google, and Apple have issued calls for a restoration of balance of the kind we are suggesting here. Tristan Harris, a former design ethicist at Google, announced the formation of a coalition called the Center for Humane Technology (CHT) (Lapowsky 2018). Among other concerns, the coalition focuses on the link between technology, addiction, and depression, with a special concern for the protection of children, as well as the appearance of rips and tears in our social fabric (Bowles 2018). Harris's group highlights important legislative initiatives, including policies that fund research on technology's impact on children and laws requiring the explicit identification of online bots. Other initiatives like All Tech is Human (2019) provide similar pathways to sustainable tech design. This overarching philosophy, newly emerging, goes by various names. CHT (2019) calls it "humane design" which, according to its website, "requires that we understand our most vulnerable human instincts so we can design compassionately to protect them from abuse."

We are not arguing that it is necessary or desirable to abandon commercial markets. As powerful tools for technical development, commercial markets have drastically reduced the costs of VR hardware for use by researchers and non-commercial developers. Rather than abandoning or cynically denouncing markets in sweeping terms, our argument is that bringing greater integrity to the digital economy requires ensuring that its commercial and non-commercial sectors work symbiotically in service of the public good.

It is possible, we believe, to construct platforms differently and in a way that understands, on the most basic level, that the human self "isn't a thing or an entity; it's a process" (Thompson 2015, p. 323). To borrow from a Buddhist author, this would mean building platforms such that "the subject of experience still exists but is no longer deluded about its nature" (Thompson 2015, p. 324). Technologies that avoid fixation on self-image, instead creating opportunities to disengage from the process of identification with the content of one's stream of thought, may allow users to move beyond "mind wandering" to "mindfulness" (Thompson 2015, pp. 349–55).

Such pronouncements may sound lofty, but there is already concrete evidence for the benefits of humane design in the development of virtual reality and augmented reality (AR), environments that attend to the somatic and kinesthetic dimensions of human perception. It has long been clear that users' awareness of their own body in physical space provides a fundamentally different sense of self-awareness and reflectiveness (Heim 1998, p. 100) and, apropos our gesture toward Buddhist mindfulness practice here, participants have reported memorable liminal experiences, comparable to meditative states, that challenge ordinary perceptual categories (Purser 2001, p. 225). On a more pragmatic note, medical researchers have more recently developed VR spaces to address autism-related anxiety (Maskey et al. 2014). One space called the Blue Room helps patients confront daily anxieties such as shopping or crossing bridges. Conventional therapy involves the use of imagination, a facility with which most with autism have trouble. VR in this context helps to catalyze the therapeutic process.

We see great potential in harnessing the immersive power of VR environments to enable somatic learning, which facilitates the development of critical-reflective capabilities: key components of what we have referred to in this book as the prophetic imagination. Somatic models of learning (storytelling, reflective dialogue, dance, theater) enable "new ways of thinking and acting" (Rigg 2016, p. 2). Engagement with the body and the affective-emotional dimensions of thought enables engagement with the shadow aspects of consciousness. Cave Automatic Virtual Environments (CAVE) that facilitate real-time communication between participants in a shared space can extend these somatic and affective benefits. Amar Bakshi's portal project, which uses virtual telepresence technology to encourage cross-cultural dialogue, is exemplary in this regard (Kravarik and Elam 2017). These experiments are a far cry from the over-the-eyes types of VR headsets (commonly known as the "falcon-hood" design) that currently dominate the consumer VR market, including Google Cardboard, HTC Vive, and Oculus Rift. Mixed-reality AR platforms and devices, including, for example, the Microsoft HaloLens, may be better for maintaining users' awareness of immediate surroundings, although currently these hardware designs are more expensive than full-surround headsets such as HTC Vive. Such cost and design limitations will likely become obsolete in the coming years.

In our discussion of authentic transparency in Chapter 8, it is worth noting that most platform architectures consist of proprietary coding that is opaque to users and other developers, and for this reason many researchers (especially those specializing in data-visualization applications) have found it useful to pair commercially available products like HTC Vive with open source development platforms like Unity. Beyond the research lab, limitations posed by closed-code environments have prompted a backlash among hackers. For example, just as Facebook has begun to explore VR technologies with its acquisition of Oculus Rift, an open-source alternative to Facebook called Minds drew support from activists and citizen journalists for its use of encryption, its emphasis on user privacy, and its use of what *Business Insider* calls a "de-mystified algorithm" (Weissman 2015). When Microsoft decided to open some of its code for the Kinect to hackers in 2013, it set a precedent underscoring the potential benefits of open-source models. Regulation may be necessary to nudge industry players toward more open platforms, as well as toward a broader commitment to interconnectivity and interoperability (Picard and Pickard 2017, pp. 20–21).

Humane design depends, of course, on the humans who populate the headquarters and local offices of tech companies, which are populations often distinctly lacking in diversity. Companies like Google have admitted to the lack of diversity among their employees, which skews toward young white men (McGregor 2014). The age bias in Silicon Valley is so acute that the region has become "a hotbed for male plastic surgery" as potential job applicants strive to appear younger and therefore, according to the common prejudice, more innovative and creative (Tiku 2014).

This prejudice has, from time to time, backfired spectacularly, as when Groupon's former CEO Andrew Mason (who was thirty-two years old at the time) was fired after what *Time* magazine described as "a tumultuous tenure pockmarked by accounting gaffes, sophomoric stunts and a whopping 77% decline in the company's share price" (Gustin 2013). After his firing, Mason recalled the culture of youth and inexperience from which he had graduated: "I managed over 12,000 people at

Groupon, most under the age of 25. One thing that surprised me was that many would arrive at orientation with minimal understanding of basic business wisdom" (Constine 2013). For such reasons, Wall Street investors have begun to shy away from companies whose chief executives are under thirty and have little experience in the areas where their company aims to specialize.

Moreover, the commonplace assumption that younger workers are more innovative is simply not supported by evidence. A transnational *Harvard Business Review* study shows that companies with greater diversity of all kinds, including national origin, gender, age, and education, are more innovative and more productive (Lorenzo and Reeves 2018). The study's authors conclude that diversity in pure numbers needs to be coupled with certain "enabling practices," which includes, for example, "a non-hostile work environment, an inclusive culture, and a culture where diverse ideas resulting from a diversity of backgrounds are free to compete" (Lorenzo and Reeves 2018). In this vein, local coding boot camps have emerged in places like Austin, Texas, to support women, African Americans, and other minorities toward the overarching goal of "creating access to technology education and resources for people who might not have had access otherwise" (Groetzinger 2017). In San Francisco, the non-profit group Code2040 similarly aims to "dismantle the structural barriers that prevent the full participation and leadership of Black and Latinx technologists in the innovation economy" (Code2040 2019).

Other initiatives focus not just on breaking into the industry as it exists but transforming the very structure of the industry itself. Tellingly, the type-writer event we described in Chapter 5 was hosted by As We Dwell, a co-working space in Los Angeles which encourages collaboration between small business owners, independent professionals, and entrepreneurs. Co-working between small businesses is a refreshing counter-point to the dynamics of digital capitalism, where technical convergence is accompanied by economic convergence. A small number of powerful companies like Amazon, Facebook, and Google have transformed an otherwise competitive marketplace into a near-oligopoly. Similar dynamics hold in the wireless telecommunications market. In the United States, many workers cannot afford smartphones due to the steep prices arising from the near-duopoly status of AT&T and Verizon (McChesney 2013, p. 112). The market is not diverse enough. Big-name players have enough disproportionate power to squash smaller competitors. In the long run, this serves only the interests of those major players but does not serve the interests of the economy as a whole. By cozying up with legislators, established digital powerhouses have undermined the possibility of genuinely free competition, which is the very thing that most pro-business legislators claim to care about in the first place. We understand this as a lack of integrity in the market.

Arguably, the integrity of the marketplace depends on initiatives like As We Dwell, without which the unique contributions of non-profits and small-scale businesses may get blended beyond recognition into a corporate soup. Sarah Jung, a founder of As We Dwell, sees her co-working space as part of a broader movement that "promotes authentic and intentional community building" ("Meet Sarah Jung" 2017). That is a small-scale start on the path to more far-reaching initiatives. Further along the path, we may consider the increasing importance of platform cooperatives (co-ops), which advocates like Cory Doctorow (2019) posit as a potential means of disrupting the corporate status quo.

Other alternative organizational structures such as the low-profit limited liability company (L3C) in the United States, the community interest company (CIC) in Britain, and various worker-owned cooperative models in the United States and abroad are aimed at enhancing workplace democracy and the promotion of the public good. The worker-owned Mondragón Cooperative Corporation in Spain, which produces computer chips and other high-tech machinery, is exemplary in terms of its size and productivity. Other industry initiatives such as Vendor Relationship Management (VRM), Customer Commons, and the Identity Commons project aim to move beyond proprietary approaches to user data exploitation toward models that prioritize user ownership and management of personal data.

Politics

To some extent we have covered politics in previous chapters. And the Ad Council, mentioned in this chapter's opening anecdote, often receives funding from the federal government for campaigns intended to raise awareness about public interest issues, including healthy tech-use habits. At the 2018 SXSW conference, the Ad Council's Anastasia Goodstein (2018) argued for a sustained conversation about ethics in digital technology, a subject of frequent blog posts at the organization's website. Other overlapping issues related to public health, such as the 2018 "Seize the Awkward" suicide awareness and prevention campaign, featured charitable donations from tech companies like Tumblr, Reddit, and Twitch.

Our broader point in highlighting the Ad Council is to underscore the potential benefits of state governmental support for public media. This umbrella includes national organizations like National Public Radio (NPR), American Public Media (APM), Public Radio International (PRI), and the Public Broadcasting Service (PBS) as well as locally based public media initiatives like the many Independent Media Centers whose constituents have formed in places like Urbana, Illinois, or larger organizations like Pacifica Radio in New York City.

These types of local, regional, publicly funded, and/or non-commercial media organizations are an important element in a thriving, competitive, and diverse media marketplace. There is substantial support for this "public goods" framework both in First Amendment legal history and in market-friendly economic theory. For decades, economists have written about the concept of market failure, which refers to specific types of valuable goods of commodities that commercial systems often fail to produce with ample quality or diversity. The concept applies especially to public goods, including media (especially news and journalistic analysis) (Pickard 2015, pp. 213–15). At the inception of the constitutional republic in the United States, James Madison argued on behalf of First Amendment protections for press freedom not because he wanted commercial organizations to secure their market power by squashing competition but because he wanted to ensure that citizens would have access to, and be able to understand, the information and arguments that an informed citizenry requires. This is in fact the basis of the concept of the consent of the governed (see McChesney and Nichols 2010, p. 2). Madison, along with Alexander Hamilton, argued on behalf of interventions into the emerging commercial markets to ensure both that newspapers would continue to publish and that the market would be sufficiently diverse and protected from undue commercial pressures (McChesney and Nichols 2010, pp. 123–24). The Founders understood the limits of markets and the role of government in ensuring that they function in service of democracy (rather than governments and legislators serving the interests of market players).

The prospect of federal- and state-level funding for public media is politically contentious in the United States but is commonplace abroad. The United States spends far less on public media than comparable developed nations. Federal subsidies cover only about ten percent of the overall operational budget for public radio in the United States. But they are important in sustaining local news reporting and the production of local programming content (Usher 2011). Per capita, the United States spends between $3 and $4 on public broadcasting per year, with some states spending much less than that overall average (Usher 2011). As one headline put it, "Americans could barely buy a coffee with what they spend per year on public media" (Coren 2018). By comparison, countries in Europe spend an average of $86 per capita on public broadcasting (Coren 2018). Yet research shows that public media organizations produce high-quality content, encourage higher levels of news consumption, and therefore cultivate better informed citizens (Usher 2011). Countries like Belgium, Finland, France, the Netherlands, Norway, and Sweden spend money to ensure that newspaper markets are thriving and competitive—the type of initiative that the Founders and other legislators in the United States once supported.

A federal-level public-media tax of one percent of net income from companies like Facebook and Google could provide nearly $3 million for local and non-commercial news initiatives (Pickard 2018). In the meantime, there are a few pioneering efforts that have gained bipartisan support. New Jersey decided to spend $5 million to support a news incubator program called the New Jersey Civic Information Consortium. As one journalist reports, "the dollars for New Jersey's anemic local news scene could mark a revival of civic-minded journalism backed by public dollars" (Coren 2018). Similar initiatives could potentially assist in leveling the playing field among Internet service providers and other telecommunication sectors, where companies like Comcast and Time Warner (in the wireless market) or Verizon and AT&T (in the wired market) hold a near-duopoly status. Prospective strategies include subsidizing the build-out of market competitors for such duopoly players including local and state support for community broadband initiatives (Pickard 2015, pp. 221–22). There is clear historical precedent for such initiatives in the early nineteenth-century newspaper industry in the United States, as well abroad as in the British Broadcasting Corporation (BBC) (see McChesney and Nichols 2010, p. 162).

According to the National Council of State Legislatures, all fifty U.S. states, the District of Columbia, Guam, Puerto Rico, and the Virgin Islands have implemented laws that require private and governmental organizations "to notify individuals of security breaches of information involving personally identifiable information" ("Security Breach Notification Laws" 2018). In terms of broad-scale, sweeping legislative initiatives aimed at curbing the power of tech companies and protecting the public's data, the European Union's General Data Protection Regulation (GDPR) has served as a model for state-level initiatives in the United States. The GDPR addresses many of the concerns outlined above, including data protection by design, data portability, high standards for user consent, and the right of data erasure. A similar measure has taken root in California, where the Consumer Privacy Act of 2018 is set become effective in 2020. As stated in the bill (Chau et al. 2018), the legislation is intended to protect the following rights for the state's citizens: the right to know what personal information is being collected about them; the right to know whether their personal information is sold or disclosed and to whom; the right to refuse the sale of personal information; the right to access personal information; and the right to equal service and price. Though this state law is not nearly as sweeping in scope as the GDPR, it is one of the most comprehensive in the United States if we consider that many existing laws place few restrictions on companies' use of consumer data (Wakabayashi 2018).

Other legislative initiatives seek to crack open the secret vaults in which proprietary code resides. Some local governments have implemented regulatory proposals that serve as auditing mechanisms for algorithms. In 2017, the New York City Council passed the first algorithmic accountability bill in the United States. It creates a task force that studies how NYC city agencies use algorithms in their decision-making processes, with an eye toward transparency and accountability.

In response to socio-economically lopsided "reputation society" (Draper 2019, p. 231), activists and legislators in the United States, and (more prominently) in the European Union, have mobilized to develop laws and software applications that "introduce ephemerality into digital content and offer opportunities to remove or bury unwanted content" as part of a strategy to "insert friction into a digital environment that has been designed to collect and remember" (Draper 2019, p. 219). The so-called "right to be forgotten" ruling from the European Union's Court of Justice directly impacts search engine providers like Google, which may return misleading and unflattering results about an individual. Such regulatory schemes aim to restrict "the length of time and purposes for which businesses can retain electronic information" (Tsesis 2014).

These legal restrictions go further than the self-regulatory approaches that tech companies prefer, and beyond the commercially friendly solutions that the reputation industry treats as a niche market. They require more corporate transparency, more secure methods of data protection, and additional legal avenues for citizens. In a way, these measures seek to restore traditional legal protections, such as procedures for erasing past criminal records. Expunging a criminal record is tantamount to declaring that an arrest never happened. Today, plaintiffs are suing to have information removed from online databases, including search records, Street View images, and social media profiles. Unlike the deregulatory, utilitarian approach of U.S.-based legal models in which users trade privacy for security and convenience, the European "right to be forgotten" model seeks to establish a rights-based framework that prioritizes the interests of consumers and citizens.

A healthy skepticism is warranted in regard to these initiatives, both because they are legally complex and because it is unclear whether they establish a sufficiently novel way of approaching the ethics of memory in the digital economy. On one hand, rights-based privacy models recognize that the achievement of an authentic life hinges not on total personal transparency or perfect memory but on control over one's reputation and identity (Margulis 2011, p. 12). This view appears to contradict the quasi-religious ideology of tech leaders such as Ray Kurzweil and Eric Schmidt (discussed in Chapter 7), in which unbounded storage capacity and processing speed may offer the possibility of immortal life beyond the flesh. On the other hand, these initiatives' focus on deletion tends to "prize efficiency and perpetuate myths of perfect memory" (Wagman 2016, p. 120).

Surprisingly, a bipartisan array of U.S. legislators have proposed what might be the most sweeping response to Silicon Valley's power over-reach: breaking up the Big Tech. They are using legislative and regulatory means to break up multi-platform companies like Facebook (which owns Instagram, What's App) or Google (which owns YouTube and many other apps) into separate entities. The philosophy here is that instead of having one company succeed in being all things for all people (precisely the race that Amazon, Google, and Facebook are all trying win), we should have many smaller companies providing different, yet symbiotic, products and services. These should fit together into a broader whole, that is, a functioning and diverse market, which is arguably what the Founders had intended in the first place. If you will recall our discussion in Chapter 2, it was none other than Adam Smith who first articulated the threat that monopoly-like entities pose in every realm from religion to the economy.

While coverage of the 2020 U.S. election is punctuated by "progressive" initiatives to break up Big Tech, conservatives have also floated such proposals. Most notable among progressives is Senator Elizabeth Warren, who argues for creating a "level playing field" so we might "get the best out of markets" (McCarthy 2019). Similar arguments have arisen from traditionally conservative sources like *Wall Street Journal* and *National Review*. Citing conservatives like Howard Taft and Ronald Reagan, columnist John Hawkins (2018) argues that "breaking these [tech] monopolies up into smaller, more focused entities" would both "reduce the power of these companies and serve the public interest." Likewise, Missouri Republican Josh Hawley sees such proposals as a means for the public to take action "to defend their rights" in the face of each "creepy new revelation" that emerges about Big Tech (McCarthy 2019). In fact, if Facebook conceives of itself as an indispensable public utility "like electricity," as one insider claimed, it bolsters arguments for regulating tech companies the way Roosevelt and Reagan reined in the Standard Oil and Ma Bell (Gillmor 2012). Writing within the auspices of the market-friendly Stigler Center at the University of Chicago Booth School of Business, media scholar Tim Wu cites historical precedent in the Gilded Age, where economic concentrations of power went hand-in-hand with anti-democratic, indeed authoritarian, upheavals in government (Schechter 2019; Wu 2018). Similar to our argument (from Chapter 2) for recovering the long-misunderstood insights of Adam Smith, Wu advocates recovering the lost principles articulated by Justice Louis Brandeis, who described the threat of economic concentration as "the curse of bigness" (Wu 2018). As the crisis of Big Tech reaches new heights, we see what the *Wall Street Journal* calls "the scrambling of the old left-right divide over government intervention in the market" (Schlesinger et al. 2019).

Our goal here is not to offer such policy initiatives as definitive solutions, but as examples of how we might go about thinking differently about markets and technologies. Regulation is important, but regulation of a particular sort. As of this writing, there is some movement on the part of major players like Facebook toward federal-level regulation in the United States. The rhetoric on behalf of such initiatives plays into public concerns but is potentially misleading. In a very real sense, companies like Facebook want to get ahead of the game just as individual states are moving to put in place much more drastic measures that are similar to new regulatory frameworks in the European Union. At this time, the main objective for concerned citizens is to avoid federal-level measures that will essentially nullify or undermine state-level work that is moving in the right direction (Draper 2019).

Civic and Professional Organizations

In this section, we highlight a range of groups who have the potential to hold corporations and governments accountable. The term Fourth Estate is apropos here, as it refers to the role of journalism and news media in providing a check on established power structures. The less common term Fifth Estate is also relevant and refers to more recent developments in civic life like the rise of social media, which celebrants often frame as a tool for revitalizing the public square. In any case, our point is to underscore the role of specialized organizations or movements who assert some degree of influence on behalf of the general public. These include grassroots, civil society, and activist groups. We also include journalism and education in this section; these are public goods insofar as they produce forms of value that commercial markets tend to neglect or fail to generate effectively. We acknowledge that these distinctions are not entirely precise since many journalistic and educational endeavors are at least partially commercial. Even in such cases, however, we aim to stress the difference it makes to structure such endeavors from the perspective of the long-term public interest rather than short-term financial gain.

Let us begin with journalism, a topic that has been a touchstone throughout this book. As "the nation's early warning system," journalism has an even more crucial role to play in critical institutional analysis. The first task of journalism is to serve as a watchdog of both corporate and governmental power. It is precisely journalism's potential to focus civic attention and spur collective action in advance of such crises that makes it "a necessary and indispensable part of our economic infrastructure" (McChesney and Nichols 2010, p. 106).

Journalists must reclaim some of their traditional gatekeeping power and their moral authority if we are sincere in our efforts to realize the Founders' vision of authentic democracy as catalyzed by a free press. More specifically, U.S.-based scholars and media reform activists must challenge the highly commercialized model of news reporting that has prevailed in recent decades in order to recapture the Founders' original vision of authentic democracy. Suffice it to say, decades of deregulatory and pro-market media policies have veered from that founding vision (McChesney and Nichols 2010).

Now let us consider a few examples of how journalism can apply the insights from the corollaries to our five proverbs. In a case demonstrating the importance of processing judiciously, ProPublica and the *New York Times* raised questions about computerized DNA analysis software that New York City had implemented. They had found glaring issues that even the inventors of the software acknowledged. For its part, ProPublica filed a motion to release the source code for the software package, which had been "a closely held secret" for years. In a dramatic move, ProPublica published the code. New York City stopped using the tool.

With regard to the ethics of memory in the digital age, despite the downward pressure that social media places on the quality of online content, journalists have done the hard work of connecting current events to their historical roots. When riots broke out in Ferguson, Missouri, after the shooting death of Michael Brown in 2014, some news reporters insisted that viewers put the spectacle of violent, fiery protests in proper historical context. Acting as gatekeepers of cultural memory, they connected the dots between Ferguson 2014 and the discriminatory housing policies put in place after World War II (Coates 2014). To their credit, social media platforms have enabled activists to demand some semblance of justice in the construction of cultural memory. U.S.-based activists, who often see themselves as citizen-journalists, have taken to Facebook and Twitter to insist that victims of police brutality have a right to be remembered (Williams 2015).

In the context of the digital economy, quality journalism avoids two major pitfalls. First, it does more than simply amplify the utopian rhetoric of technologists through undue deference (e.g., a "gee whiz" approach to technology reporting). Second, it avoids excessive skepticism or cynicism with regard to new technologies (e.g., sensational headlines such as "Facebook Causes Depression," which typically distort the nuances of social-scientific research). The fact that technology news is generally geared toward a business audience lends itself to the problem of deference, while the speed of development and lack of technical expertise among reporters (not to mention readers) lends itself to the problem of cynicism.

Tech reporting is no easy task. Journalists must understand not only how new technologies work but what their broader socio-economic impacts might be, including those impacts rendered invisible by the self-serving optimism of technology leaders. The utopian ideology of technologists has yielded aggressive development campaigns that defy the cautionary pronouncements of legal authorities and consumer groups. This problem is compounded by the fact that tech leaders often do not distinguish their assumptions as ideological in nature, never mind as quasi-religious. Therefore, journalists have a special role in uncovering the hidden assumptions in pro-technology rhetoric, challenging tech leaders in their powerful gatekeeping roles, and clarifying the importance of regulation and policymaking in generating a more equitable digital future.

As noted in Chapter 8, in terms of improving the quality of tech journalism, a key priority is to move beyond narrow and outdated definitions of objectivity that place a stranglehold on reporters' capacity to serve as watchdogs. Journalists are charged with informing the public wisely, which means they must actively exercise judgment rather than being "neutral" or "objective" in a passive sense (e.g., simply relaying the self-serving statements of executives or legislators to the public without context or question). Journalists need to be objective with facts. But journalism is much more than fact reporting. Indeed, the very decision about what to cover today, and what to leave unreported, is ethically and morally charged.

Notions of objectivity that emerged in the twentieth century served in part to protect the commercial interests of news organizations, who feared retaliation from powerful elites and advertisers for unflattering coverage or commentary. Early on, the emerging public relations industry produced corporate-friendly "filler" that now accounts for a large percentage of news content (McChesney 2004, pp. 71–72). When ad revenues dwindle, such content subsidizes a struggling industry, creating a downward spiral that undermines the capacity of journalism to serve the public interest despite the best intentions of individual reporters.

And yet insightful analysis is more important than ever. The purpose of a robust system of independent investigative journalism is precisely to fulfill this task. Journalism at its best provides the necessary elements of discernment and self-control by vetting the authenticity of citizen-sourced materials, leveraging resources to uncover and access additional information and material, and providing context and analysis in a sustained manner over time.

Understanding news as a public good provides a level of protection for reporters and journalists who, by the nature of their work, must assume some level of risk in reporting on contentious issues. Digital platforms have amplified tribal, partisan rhetoric that is often misleading (if not outright false), and that plays into the anger and fear of readers. Journalists have the difficult task of holding politicians' and activists' feet to the fire when they make such questionable statements. They operate now in an environment where honesty and sincerity are no longer taken-for-granted background assumptions of public conversations. Journalists are in a sense like lifeguards who must, at times, descend from their watchful perch and enter the moral rip tides of public debate.

A vibrant marketplace of ideas requires more than a binary choice between traditional-style "just-the-facts-ma'am" reporting, on one hand, and the hot-headed sophistry of cable news pundits, on the other. This is especially true in the context of new information activists like Anonymous and WikiLeaks, which may have little interest or incentive to exercise the kind of prudent judgment that once characterized professional news analysts. WikiLeaks' tendency to err on the side of raw data collection and dissemination is "symptomatic of a brand of open-access ideology" in which "the crisis in investigative journalism is neither understood nor recognized" (Lovink and Riemens 2013, p. 248). (We discussed some potential solutions to this impasse in the section above on politics.)

For their part, journalists have begun to develop new approaches to reporting that move us closer toward productive conversations about important issues. Exemplary in this regard is the Solutions Journalism Network, with whom we have worked directly in recent semesters. The goal of solutions journalism is to provide comprehensive and sustained coverage of social and economic problems in a way that enables "constructive, de-polarizing public conversations" ("Who We Are" 2019). In the past year, we worked directly with representatives of the Solutions Journalism Network to bring the Solutions U® initiative into an undergraduate class titled Digital Democracies. The latter initiative allowed our students to access a growing and well-curated database of solutions-based news reports. Representatives from Solutions U® worked directly with us to locate relevant content and assist students in creating their own portfolios as they conducted research projects over the course of the semester.

Education

The example of Solutions U® brings us to education, another important dimension of civic life. We have argued elsewhere in this book that by integrating contemplative studies and media scholarship, researchers can harness the power of contemplative practice for the cause of media reform (Healey 2013, 2015). Employing such practices as methodological tools, contemplative scholarship examines media platforms and devices as intellectual technologies. In doing so, it critiques the impact of digital power structures on the formation of self-identity and the perception of reality, while providing a moral compass for the development of technologies built upon values of justice, stewardship, and openness.

We are heartened by the work of exemplary organizations like the Association for Contemplative Mind in Higher Education, whose members have begun to forge this path. In applying contemplative concepts to the field of education, these scholars demonstrate how teachers and administrators can bring greater integrity to their institutions' pedagogical commitments. Beyond adding "a desirable frill" to course offerings, universities' incorporation of contemplative principles fulfills "their duty to provide a liberal, that is, a liberating and empowering, education" (Thurman 1994, p. 8).

In applying contemplative principles to economics, mindfulness can help citizens understand their long-term self-interest, and thereby avoid the mistaken assumptions that led to the recent economic collapse (Bush 2011, p. 195). Practices aimed at fostering empathy and compassion can cultivate the human capacities for cooperation and connection that are increasingly important as we face complex global issues, like economic inequality and climate change (Barbezat and Bush 2014, p. 29). Such practices help individuals move beyond "habitual modes of engaging with injustice and suffering," creating opportunities for renewed engagement (Barbezat and Bush

2014, p. 183). In a course on Meditation and Media Violence at the University of California, Davis, one professor found that compassion meditation helped his students move beyond the disempowering view of mass media as merely a source of compassion fatigue. Students were able to view familiar scenes of violence in a different, ethically engaged manner that opened up possibilities for "making change in the world" (Barbezat and Bush 2014, p. 184).

Similar benefits accrue from the integration of arts-based research (ABR) into the classroom. These two areas, contemplative and arts-based scholarship, overlap considerably since both embrace uncertainty and ambiguity as an avenue to transformation (Gerber and Myers-Coffman 2018, p. 594). Contemplative, arts-based pedagogy can enable students (as future users, developers, and citizens) to exercise greater responsibility in shaping our socio-technical future. The types of practices described in each of this book's proverb chapters can cultivate not just informational awareness, but also empathy and compassion—a holistic engagement with news content that is too often lacking in the social media ecosystem. The point is not for students to create "great" works of art. The process matters more than the product. At its best ABR "invites people to imagine new possible entanglements with the professions and social challenges of our day" (Rosiek 2018, p. 644).

The pedagogical goal here is to displace and subvert the gatekeeping power of the human engineers and business operators of digital platforms, as well as the material affordances of the platforms themselves. Young people are exposed to plenty of news and often express a positive regard for the role of social media in aiding their understanding of current events. Yet research shows that emotional and cognitive responses to news usually occur without students' awareness. Upon reflection, younger viewers recognize the level of exposure they face, and only then do they realize they do not process news consciously (Sivek 2018, p. 131; see also Klurfeld and Schneider 2014). The constant need for news scoops and up-to-the-second personal updates has been shown to "reduce the opportunity for analytic deliberation … allowing affective considerations free rein" (Sivek 2018, p. 129).

The dynamics of social media favor not a balanced integration of heart and mind but a mindless provocation of emotion by means opaque to users, and for purposes that are arguably at odds with users' best intentions and interests. Contrary to the declarations of people like Facebook's Mark Zuckerberg and Sheryl Sandberg, platforms like Facebook do not reliably cultivate authenticity among users—not unless we define an authentic life as one in which our every thought and emotion is posted online, captured for analysis, and sold to marketers. When news consumption is reduced to "engagement" via likes, retweets, and comments, we lose meaningful engagement in favor of the fleeting experience of moral sanctimony or performative morality. In this way, as theologian Walter Brueggemann (2001) argues, the "ethos of consumerism" amounts to a program of "achievable satiation," one which appeals to our moral sensibility but is ultimately "concerned only with self-satisfaction" and as such tends to leave the political status quo intact (pp. 41–42).

Recent scholarship in media literacy, specifically news literacy, argues that mindfulness can serve as an effective tool for "increasing news consumers' awareness of their emotions and reducing their 'cognitive failures' regarding the information they see" (Sivek 2018, p. 131). Instructors can design assignments and exercises to "encourage students' awareness of news exposure and of their emotional responses to it, thereby encouraging further analysis of emotions spurred by provocative real or fake news content" (Sivek 2018, p. 132). What such exercises aim to cultivate is not simply knowledge about media institutions, or facility in media production, but what some Thai educators call "media wisdom" (Sivek 2018, p. 131).

Contemplative and arts-based pedagogy can facilitate a more nuanced definition of media and news literacy. Emotion has the ability to "lubricate reason" in a way that is both wondrous in its speed and subtlety and frightening in its potential to render us vulnerable to manipulation (Slovic et al. 2007, p. 1349). We need to develop special practices so that "when we see emotionally provocative news content and realize that emotional manipulation may be occurring, we can attempt to short-circuit that process and engage that information in a more cognizant manner" (Sivek 2018, p. 134). Insofar as they include a contemplative dimension, such practices enable the "prophetic imagination," or a mode of thinking and being that challenges established structures of authority (Brueggemann 2001, p. 11). Rather than resignation, such imagination cultivates a radical hope.

Conclusion

The current critical juncture has implications on many levels: from the ethical standards of media professionals, to the culture and practices of users and audiences, to the development of media technologies themselves. What is at stake at any such juncture is more than the partisan concerns of the moment, rather, it is the universal values of human solidarity and authentic being. As we have argued throughout this book, religious tradition has much to offer to the kind of prophetic imagination needed to bring about wholesale institutional change (see especially Chapter 3). Religious and political institutions have traditionally guided citizens' understanding of how general (and universal) ethical principles should be applied in day-to-day life. One's close identification with the Republican Party or the Catholic Church, for example, might lead to a particular understanding of how charity or compassion might be expressed through personal action or policy initiatives (Hinck 2016, p. 10). Postmodern trends toward fluidity of identity, driven in part by the dynamics of commercial media, have disrupted these relationships.

As professor and activist Cornel West suggested three decades ago, our "utopian energies" must be channeled into various "reformist strategies that oppose the status quo of our day" (1989, p. 229). Media reform activism therefore has a significant role to play. However, as West suggests, these strategies "are never to become ends-in-themselves" (p. 229). As Professor Emeritus at the University of Illinois, Champaign-Urbana Clifford G. Christians argues, we must encourage responsible technological development "while witnessing to the darker side of the technological process with tears" (1989, p. 137). We must stand in a space of uncomfortable, dialectical tension between the "yes" of iterative reform and engagement with popular media, and the "no" of an unrelenting refusal to succumb to the onslaught of what Jacques Ellul describes as *la technique* (Ellul [1948] 1967, p. 79; Ellul 1971, p. 25). The call for prophetic witness that we have issued in this book serves not merely as a call for technical and legislative reform, but as a demand that such activism avoid devolving into the idolatrous worship of technology itself as the source of human salvation.

We live in an era where moral risk-taking is a necessity. Being courageous means becoming vulnerable. Disruption without risk and vulnerability is just hubris and recklessness. On the path to integrity, the tiny moral bubbles of Silicon Valley must burst. To the extent that our strategies embrace a holistic commitment to both personal and civic mindfulness, the emerging digital economy may yet fulfill what one scholar describes as the primary goal of every economic system, namely, "to promote widespread and sustainable human flourishing" (Loy 2013, p. 420).

References

All Tech is Human. "History." 2019. https://www.alltechishuman.com/history.

Barbezat, Dan, and Mirabai Bush. *Contemplative Practices in Higher Education: Powerful Methods to Transform Teaching and Learning.* San Francisco: Jossey-Boss, 2014.

Bowles, Nellie. "Early Facebook and Google Employees Form Coalition to Fight What They Built." *New York Times,* February 4, 2018. https://www.nytimes.com/2018/02/04/technology/early-facebook-google-employees-fight-tech.html.

Brueggemann, Walter. *Sabbath as Resistance: Saying No to the Culture of Now.* Louisville, KY: Westminster John Knox Press, 2014.

———. *The Prophetic Imagination.* 2nd ed. Minneapolis, MN: Fortress Press, 2001.

Buber, Martin. *I and Thou.* 2nd ed. New York: Charles Scribner's Sons, 1958.

Bush, Mirabai. "Mindfulness in Higher Education." *Contemporary Buddhism* 12, no. 1 (June 14, 2011): 183–97.

Center for Humane Technology. "Problem." 2019. https://humanetech.com/problem/.

Chau, Edwin, Robert Hertzberg, and William Dodd. H. R. Res. 375, Sess. of 2018 (CA 2018). https://leginfo.legislature.ca.gov/faces/billTextClient.xhtml?bill_id=201720180AB375.

Christians, Clifford G. "A Theory of Normative Technology." In *Technological Transformation: Contextual and Conceptual Implications,* edited by Edmund F. Byrne and Joseph C. Pitts, 123–40. Boston, MA: Kluwer Academic, 1989.

Coates, Ta-Nehisi. "The Racist Housing Policies That Built Ferguson." *The Atlantic,* October 17, 2014. https://www.theatlantic.com/business/archive/2014/10/the-racist-housing-policies-that-built-ferguson/381595/.

Code2040. "Our Mission." 2019. http://www.code2040.org/mission.

Constine, Josh. "For Real, Ex-Groupon CEO Andrew Mason Is Releasing an Album of Motivational Music." TechCrunch. May 16, 2013. https://techcrunch.com/2013/05/16/andrew-mason-hardly-workin/.

Coren, Michael J. "Americans Could Barely Buy a Coffee with What They Spend Per Year on Public Media." Quartz. September 9, 2018. https://qz.com/1383503/americans-could-barely-buy-a-coffee-with-what-they-spend-per-year-on-public-media/.

Doctorow, Cory. "Disruption for Thee, But Not for Me." *Locus.* January 7, 2019. http://locusmag.com/2019/01/cory-doctorow-disruption-for-thee-but-not-for-me/.

Draper, Nora A. *The Identity Trade: Selling Privacy and Reputation Online.* New York: New York University Press, 2019.

———. Personal conversation. University of New Hampshire, Durham, NH, May 7, 2019.

Draper, Nora A., and Joseph Turow. "The Corporate Cultivation of Digital Resignation." *New Media & Society* 21, no 8 (2019): 1824–39.

Einstein, Mara. *Compassion, Inc.: How Corporate America Blurs the Line between What We Buy, Who We Are, and Those We Help*. Berkeley, CA: University of California Press, 2012.

Ellul, Jacques. *Presence of the Kingdom*. 1948. Reprint ed., New York: Seabury, 1967.

———. *Propaganda: The Formation of Men's Attitudes*. New York: Knopf, 1971.

Fishbane, Michael. *Sacred Attunement: A Jewish Theology*. Chicago, IL: Chicago University Press, 2008.

Forbes, David. *Mindfulness and Its Discontents: Education, Self, and Social Transformation*. Black Point, Nova Scotia: Fernwood Publishing, 2019.

Gerber, Nancy, and Katherine Myers-Coffman. In *Handbook of Arts-Based Research*, edited by Patricia Leavy, 587–607. New York: Guilford Press, 2018.

Gillmor, Dan. "Facebook's New Business Plan: From Utility to Monopoly." *The Guardian*, October 8, 2012. https://www.theguardian.com/commentisfree/2012/oct/08/facebook-business-plan-utility-monopoly.

Goodstein, Anastasia. "SXSW 2018: It's Time for a Real Conversation about Ethics in Technology." AdLibbing. March 22, 2018. https://www.adlibbing.org/2018/03/22/sxsw-2018-its-time-for-a-real-conversation-about-ethics-in-technology/.

Groetzinger, Kate. "Coding Boot Camps Aim to Help Solve Diversity Problem in Tech Sector." KUT 90.5 FM [Austin, TX]. March 31, 2017. https://www.kut.org/post/coding-boot-camps-aim-help-solve-diversity-problem-tech-sector.

Gustin, Sam. "Groupon Fires CEO Andrew Mason: The Rise and Fall of Tech's Enfant Terrible." *Time*, March 1, 2013. http://business.time.com/2013/03/01/groupon-fires-ceo-andrew-mason-the-rise-and-fall-of-techs-enfant-terrible/.

Hawkins, John. "The Conservative Case for Breaking Up Big Tech." *National Review*, March 28, 2018. https://www.nationalreview.com/2018/05/breaking-up-tech-giants-conservative-case/.

Healey, Kevin. "Searching for Integrity: The Politics of Mindfulness in the Digital Economy." *Nomos Journal*, August 5, 2013. http://nomosjournal.org/2013/08/searching-for-integrity/.

———. "Contemplative Media Studies." *Religions* 6, no. 3 (August 5, 2015): 948–68.

Heim, Michael. *Virtual Realism*. Oxford: Oxford University Press, 1998.

Hinck, Ashley. "Ethical Frameworks and Ethical Modalities: Theorizing Communication and Citizenship in a Fluid World." *Communication Theory* 26, no. 1 (February 2016): 1–20.

Klurfeld, James, and Howard Schneider. "News Literacy: Teaching the Internet Generation to Make Reliable Information Choices." Washington, DC: Center for Effective Public Management at Brookings. July 3, 2014. https://www.brookings.edu/research/news-literacy-teaching-the-internet-generation-to-make-reliable-information-choices/.

Kravarik, Jason, and Stephanie Elam. "The Portals Project: This Gold Box Is 'Better Than Facebook.'" CNN. April 23, 2017. https://www.cnn.com/style/article/portals-project-los-angeles/index.html.

Lanier, Jaron. *You Are Not a Gadget: A Manifesto*. New York: Vintage Books, 2011.

Lapowsky, Issie. "Ethical Tech Will Require a Grassroots Revolution." *Wired*, February 8, 2018. https://www.wired.com/story/center-for-humane-technology-tech-addiction/.

Levy, David. "More, Faster, Better: Governance in an Age of Overload, Busyness, and Speed." *First Monday*. Special issue no. 7. September 2006. http://firstmonday.org/issues/special11_9/levy/index.html.

Lorenzo, Rocio, and Martin Reeves. "How and Where Diversity Drives Financial Performance." *Harvard Business Review*, January 30, 2018. https://hbr.org/2018/01/how-and-where-diversity-drives-financial-performance.

Lovink, Geert, and Patrice Riemens. "Twelve Theses on WikiLeaks." In *Beyond WikiLeaks: Implications for the Future of Communications, Journalism and Society*, edited by Benedetta Brevini, Aren Hintz, and Patrick McCurdy, 245–53. New York: Palgrave Macmillan, 2013.

Loy, David R. "Why Buddhism and the West Need Each Other: On the Interdependence of Personal and Social Transformation." *Journal of Buddhist Ethics* 20 (2013): 401–21.

Margulis, Stephen T. "Three Theories of Privacy: An Overview." In *Privacy Online: Perspectives on Privacy and Self-disclosure in the Social Web*, edited by Sabine Trepte and Leonard Reinecke, 9–17. New York: Springer, 2011.

Maskey, Morag, Jessica Lowry, Jacqui Rodgers, Helen McConachie, and Jeremy R. Parr. "Reducing Specific Phobia/Fear in Young People with Autism Spectrum Disorders (ASDs) through a Virtual Reality Environment Intervention." *Plos One*, (July 2, 2014). e100374. doi:10.1371/journal.pone.0100374.

McCarthy, Tom. "'A Cop on the Beat': Elizabeth Warren Defends Plan to Break Up Tech Giants." *The Guardian*, March 10, 2019. https://www.theguardian.com/us-news/2019/mar/10/elizabeth-warren-break-up-amazon-google-facebook-socialism-capitalism.

McChesney, Robert. *The Problem of the Media: U.S. Communication Politics in the 21st Century*. New York: Monthly Review Press, 2004.

———. *Digital Disconnect: How Capitalism Is Turning the Internet against Democracy*. New York: The New Press, 2013.

McChesney, Robert, and John Nichols. *The Death and Life of American Journalism*. Philadelphia: Nation Books, 2010.

McGregor, Jena. "Google Admits It Has a Diversity Problem." *Washington Post*, May 29, 2014. https://www.washingtonpost.com/news/on-leadership/wp/2014/05/29/google-admits-it-has-a-diversity-problem/.

"Meet Sarah Jung of Faithful Artisans in Downtown Los Angeles." VoyageLA. February 6, 2017. http://voyagela.com/interview/meet-sarah-jung-faithful-artisans-downtown-los-angeles-arts-district/.

Nhat Hanh, Thich. *Being Peace*. Berkeley, CA: Parallax, 2005.

Ng, Ed. "Using an Analytic of Governmentality to Understand the Role of Mindfulness in the Production (and Potentially, the Refusal) of Neoliberal Subjectivity." Paper presented at the European Group for Organizational Studies, Naples, Italy, July 2016.

Picard, Robert G., and Victor Pickard. "Essential Principles for Contemporary Media and Communications Policy," 1–48. Oxford: Reuters Institute for the Study of Journalism, 2017.

Pickard, Victor. *America's Battle for Media Democracy: The Triumph of Corporate Libertarianism and the Future of Media Reform*. New York: Cambridge University Press, 2015.

———. "Break Facebook's Power and Renew Journalism." *The Nation*, April 18, 2018. https://www.thenation.com/article/break-facebooks-power-and-renew-journalism/.

Purser, Ron. "The Cultural Aesthetic of Virtual Reality: Simulation or Transparency?" In *Human Computer Interaction: Issues and Challenges*, edited by Qiyang Chen, 214–31. Hershey, PA: IGI Global, 2001.

Rigg, Clare. "Being in the World, Not Just in the Mind: Considering Contrasting Traditions of Mindfulness for Critical Reflection." Paper presented at the European Group for Organizational Studies, Naples, Italy, July 2016.

Rosiek, Jerry. "Art, Agency, and Ethics in Research: How the New Materialisms Will Require and Transform Arts-Based Research." In *Handbook of Arts-Based Research*, edited by Patricia Leavy, 632–48. New York, Guilford Press, 2018.

Schechter, Asher. "It's Crucial to Break Up Facebook." ProMarket. January 4, 2019. https://promarket.org/crucial-break-up-facebook.

Schlesinger, Jacob M., Brent Kendall, and John D. McKinnon. "Tech Giants Google, Facebook and Amazon Intensify Antitrust Debate." *Wall Street Journal*, June 8, 2019. https://www.wsj.com/articles/tech-giants-google-facebook-and-amazon-intensify-antitrust-debate-11559966461.

"Security Breach Notification Laws." National Council of State Legislatures. September 29, 2018. http://www.ncsl.org/research/telecommunications-and-information-technology/security-breach-notification-laws.aspx.

Sivek, Susan Currie. "Both Facts and Feelings: Emotion and News Literacy." *Journal of Media Literacy Education* 10, no. 2 (December 14, 2018): 123–38.

Slovic, Paul, Melissa L. Finucane, Ellen Peters, and Donald G. MacGregor. "The Affect Heuristic." *European Journal of Operational Research* 177 (2007): 1333–52. doi: 10.1016/j.ejor.2005.04.006.

Strain, Charles R. *The Prophet and the Bodhisattva: Daniel Berrigan, Thich Nhat Hanh, and the Ethics of Peace and Justice.* Eugene, OR: Wipf and Stock, 2014.

Thompson, Evan. *Waking, Dreaming, Being: Self and Consciousness in Meditation, Neuroscience, and Philosophy.* New York: Columbia University Press, 2015.

Thurman, Robert A. F. "Meditation and Education: Buddhist India, Tibet and Modern America." Paper for the Working Group of the Contemplative Mind in Society, Pocantico, NY, October 2, 1994.

Tiku, Nitasha. "Ageism Turned Silicon Valley into a Hotbed for Male Plastic Surgery." Valleywag. March 24, 2014. http://valleywag.gawker.com/ageism-turned-silicon-valley-into-a-hot-bed-for-male-pl-1550347156.

Tsesis, Alexander. "The Right to Erasure: Privacy, Data Brokers, and the Indefinite Retention of Data." *Wake Forest Law Review* 49 (2014): 433–84.

Usher, Nikki. "Funding Public Media: How the US Compares to the Rest of the World." NiemanLab. March 11, 2011. https://www.niemanlab.org/2011/03/funding-public-media-how-the-us-compares-to-the-rest-of-the-world/.

Wagman, Ira. "Forgiving without Forgetting: Contending with Digital Memory." In *Image, Ethics, Technology*, edited by Sharrona Pearl, 111–25. New York: Routledge, 2016.

Wakabayashi, Daisuke. "California Passes Sweeping Law to Protect Online Privacy." *New York Times*, June 28, 2018. https://www.nytimes.com/2018/06/28/technology/california-online-privacy-law.html.

Weissman, Cale Guthrie. "Anonymous Is Supporting a New Privacy-focused Social Network That Takes Aim at Facebook's Shady Practices." *Business Insider*, June 15, 2015. http://www.businessinsider.com/facebook-competitor-mindscom-launches-with-help-from-anonymous-2015-6.

West, Cornel. *The American Evasion of Philosophy: A Genealogy of Pragmatism.* Madison: University of Wisconsin Press, 1989.

"Who We Are." Solutions Journalism Network. 2019. https://www.solutionsjournalism.org/who-we-are/mission.

Williams, Stereo. "The Power of Black Twitter." *The Daily Beast*, July 6, 2015. https://www.thedailybeast.com/the-power-of-black-twitter.

Wu, Tim. *The Curse of Bigness: Antitrust in the New Gilded Age.* New York: Columbia Global Reports, 2018.

Zajonc, Arthur. *Meditation as Contemplative Inquiry.* Great Barrington, MA: Lindisfarne Books, 2010.

CONCLUSION

An Ethic of Non-Violence for the Digital Age

Believing he was on a collision course with another ship, a battleship captain signaled the second vessel to change course. When his request was denied, the captain grew angry and demanded compliance, adding "I'm a battleship." His message was met with a simple reply: "I'm a lighthouse" (Amichai-Hamburger 2009, p. 261). Unsurprisingly, the captain quickly changed course. The lighthouse here represents "permanent values which are necessary to protect us and prevent our hazardous collision with the rocks" (p. 266). Unfortunately, in the age of digital media an "excessive belief in technology" has created "a situation in which there is a lack of genuine leadership and a fading of the real 'lighthouse' values" (pp. 263–65).

Throughout this book, we have articulated a set of lighthouse values (or virtues) whose continued importance we hope to underscore: wisdom, authenticity, integrity, judgment, and memory. Our concerns are echoed by numerous critical scholars. The pervasiveness of "blind faith in technology and market fundamentalism" calls for guiding principles that prioritize the human over the technological (Vaidhyanathan 2011, p. xiii). "Another futurism is possible" beyond the celebratory presentations at the latest TED talk, provided that we avoid a complacent "placebo techno-radicalism" that amounts to little more than "toying with risk so as to reaffirm the comfortable" (Bratton 2013).

It is somewhat reassuring that efforts to "comfort the afflicted and afflict the comfortable" have become more commonplace in Silicon Valley. In a speech that one commentator described as a "fiery sermon" at a recent Wisdom 2.0 conference, author and spiritual leader Marianne Williamson invoked that very phrase, insisting that she would not "be a dancing monkey" to entertain "a bunch of rich capitalists" (Drda 2014). She further critiqued the conference's focus on mindfulness with a cutting comment: "Only in America," she said, "could we come up with some ersatz version of spirituality that gives us a pass on addressing the unnecessary human suffering in our midst" (Drda 2014). Surprisingly, her audience of well-to-do tech elites agreed and cheered her on. There is, perhaps, a growing awareness (or lack of awareness in this case?) among technology leaders that, as one insider insists, "we technologists ought to be serving [hu]mankind, not turning ourselves into a privileged class" (Lanier 2013, pp. 306–7). While Williamson has a point about the rampant materialism of American culture, it is also the case that out of its very divisive racial tensions, American culture produced a spiritual leader whose philosophy of non-violent activism catalyzed a transformation that continues to unfold today.

In this chapter, we revisit Martin Luther King Jr.'s (MLK) six principles of non-violent resistance and offer a framework for applying them to a digital economy whose dynamics King could not have foreseen. In his 1961 speech "Love, Law and Civil Disobedience," King articulated an approach based on a basic commitment to human dignity, self-respect, compassion, and hope. In summary, here are the six guiding principles he outlines in that speech (King [1961] 1986, 45–47):

1. The end does not justify the means. The means "must be as pure as the end."
2. We need to follow "a consistent principle of non-injury" by avoiding both physical violence and "internal violence of spirit."
3. The "ethic of love," which means understanding and good will for all, must be the foundation of all action.
4. We need to target "the unjust system, rather than individuals who are caught in that system."
5. We must accept the suffering that results from our resistance, as it "may serve to transform the social situation."
6. We need to appeal to the "amazing potential for goodness" that exists in all people.

At some level, all of the stakeholder groups we have discussed throughout this book have fallen short in fulfilling these principles: from Silicon Valley executives, to political opportunists, to anti-capitalist hacktivists. Nevertheless, we remain encouraged by the initiatives we describe in Chapter 9 and in the ongoing grassroots work, political leadership, and industry stewardship we see emerging from a new generation of students and future professionals. Let us turn now to each of King's six principles.

Principle One: Understanding Means and Ends

King insists that the means of any social movement must be pure. He opposes the idea, articulated by some of his own civil rights contemporaries, that the ends justify the means. For our end goals to be morally justified, so must be our actions that lead up to it. We extend this principle here by offering an understanding of means and ends in the context of the digital economy.

Perhaps the most egregious violation of this first principle is the phenomenon of cyber-vigilantism. The movement Anonymous exemplifies this development. The group is known for leveraging social media to mobilize support for the Arab Spring, U.S.-based and international Occupy networks, and WikiLeaks (Coleman 2012,

p. 94). In its anti-corporate campaigns, Anonymous seeks to reverse the one-way transparency of corporate and military surveillance by turning digital networks into citizen-wielded tools of vigilance that expose corporate and political malfeasance while protecting the privacy of activists, symbolized by its use of the iconic Guy Fawkes mask (Coleman 2012, p. 87). Yet its history is replete with malicious attacks.

Emerging in the early 2000s from the online image board 4chan, Anonymous came to be known for its mischievousness. It trolled its critics, making prank calls and coordinating dedicated denial-of-service (DDoS) attacks on its adversaries. Its focus become political over time, including issues of free speech and corporate or government deception (Coleman 2012, p. 87). Through actions that resulted in numerous arrests in the United States and abroad, Anonymous aligned itself closely with WikiLeaks. When PayPal, Visa, MasterCard, and Amazon refused to handle financial transactions or Internet traffic for WikiLeaks after the latter's 2010 release of the secret Afghanistan war logs, Anonymous coordinated DDoS attacks against these organizations, causing millions of dollars in financial damages. Even some Anonymous members "took issue with the collateral damage wrought" by some of the groups' more malicious campaigns, noting that the "the necessarily clandestine nature of such hacks" often runs "counter to the [group's own] ethos of transparency" (Coleman 2012, p. 91). By taking a by-any-means-necessary approach to activism, Anonymous had arguably lost its integrity, and thereby lost many of its own supporters.

Even if our intentions and behaviors are benevolent rather than malicious, they can still be misguided in a way that causes long-term harm. A variation on the first of King's principles is that we need to be clear about what our means and ends are, so we do not mistake one for the other. The goal of "creating a new digital humanism" (Lanier 2011, p. 23) is to reverse the trend of putting the proverbial cart before the horse. For their part, tech companies often see users as a means to an end. This is a core issue in digital capitalism, where users are not customers but products or commodities to be bought and sold to advertisers and marketers. But the benefits of ad personalization, or more effective social networking services, do not justify tech executives' violations of user privacy and basic norms of consent. We have covered this issue in various ways throughout this book. Our main argument has been that the catechism of Silicon Valley sees concepts like information, convergence, and transparency as ends in themselves. Instead, these technical concepts should be understood as a means toward the greater ends of wisdom, integrity, authenticity, and other human virtues.

When thinking about solutions to ongoing social, political, or economic problems, this confusion of ends and means often arises in the form of technological solutionism, a strategy whereby we create new technologies to fix the problems caused by old technologies. We are not saying that technology has no role to play in addressing issues like climate change or cyber terrorism. But technical solutions work best when they are one tool among others in a toolkit. This is due in part to the unpredictable, systemic impacts of technical development. We never know for sure what the long-term impacts of a new technical innovation might be. We might end up creating a whole new set of problems in our attempts to solve an older set of problems.

The Arab Spring, briefly mentioned above, consisted of a series of revolutionary actions that began in 2010 and swept through the Middle East. Social media technologies like Facebook and Twitter played an important role in these developments. But it was ultimately flesh-and-blood human beings who enabled such developments. The initial impetus for these revolutions lay in the self-immolation of Mohamed Bouazizi, a Tunisian street vendor who set himself on fire in response to the repressive policies of local authorities. The sources of the Arab Spring had been developing for some time before such tragic actions finally set off a wave of public protest. Social media catalyzed these movements but did not "cause" them any more than the proliferation of fax machines "caused" the democratic movements of 1989 in China's Tiananmen Square. In the aftermath of these protests, many governments used the same technologies as surveillance tools to monitor activists.

While it is important to recognize the role technologies play in social change, it is essential not to discount "the remarkable human struggle, raw courage, and ideological effort that were more instrumental in the overthrow of oppressive regimes" (Vaidhyanathan 2011, p. 122). As *The New Yorker*'s Malcolm Gladwell (2010) notes, "the revolution," as it were, "will not be tweeted." If we assume too much, tech becomes an end in itself, and this mistake will lead to unforeseen and possibly dangerous consequences. As we argued in Chapter 9, integrity in the tech industry involves a range of ethical "means" including fair labor practices, environmental sustainability, and emerging social innovation programs.

Politicians, activists, and scholars must likewise avoid the confusion of ends and means. Policy-oriented strategies must be launched with an attitude of realism. In his discussion of prophetic pragmatism, author and professor Cornel West recognizes that "utopian energies" must be channeled into various "reformist strategies that oppose the status quo of our day." But these strategies "are never to become ends-in-themselves"; rather, they are a means through which to channel moral outrage against the evil of human suffering (1989, p. 229). We must encourage responsible technological development "while witnessing to the darker side of the technological process with tears" (Christians 1989, p. 137).

Principle Two: Embracing Non-Violence

After his house was bombed in January of 1956, King issued a warning to his fellow activists: "We believe in law and order. Don't get panicky. Don't do anything panicky at all. Don't get your weapons. He who lives by the sword will perish by the sword" (Azbell 1956).

King believes that we must avoid physical violence at all costs, even when violence is inflicted upon us. But non-violence is not passivity. In fact, he makes a crucial distinction between the "negative peace" of complacency with the status quo, and the "positive peace" of non-violent resistance to injustice (King [1961] 1986, pp. 50–51). We should be active and engaged, but that manner and quality of our engagement matters. It follows that we must also seek to avoid what he calls the "internal violence of spirit" (p. 46). Violence in this broad sense is anything that indulges our vices, especially of anger and fear, and thereby undermines the development of our higher virtues.

Recalling the above examples about Anonymous and WikiLeaks, we argue that the spirit of vengeance and retaliation that drives cyber-vigilantism is a kind of internal violence of the spirit. In addition to their DDoS attacks on servers, Anonymous also directly targeted its critics. Former Anonymous activist Jennifer Emick describes how the group's members sent her highly misogynistic and sexual threats after she broke from the group (Swash 2013).

Contrary to King's warning, Anonymous and other third parties have weaponized WikiLeaks as a tool for retaliation and malicious attacks. As such, it is a threat to, rather than a guardian of, public discourse.

Popular social media platforms like Twitter and Facebook have contributed to the cynical degradation of public discourse in a way that has done great internal violence to the spirit of personal communication and democratic debate. Such platforms further contribute to our culture's growing incivility and ideological divisions by prompting slogans and memes of tribal superiority as we attack and demonize those who do not share our views. Users and platform developers alike share the blame for this situation. For their part, all users, and not just cyber-vigilante activists, can avoid trolling and cyber-bullying. But perhaps more importantly, site developers must attend to the consequences of their platform architectures including how personalization algorithms amplify fear, anger, domestic conspiracy theories, and foreign propaganda (Vaidhyanathan 2018).

In a short article on TechCrunch, author and tech executive Jon Evans (2016) notes that compassion is "the human instinct most quickly and easily leached out by social media," an always scarce resource whose absence "seems to render us all a little bit more sociopathic." Evans argues that we should treat Internet trolls with compassion, rather than responding with anger even when the troll is a powerful individual. His reasons for responding with compassion are consistent with King's philosophy of non-violence as a path to social transformation: not because it is the right thing to do in an abstract sense, but "because it *works*" (Evans 2016, emphasis original). "Nothing is more effective when reacting to a sick or hurt person who is lashing out" than a compassionate response Evans says, adding, "and I think (and/or hope) that describes a lot of the apparently terrible people out there." The eye-for-an-eye response to online harassment and bullying is not just a damaging habit for us personally, but in the long run it also undermines the collective search for equity and justice. Compassion is a harder path to tread, but it is the surer path to lives well lived with each other.

Principle Three: Understanding Love as an Ethical Principle

King argues that the ethic of love must serve as the foundation of the civil rights movement. The type of *agape* love that King describes transcends our approval or disapproval of someone's actions and beliefs. In theological terms, King argues that *agape* love sees an evil person, a doer of evil deeds, as someone who is profoundly misled, but whom God still loves and forgives. In a speech to the Association for Contemplative Mind in Higher Education, physics professor and Mind & Life Institute president Arthur Zajonc (2016) argued that we all need to "find the MLK in each of us." We need to "find our way again and again to that place" where we can meet challenges "without anger, but with love," Zajonc told his listeners.

This goal is clearly connected to the principles of non-violence and the purity of means. The ethic of love, however, often takes subtle, mundane, and everyday forms that are harder to recognize and therefore easier to undermine. If tech companies treat users (or user data) as a product or commodity, or a means to an end for profit, then over time this enables an attitude of cynicism and contempt with regard to users' concerns. Attitudes of contempt are pervasive among tech elites. The disdain with which Mark Zuckerberg dismissed the "dumb fucks" at Harvard who trusted him with their personal data is echoed in similar statements from executives at Apple, OkCupid, and Uber (Healey 2015, p. 959). As one spectator reminds us, "showing contempt doesn't have to be a deliberate or intentional act—one can also show contempt simply by failing to take into account people or things that should, in fact, count" (Hoffmann 2014). To the extent that this ethos of unreflective privilege informs design and policy decisions, commercial platforms like Facebook constitute "architectures of contempt" (Healey 2015, p. 958).

The tendency toward individualism, both in consumer markets and in solutions thinking, also undermines the ethic of love. Market systems tend to emphasize the duties, responsibilities, and preferences of individual consumers. Products and services are targeted to individuals or households. This dynamic reflects a broader philosophy that manifests itself in commercial markets but has deep roots in Enlightenment philosophy, a whole taken-for-granted framework that drives modern and post-modern political systems. This philosophy further posits the individual as a discreet entity or unit with its own agency. It is an entity that is primarily responsible for itself, its own well-being and livelihood. To the extent that the Enlightenment self has moral responsibility to others, the primary stage of moral action and behavior is local: for example, how I treat my co-workers, my family, my friends; whether I do my taxes; whether I recycle my garbage; and whether I turn the faucet off when I brush my teeth.

It is not surprising, therefore, that corporate mindfulness programs like Wisdom 2.0 or Google's Search Inside Yourself programs focus on reducing the stresses and anxieties of individual employees while neglecting their systemic root causes. These are issues we discuss in Chapters 2 and 5. The problem is not that self-love or self-care is without merit. It just does not go far enough, because it misunderstands the self as separate from others. The key insight of contemplative practice including King's philosophy of non-violence is that our separateness as individuals is ultimately an illusion. Caring for others and caring for the self are two sides of the same coin.

By refusing a hard-and-fast distinction between self and other, by insisting on the interdependence of all living things, and by therefore underscoring our mutual responsibility to each other, the ethic of love challenges the individualist foundations of consumer capitalism.

Agape love is social and relational in nature and therefore has broad political implications. It is not a stress-reduction technique, nor is it an ethic of negative or complacent peace within status-quo systems. It is instead an ethic of positive, engaged peace that serves to transform those systems.

Principle Four: Targeting Systems, Not Individuals

The fourth principle extends this systemic, anti-individualist thinking. King argued that the civil rights movement should target the system itself and not specific individuals. Here again, cyber-vigilante campaigns violate this principle by maliciously targeting individuals rather than unjust systems. In 2011, Anonymous launched Operation HBGary against CEO Aaron Barr of the security firm HBGary Federal. Internal documents revealed that Barr, in conjunction with Bank of America, had planned to undermine WikiLeaks by submitting fake documents and subsequently exposing them. Hacking into Barr's accounts, Anonymous released his private e-mails through the Pirate Bay bit torrent website and defaced his Twitter feed while publicizing its actions in separate tweets. Reflecting on Operation HBGary, one observer remarked, "there is something deeply ironic and troubling about … unveiling a person's identity, name, phone number, social security number" in order to make a point about the need for privacy and anonymity (Coleman 2012, p. 92). This targeting of individual actors is troubling precisely because it perpetuates the very problem such activists claim to care so much about. As such actions escalate public anxiety about data privacy, they erode public trust in the very possibility of civil discourse and institutional integrity. They may even backfire by lending more legitimacy to arguments for increased surveillance of activists and of the general public.

This does not mean that activists, scholars, politicians, or other stakeholders should avoid holding corporate executives accountable. For example, there may be good reasons for calling on executives to step down, just as there may be good reasons to impeach a federal judge or a president if their actions appear to be corrupt or illegal. Within the constraints of an equitable legal system, such procedural safeguards can hold individuals accountable in ways that are fair and non-violent. But without an eye toward systemic root causes, an excessive focus on individual bad actors may ultimately serve the system that produced them in the first place.

A similar problem of individualism dominates public conversations when well-meaning experts, policy-makers, and news reporters place too much burden on the shoulders of users for issues like privacy and Internet addiction. An excessive focus on individual behavior and personal responsibility ultimately serves the integrity of the system at the expense of the people who live within it. We sometimes ask students to read a chapter or two from Clay Johnson's (2012) *The Information Diet: A Case for Conscious Consumption*. The book is good, and the analogy to food consumption and nutrition goes a long way with students. But it only goes so far, and in fact it shares one of the main limitations, namely, that dieting of either kind (informational or nutritional) puts the burden on the individual while neglecting the systemic issues that lead to over-consumption in the first place.

Nora A. Draper (2019), a colleague of ours who studies online reputation and data privacy issues, suggests thinking about technological problems as analogous to (and intertwined with) environmental issues. Both are systemic, and both require something beyond individualist actions that fall within the parameters of the political-economic status quo. Even actions that appear to be collective, like users' response to the trending hashtag #DeleteFacebook, do not represent a long-term solution even if it feels satisfying to follow the trend. Facebook is a major player, but the problems it represents go beyond one company. We may decide to take actions or even create new regulations that aim primarily at one target like Facebook. Doing so may miss the systemic issues in the same way that recycling is good but cannot by itself fix the problems of climate change (Draper 2019). The easiest solutions are good but not good enough. This does not mean they are pointless, but they cannot stand alone and must instead be coupled with other strategies as part of a holistic plan.

Principle Five: Accepting Suffering

King argues that self-suffering is intrinsic to non-violent activism. One must accept suffering while refusing to inflict it upon others. It is worth noting that King's civil rights marchers managed to transform their social situation by willingly facing jail time or worse. This willingness to face the consequences of resisting injustice publicly is an essential element of non-violent activism.

Once again we note that malicious hacking campaigns violate this principle insofar as participants seek to "get away with" acts of physical or spiritual violence by leveraging tools that enable online anonymity. The very name Anonymous, and its trademark Guy Fawkes mask, highlight how central anonymity is to the political ideology of the group. We agree that anonymity and secrecy are important in certain contexts. They enable social minorities to establish meaningful relationships, seek support, and organize on behalf of social change. But they can also be a strategy for avoiding accountability. Online anonymity involves a temptation toward vengeance that can cause the pursuit of justice to backfire.

Recall here our discussions of authentic transparency in Chapter 8. An ethos of authentic transparency would mean that different and potentially competing groups would consent to disclosing relevant information for the sake of productive, legitimate critique, and oversight. This is a fine line to navigate, and Helen Nissenbaum's (2010) principle of contextual integrity (discussed in Chapter 8) provides a helpful rubric for understanding when anonymity and secrecy are appropriate versus when they amplify systemic injustice or simply enable maliciousness.

When it comes to the distribution of responsibility and risk, the burden is too often carried by users and consumers. User-end agreements and privacy policies are typically written to protect companies from liability. The dangers of information disclosure are unevenly distributed. Legislation of the kind we discuss in Chapter 8 demands a level of risk and accountability from industry players, not just from consumers. Commercial organizations must accept the possibility that, in response to the concerns of consumers and their elected representatives, they may need to make structural adjustments that impact their bottom line or market dominance. Consumers have begun to voice legitimate complaints that while they pay more than their fair share of taxes, companies like Amazon, Netflix, and IBM pay no taxes at all and in some cases receive a tax rebate (Saul and Cohen 2019). Within the year preceding the publication of this book, the number of U.S. companies who paid no taxes doubled, according to the non-partisan Institute on Taxation and Economic Policy (Gardner et al. 2019). Restoring balance to this lop-sided system requires courage from business executives and especially from politicians, the latter of whom may suffer a loss of support from corporate lobbyists, if not electoral defeat.

On a more seemingly mundane level, users need to break out of their habitual patterns of using digital tech to self-soothe and distract themselves from the stresses of everyday life or, for that matter, engaging in contemplative practices like yoga and meditation merely for the purpose of stress relief. As Walter Brueggemann (2001) explains, the culture of "achievable satiation" is about being complacent within a scheme of convenience and comfortability (p. 42). Such complacency often amounts to complicity. As we have made clear throughout this book, we embrace digital media and contemplative practices. We have insisted on embracing these in ways that catalyze our prophetic imagination and our willingness to challenge the status quo and serves others. The Buddhist roots of contemplative practices like meditation emphasize social ethics, not just stress relief (Forbes 2019, pp. 58–60). We have attended weekend-long conferences specifically dedicated to this insight, under the banner of "integrity of practice" ("Integrity of Practice" 2013). The purpose of such practices is not to distract or soothe us into complacency but to allow us to remain grounded even as we consciously enter into situations where we know we may suffer.

The goal of mindfulness from a Judeo-Christian perspective is not to empty the mind but to fill it; to re-focus away from the clutter of one's life to the gift of the moment, or the gift of the presence of the grace that engulfs us; to encounter reality through God's eyes, with His ears, and all of His senses as part of a faithful and connected community. Christian mindfulness like this, to borrow a phrase from Rabbi Abraham Joshua Heschel, reminds us that "there is something sacred in every moment" (Heschel 1955, p. 74). As a type of human-divine perspective taking, Christian mindfulness makes us more ourselves, or more who God intended us to be, while helping us avoid the kind of self-indulgence or hyper-individualism that often accompanies our consumption of media and technology.

As Richard J. Foster explains in his classic book *Celebration of Discipline*,

> There is need for detachment—a "sabbath of contemplation" … But there is a danger in thinking only in terms of detachment as Jesus indicates in his story of the man who had been emptied of evil but not filled with good … No, detachment is not enough; we must go on to *attachment*. The detachment from the confusion all around us is in order to have a richer attachment to God.
>
> (Foster [1978] 1998, p. 21)

Experiencing the kind of mindful attachment described above is easier said than done. Most of us tend to lack a habit-forming lifestyle that cultivates sustained attachment in meaningful ways when faced with the readily accessible flood of digital distractions. We are lost when it comes to finding daily rituals and practices to promote the kind of everyday Sabbath we seek.

The capacity to maintain an active, positive peace in the face of (digital) risk and suffering is called equanimity. We must demand it from ourselves if we are to demand it from our elected representatives and business leaders. It is the active dimension of love. Writing in *Journey to the Common Good*, Brueggemann describes how the collective movement from anxiety, fear, and scarcity toward a spirit of "neighborhood" is "the key journey that Jews must make, that Christians must make, and that all humans must make in order to be maximally human" (2010, p. 31). It is a journey that requires "steadfast love," and, most importantly, it is one that "must be taken again and again" (p. 31).

Principle Six: Recognizing the Good in People

In the fall of 1967, just six months before he was assassinated, King told a gathering of Philadelphia high school students,

> in your life's blueprint, [there] must be a commitment to the eternal principles of beauty, love, and justice. Don't allow anybody to pull you so low as to make you hate them. Don't allow anybody to cause you to lose your self-respect to the point that you do not struggle for justice.
>
> (King [1967] 2016, p. 68)

King believes that within human nature there is potential for both good and evil. Non-violent activists have an obligation to appeal to the good that exists within all people, including even the most stubborn opponents. King understood the deeper meaning of authenticity. It is an aspiration toward virtue. It is about what we have *yet* to become. From King's theological standpoint, we are all imprinted with the image of God. Violence and hatred interfere with our ability and willingness to see that image in ourselves and in others (see Genesis 1:26–28).

Examples of this type of compassionate response, of willingness to see good even in those who appear to hate us, sometimes come from unexpected places. Recall for a moment Jon Evans's argument that we should respond to online trolls with compassion, on the premise that it is a more effective strategy for diffusing their anger and stalling their attacks. A helpful illustration of this involves comedian Sarah Silverman, whose response to one online troll is described by one reporter as "a master class in compassion" (Van Evra 2018). When a man named Jeremy insulted her with profanity on Twitter, Silverman (2017) speculated that his anger was really "thinly veiled pain." Apropos King's principle of seeing the good in all people, Silverman tweeted in reply to Jeremy, "I believe in you … see what happens when u choose love. I see it in you." At this gesture of sympathy, the man's guard fell and he confessed to having suffered abuse as a child and having too little money to pay for medical treatment for his ongoing back issues. Silverman continued her campaign of support, calling on readers to rally on his behalf. The interaction drew attention across the Twittersphere, and soon a spinal pain treatment clinic in Jeremy's home city of San Antonio reached out to him directly. In a subsequent interview, Silverman reflected on the state of public discourse in the United States, saying, "Screaming at each other has never caused change. ... So we need to try and understand each other" (Husband 2017).

Reflect for a moment on the true purpose of an acorn. What is its authentic nature? What does it look like for an acorn to live authentically? When we ask this question of students in our seminars on ethics, someone eventually observes that—as long as it gets sunlight and good soil—an acorn will become a tree. The authentic nature of the acorn, or its blueprint, to use King's phrase, is an image of something altogether different.

Now consider this question: What if acorns refuse to become trees? What if one of them fashions himself a Leader of Acorns, convincing the others they should be proud of their acorn nature? Unfortunately, our culture has long been steeped in a notion of authenticity that is strident and stubborn in this way, what philosopher Charles Taylor called a "flat" notion of authenticity (1991, p. 94). Digital technologies, at least in their current form, have exacerbated this misunderstanding by elevating the social media profiles of those who speak, or tweet, without thinking. Crass, unfiltered, imprudent speech has come to be seen as a mark of authenticity among politicians. This is one reason why American politics and public discourse more generally is moving in a more tribal, partisan direction. Personalization algorithms indulge our fears and anxieties, our partisan and tribal instincts, our desire to blame and lash out at others.

When King says we should appeal to the good that is in all people, he is saying that we should see even our worst enemies not for who they are now, but for who and what they are capable of becoming. See the tree, not the acorn. In this space of compassion, the acorn we see may let go of its pride, and in this way it can become what it truly is: something far grander and more deeply rooted. The seedling for some grand sequoia may right now be resting on fertile soil, if not sprouting from its protective shell! Do we have the wherewithal to nurture it? Will we, too, become so humble and wise?

Conclusion

King's principles of non-violence suggest that we must go beyond personal spiritual practices that help us maintain our individual sense of well-being. What are we practicing for? We practice to establish the equanimity we need as we "fight the good fight," with love, in the arena of public opinion and civic engagement. We need that equanimity, that prudent foresight, now more than ever because of the increasing speed with which our technical environment is changing and changing us. Grounded with equanimity, we stretch out within the space of prophetic imagination.

In a speech about technology to the Bavaraian Academy, the German philosopher Martin Heidegger (1971) offered a vision: If humans are language-bearing people, and if language is taken over by the technocratic mind, we need artists, literary people, and fiction writers to create a new poetry, a new language system. We are the artists that Heidegger describes. You, the reader, are the poet. One of the goals we have in offering this book has been not only to offer distinctions of our own between information and wisdom but to prompt prophetic thinking about other distinctions we have not even conceived of.

The technical space we are developing now, as consumers and software engineers, is more entertaining and spectacular than anything that has come before. A language of magic and mystery surrounds this technology. We are speaking here about virtual reality (VR) and augmented reality (AR) systems. In 1990, long before the HTV Vive or the Microsoft HaloLens, a narrator in the documentary film *Cyberpunk* describes the implications of VR as follows: "Never before in the history of mankind has there been an alternative universe one could actually inhabit. Now that anyone can experience them, alternate universes are no longer the province of physicists, theologians, and supernaturalists. It is a matter of the creator and the creation" (*Cyberpunk* 1990).

More recently, in an exemplary tweet, Unity Technologies CEO John Riccitiello likewise frames the technology as revolutionary: "VR is going to be driven by mobile. Dream 'em, build 'em, life will never be the same" (Google AR & VR 2016).

In similar language, Zuckerberg (2014) noted that the mission of Facebook's newly acquired Oculus technology is "to enable you to experience the impossible." Regarding Facebook's acquisition of Oculus, Zuckerberg pontificated that "One day, we believe this kind of immersive, augmented reality will become a part of daily life for billions of people."

If King had a dream, so do these engineers and CEOs. Whose vision of humanity should we trust? Who will dream our digital future? As professor of journalism and environmental activist Robert Jensen (2013) argues, "We are all prophets now" (p. 20). We must be the dreamers. But we must dream consciously and mindfully, otherwise our shadow selves will drag us down into dystopian scenarios of the kind that Hollywood film producers envision. As the Sufi poet Hakim Sanai once remarked, "humanity is asleep, concerned only with what is useless, living in a wrong world" (Shah 1971, p. xxviii). As long as Silicon Valley's techno-romantic ideology drives technical development, we may remain trapped by the nightmare of greed and delusion. To awaken technologically requires that we awaken spiritually as well. Let us become dreamers and poets. It is they who see the lighthouse for what it is and steer the ship to safer shores.

References

Amichai-Hamburger, Yair. "Technology and Well-Being: Designing the Future." In *Technology and Psychological Well-being*, edited by Yair Amichai-Hamburger, 260–78. New York: Cambridge University Press, 2009.

Azbell, Joe. "Blast Rocks Residence of Bus Boycott Leader." *Montgomery Advertiser* [Alabama], January 31, 1956. http://kinginstitute.stanford.edu/king-papers/documents/blast-rocks-residence-bus-boycott-leader-joe-azbell.

Bratton, Benjamin. "We Need to Talk about TED." *The Guardian*, December 30, 2013. https://www.theguardian.com/commentisfree/2013/dec/30/we-need-to-talk-about-ted.

Brueggemann, Walter. *The Prophetic Imagination*. 2nd ed. Minneapolis, MN: Fortress Press, 2001.

————. *Journey to the Common Good*. Louisville, KY: Westminster John Knox Press, 2010.

Christians, Clifford G. "A Theory of Normative Technology." In *Technological Transformation: Contextual and Conceptual Implications*, edited by Edmund F. Byrne and Joseph C. Pitts, 123–40. Boston, MA: Kluwer Academic, 1989.

Coleman, Gabriella. "Our Weirdness Is Free." *May* 9 (2012): 83–95.

Cyberpunk. Directed by Marianne Schaefer Trench. Produced by Peter von Brandenburg. New York, NY: Intercon Productions, 1990.

Draper, Nora A. Personal conversation with Kevin Healey. University of New Hampshire. Durham, NH, May 7, 2019.

Drda, Darrin. "The Selective Awareness of Wisdom 2.0." OpenDemocracy. April 16, 2014. https://www.opendemocracy.net/en/transformation/selective-awareness-of-wisdom-20/.

Evans, Jon. "Let's Have a Little Compassion for (Some of) the Trolls." TechCrunch. October 15, 2016. https://techcrunch.com/2016/10/15/lets-have-a-little-compassion-for-some-of-the-trolls/.

Forbes, David. *Mindfulness and Its Discontents: Education, Self, and Social Transformation*. Black Point, Nova Scotia: Fernwood Publishing, 2019.

Foster, Richard J. *Celebration of Discipline: The Path to Spiritual Growth*. 1978. Reprint ed., New York: Harper One, 1998.

Gardner, Matthew, Steve Wamhoff, Mary Martellotta, and Lorena Roque. "Corporate Tax Avoidance Remains Rampant Under New Tax Law." Institute on Taxation and Economic Policy. April 11, 2019. https://itep.org/notadime/.

Gladwell, Malcolm. "Small Change: Why the Revolution Will Not Be Tweeted." *New Yorker*, September 27, 2010. https://www.newyorker.com/magazine/2010/10/04/small-change-malcolm-gladwell.

Google AR and VR via Twitter. May 19, 2016.

Healey, Kevin. "Contemplative Media Studies." *Religions* 6, no. 3 (August 5, 2015): 948–68.

Heschel, Abraham Joshua. *God in Search of Man: A Philosophy of Judaism*. New York: Harper and Row, 1955.

Heidegger, Martin. *Poetry, Language, Thought*, translated by Albert Hofstadter. New York: Harper & Row, 1971.

Hoffmann, Anna. "Reckoning with a Decade of Breaking Things." *Model View Culture*, June 30, 2014. https://modelviewculture.com/pieces/reckoning-with-a-decade-of-breaking-things.

Husband, Andrew. "Sarah Silverman on Why It's Important to Understand Each Other, Now More Than Ever." Uproxx. May 31, 2017. https://uproxx.com/tv/sarah-silverman-netflix-interview/.

"Integrity of Practice: A Contemplative Vision for Higher Education." The Fifth Annual ACMHE Conference, Amherst College, Amherst, MA, November 8–10, 2013. http://www.contemplativemind.org/admin/wp-content/uploads/2013program.pdf.

Jensen, Robert. "Our Challenge: Prophetic Voices." In *Prophetic Critique and Popular Media*, edited by Robert H. Woods Jr. and Kevin Healey, 19–32. New York: Peter Lang, 2013.

King, Martin Luther, Jr. "Love, Law, and Civil Disobedience." In *A Testament of Hope: The Essential Writings of Martin Luther King, Jr.*, edited by James M. Washington, 43–53. 1961. Reprint ed., San Francisco: Harper & Row, 1986.

———. "What Is Your Life's Blueprint?" In *The Radical King*, edited by Cornel West, 65–72. 1967. Reprint ed., Boston, MA: Beacon Press, 2016.

Johnson, Clay. *The Information Diet: A Case for Conscious Consumption.* Sebastopol, CA: O'Reilly Media, 2012.

Lanier, Jaron. *You Are Not a Gadget: A Manifesto.* New York: Vintage Books, 2011.

———. *Who Owns the Future?* New York: Simon and Schuster, 2013.

Nissenbaum, Helen. *Privacy in Context: Technology, Policy, and the Integrity of Social Life.* Stanford, CA: Stanford University Press, 2010.

Saul, Stephanie, and Patricia Cohen. "Profitable Giants Like Amazon Pay $0 in Corporate Taxes. Some Voters Are Sick of It." *New York Times*, April 29, 2019. https://www.nytimes.com/2019/04/29/us/politics/democrats-taxes-2020.html.

Shah, Idries. *The Sufis.* New York: First Anchor Books, 1971.

Silverman, Sarah. Untitled tweet, December 28, 2017. https://twitter.com/SarahKSilverman/status/946555534768979969.

Swash, Rosie. "Is Hacktivism on Behalf of Rehtaeh Parsons a Revolution in Rape Campaigning?" *The Guardian*, April 15, 2013. https://www.theguardian.com/lifeandstyle/2013/apr/15/hacktivism-rehtaeh-parsons-rape.

Taylor, Charles. *The Ethics of Authenticity.* Cambridge, MA: Harvard University Press, 1991.

Vaidhyanathan, Siva. *The Googlization of Everything (And Why We Should Worry).* Berkeley: University of California Press, 2011.

———. *Anti-Social Media: How Facebook Disconnects Us and Undermines Democracy.* New York: Oxford University Press, 2018.

Van Evra, Jennifer. "Sarah Silverman's Response to a Twitter Troll Is a Master Class in Compassion." CBC. January 3, 2018. https://www.cbc.ca/radio/q/blog/sarah-silverman-s-response-to-a-twitter-troll-is-a-master-class-in-compassion-1.4471337.

West, Cornel. *The American Evasion of Philosophy: A Genealogy of Pragmatism.* Madison: The University of Wisconsin Press, 1989.

Zajonc, Arthur. "Contemplative Inquiry." Paper presented at the 2016 Summer Session on Contemplative Higher Education, Amherst, MA, August 20, 2016.

Zuckerberg, Mark. Untitled post to Facebook. March 25, 2014. https://www.facebook.com/zuck/posts/10101319050523971.

INDEX